UNCONSCIOUS STRUCTURE IN *THE IDIOT*

UNCONSCIOUS STRUCTURE IN *THE IDIOT*

A Study in Literature and Psychoanalysis

Elizabeth Dalton

PRINCETON UNIVERSITY PRESS
Princeton, New Jersey

Copyright © 1979 by Princeton University Press

Published by Princeton University Press, Princeton, New Jersey
In the United Kingdom: Princeton University Press,
Guildford, Surrey

ALL RIGHTS RESERVED

Library of Congress Cataloging in Publication Data will be
found on the last printed page of this book

Publication of this book has been aided by a grant from
The Andrew W. Mellon Foundation

This book has been composed in VIP Baskerville
Designed by Laury A. Egan
Clothbound editions of Princeton University Press books
are printed on acid-free paper, and binding materials are
chosen for strength and durability

Printed in the United States of America by Princeton
University Press, Princeton, New Jersey

For Jimmy, Julie, and Rory

Contents

Preface

This book grew out of my sense of psychoanalytic method as a subtle and powerful instrument for the examination of literary meaning, and my fascination with a particular literary text, Dostoevsky's *The Idiot*. In Part One, entitled "Psychoanalytic Method and the Study of Literature," I have tried to rethink the relationship between psychoanalysis and literature, beginning with *The Interpretation of Dreams*, and to deal with some of the principal issues and problems in psychoanalytic criticism. The ideas developed in Part One are demonstrated in Part Two, a study of *The Idiot*. The novel is a brilliant and problematic work, rich in the sense of lived experience, yet revolving about a core of mystery in the person of the enigmatic and almost unearthly Myshkin. Critics seem by and large to have been baffled and kept at a distance by *The Idiot*. Some consider it Dostoevsky's greatest novel, largely because of the beauty and originality of the conception, while others think it the least successful because of failures of execution. It is a rich subject for analysis—especially psychoanalysis.

In studying *The Idiot*, I have avoided using biographical material. Psychoanalytic critics frequently seem to compromise the autonomy of the work of literature as well as its meaning by interpreting it in terms of the author's life, rather than according to the unconscious patterns it can be shown to contain in itself. Because I wanted to demonstrate that unconscious meaning can be derived from analysis of the text alone, information about the author has been kept to a minimum. In a few instances, Dostoevsky's own experience is so obviously relevant to the novel that not to mention it would seem perverse. But this material is confined almost entirely to footnotes in order to show that the interpretation does not depend on it. In the text only a few pages deal with the author's life, and this information is used not to interpret the novel, but to remind the reader of well-known facts that provide some background for the interpretation. Material from Dostoevsky's notebooks for the novel has also been almost entirely excluded from the body of this study, and is treated separately in an appendix. Although both Parts One and Two are meant to suggest the possibilities of a certain use of psychoanalysis, the method here cannot be codified in a systematic way. The encounter between the work and the critic is bound to be personal and not entirely replicable; in any kind of criticism, what one finds in the work is partly the result of what one brings to it. Indeed, if one takes seriously the conception of mental functioning on which psychoanalytic criticism is based, it is clear that even the choice of a work to criticize is in part unconsciously determined. The purpose of psychoanalytic criticism, however, is not to project one's own fantasies into the work, but to find in it the objective psychological order that evokes fantasy and emotion in all readers. The critic must use his or her subjective response to find a way into the unconscious life of the text itself, the latent dimension of the work that neither reader nor writer is explicitly aware of, but that is nonetheless part of its deepest meaning. In the exploration of this unconscious dimension, concealed and yet present in every aspect of the text, psychoanalysis should be used not to provide interpretive formulas that reduce the literary work to a single meaning, but on the contrary to enlarge and enrich our sense of the possibilities of meaning in literature.

Acknowledgments

I would like to thank a number of friends and colleagues. I am especially grateful to Professor Steven Marcus for his support of my work, and for the scrupulous attention with which he read this manuscript. Professor George Stade, Professor Robert Belknap, and Dr. Arnold Cooper also read and commented helpfully on the manuscript. George Stade's response to my original project for the book was most encouraging. I am grateful as well to the late Lionel Trilling, not only for his generous response to this effort but for the example of his own luminous understanding of psychoanalysis and its possible uses.

As I do not know Russian, I have worked with a translation of *The Idiot*. Robin Miller has helped me by providing translations of passages from Dostoevsky's letters and by checking all quotations from the Garnett translation of *The Idiot* against the Russian text. Where the translation departs significantly from the Russian, I have amended it to bring it closer to the literal meaning.

Finally, my sister Julie proofread and corrected the manuscript, and helped me in many other ways.

1
THEORY
Psychoanalytic Method and the Study of Literature

I. INTRODUCTION

The affinity between psychoanalysis and literature, persistently challenged and denied, continues to assert itself, with the tenacity of an idea that will not succumb to repression. Freud himself began the application of psychoanalytic concepts to literature in *The Interpretation of Dreams* with his observations on *Oedipus Rex* and on Shakespeare's tragedies; later he turned his attention more directly to literature in studies of *King Lear* and of Wilhelm Jensen's *Gradiva*, and in essays on the writer and daydreaming, on Dostoevsky, and on other literary subjects. But even in Freud's first book, *Studies on Hysteria*, written in collaboration with Josef Breuer, it was apparent that Freud's fundamental conception of human experience owed a great deal to literature as well as to science. Although the psychoanalytic methods for the study of personality differed from those of literature, the conception of the object to be studied was and still is in many ways the same: psychoanalysis shares with literature its interest in subjectivity and interiority, its vision of the complexity of mind and personality, and its search for coherence and meaningful structure—a "story" of some kind—in every life.

In dealing with his first cases of hysteria, Freud soon moved away from theories of physiological and hereditary causation, and began to inquire into the histories, the life circumstances, and the emotions of his patients. In *Studies on Hysteria*, in the vignettes of Elisabeth von R., Emmy von N., and Lucy R., one begins to catch glimpses of a dense, ambiguous, and richly detailed human reality. Freud's repressed, morally ambitious young women bring to mind nineteenth-century literary heroines—Jane Eyre and Lucy Snowe, Dorothea Brooke, Sue Bridehead, Isabel Archer. The presentation and the sense of experience in all of Freud's case studies are intensely literary: there is the conflict between appearance and reality, the fascination with the inexhaustible richness of personality, the sense of the hidden motive and the secret guilt in every soul, even the evocation of a larger social ambiance in which these painfully interesting lives are lived—a decadent and hypocritical world in which natural impulse, stigmatized and denied, can only express itself in illness.[1]

Freud himself was uneasily aware of the literary quality of his case studies:

> it still strikes me myself as strange that the case histories I wrote should read like short stories and that, as one might say, they lack the serious stamp of science. I must console myself with the reflection that the nature of the subject is evidently responsible for this, rather than any preference of my own. The fact is that local diagnosis and electrical reactions lead nowhere in the study of hysteria, whereas a detailed description of mental processes such as we are accustomed to find in the works of imaginative writers enables me, with the use of a few psychological formulas, to obtain at least some kind of insight into the course of that affection.[2]

The novelistic fascination of Freud's accounts of his patients is not due to any lack of scientific exactitude on his part—there never was a more arduous and self-abnegating pursuit of truth—nor even to his extraordinary literary powers, but rather to his conception of his subject. For Freud, the significant experiences were not those that could be quantified and verified in the laboratory, but rather the complex and obscure phenomena of subjective states—the self's encounter with its own nature in desire, suffering, and fantasy—and the characteristic patterns of action that over the years and often against all conscious intent assume the shape of a destiny. Freud shares with the great writers of literature the sense of the deepest sources of character and action as alien to conscious understanding and ultimately mysterious, and he drew frequently on the psychological insights of writers to confirm his own obser-

vations. When Freud was praised at his seventieth birthday
celebration as the discoverer of the unconscious, he dis-
claimed the honor. "The poets and philosophers before me
discovered the unconscious," he said. "What I discovered
was the scientific method by which the unconscious can be
studied."[3]

As a way of understanding human life and personality,
psychoanalysis has, then, a certain affinity with literature.
But by itself this affinity would not necessarily justify the
study of literature in conjunction with psychoanalysis or
the application of psychoanalytic concepts to literary works.
Rather, the validity of psychoanalytic criticism must rest on
the specific contributions psychoanalysis can make to the
understanding of literature. In fact psychoanalysis has
opened new possibilities for literary study if we know how
to use them: it offers us an expanded and deepened interpretive method and a new conception of the text, an
understanding of the unconscious dimension of literary
structure and meaning, and valuable insights into the nature of literary language and of the creative process.

There is, of course, considerable resistance to the application of psychoanalytic ideas to literature, often on the
grounds that psychoanalysis was developed to deal with the
phenomena of neurosis and should not be applied to the
productions of the creative mind. According to this line of
argument, psychoanalytic method, when applied to works
of genius, reduces them to the level of neurotic symptoms.
Freud, however, never intended that psychoanalysis be
limited to the subject of neurosis; in *The Interpretation of
Dreams* and *The Psychopathology of Everyday Life* he made it
clear that psychoanalysis was to be considered a general
psychology applicable not only to neurosis but to all aspects
of mental functioning. In fact a large part of Freud's own
work is devoted to the study of human mental life as it is
expressed in society, culture, and art.

Freud once told Ernest Jones that he would like to retire
from the practice of medicine in order to spend his time

unraveling cultural and historical problems—"ultimately
the great problem of how man came to be what he is."[4] The
study of neurosis was interesting to Freud not only in itself
but as one of the paths to that greater problem—one of the
irregularities or fissures in the façade of human life
through which the hidden reality may be approached.
There is no sharp division in this respect between Freud's
clinical and technical papers and his studies of art and society; it is hard to think of any of his papers that does not at
some point open out onto the broadest vista of human interest and possibility. In any case, it is difficult to understand how art or the artist could be somehow sullied by
psychological analysis. In his essay on Leonardo da Vinci,
Freud writes, "there is no one so great as to be disgraced by
being subject to the laws which govern both normal and
pathological activity with equal cogency."[5] One of the most
liberating and stimulating aspects of Freud's work is his
fascination with every kind of human production, from the
great achievements of art and thought to the painful and
distorted creations of pathology, and his sense of the subterranean connections that unite all forms of human
experience—the continuities, oppositions, and transformations that show "how man came to be what he is."

II. PSYCHOANALYSIS AND
THE INTERPRETATION OF THE TEXT

Freud's most valuable contributions to the study of the
literary text come directly from the fundamental assumptions implicit in his psychology and his interpretive
method. In the manifestations of nervous illness considered random and senseless by other investigators—for
example, the somatic symptoms of hysteria or the compulsive thoughts and rituals of obsessional patients—Freud
saw meaningful communications. In those aspects of mental life such as mistakes and dreams that had seemed to

other psychologists simply the disordered activities of an improperly functioning mechanism, Freud found expressive utterances, although in a language whose meaning was unknown to the subject himself as well as to the physician. To understand the patient's illness, then, it was necessary to transcribe this archaic and fragmented language of dream, symptom, and gesture into the comprehensible language of rational speech. Freud uses the analogies of translation, language, and text again and again, particularly with regard to dreams:

> The dream-thoughts and the dream-content are presented to us like two versions of the same subject-matter in two different languages. Or, more properly, the dream-content seems like a transcript of the dream-thoughts into another mode of expression, whose characters and syntactic laws it is our business to discover by comparing the original and the translation. The dream-thoughts are immediately comprehensible, as soon as we have learnt them. The dream-content, on the other hand, is expressed as it were in a pictographic script, the characters of which have to be transposed individually into the language of the dream-thoughts.[1]

The task of the psychoanalyst, then, becomes in one sense the *interpretation of a text*.[2]

The arcane dream-script is the language of an unknown part of the mind; the hieroglyphs of the dream-text, when deciphered, reveal a whole buried mental content, a lost story of the passions of childhood. The trivial fragments of current life that appear in the dream lead back by threads of allusion to more powerful memories repressed in waking life. These memories regularly involve the child's experiences of sexual excitement, his curiosity about the sexual life of his parents, his rivalry with siblings, and the mixture of erotic and aggressive wishes toward the mother and father that culminate in the Oedipus complex. Under the

cover of the interests of current life, the dream re-stages
the drama of the early years in the form of the fulfillment
of a wish.

What Freud discovered through the interpretation of
the dream-text was the unconscious, the part of the mind
in which the interests of childhood, particularly the wishes
and fears associated with the child's sexuality, are still active. The ego, which deals with external reality, opposes
these infantile wishes; it keeps them from waking awareness by a sort of language barrier, the repression that helps
to make the dream-idiom unintelligible. The peculiar and
archaic "script" in which the dream reaches consciousness,
the dream-images themselves, revealed the workings within
the unconscious of a mode of mental function quite different from that of waking thought, a "primary process" that
ignores the realistic considerations of time and space and
the elementary logical principles that operate in conscious
thinking. Despite its deficiencies, this primitive mode of
mental function is in some ways more immediate, more
rapid and economical, than the "secondary process" associated with consciousness. Through condensation and displacement, two of its most significant operations, it can
represent a cluster of related figures or a whole train of
thought in a single image, or displace the affect belonging
to one element of the dream content onto another less significant element. Some of the fragmentary and apparently
chaotic quality of the dream is due to the nature of the
primary process, which dominates unconscious thinking.
But gaps and distortions are also attributable to the censorship, the repressive operation that keeps the meaning of
the dream from reaching awareness. Freud compares the
dream remembered in consciousness to a newspaper from
which a government censor has excised certain words in
order to conceal sensitive information. It is the task of the
analytic interpreter to restore the integrity and the original
meaning of this mutilated text.

Freud's discovery of the meaningfulness of the dream
changed radically and irrevocably our understanding of

the nature of mental life and of all mental productions. The dream, after all, is a universal mental event. The principles of dream formation and the dominant motifs of dream life are the same in neurotics and in "normal" persons. Moreover, in applying his interpretive method to a broad range of other phenomena—the nonverbal mimetic performances of hysteria or the dozens of minute deviations from conscious intent, the slips, forgettings, and mistakes in the daily lives of normal persons—Freud saw again a kind of language or text that gave utterance to unconscious meaning. In doing so, he opened to understanding a new area of the mind; he made us aware of new orders of meaning; and finally, he changed our conception of what a' text may be.

Freud's discovery of unconscious meaning in the whole range of human expression was bound to affect our understanding of the literary text. Freud himself began this extension of psychoanalytic method to literature. He found in the *Oedipus Rex* of Sophocles, in the crimes that Oedipus commits unknowingly and for which he punishes himself so cruelly, not only the story of the crucial episode in human psychosexual development but also the very pattern of the expression of unconscious meaning. As in dreams or neurotic symptoms, there is the forbidden infantile wish, its fulfillment in disguised form, and the operation of the censorship, which punishes the crime and bars its true meaning from consciousness. In *Hamlet* and *Macbeth*, and later in *King Lear* and other works, Freud found again patterns of unconscious meaning. It is, in fact, from just this power to represent in disguised form the buried life of the mind that the poet draws his great power over the minds of others. Of *Oedipus* Freud writes that it is not the conflict between destiny and human will that so moves us, but the material in which that contrast is exemplified.

There must be something which makes a voice within us ready to recognize the compelling force of destiny

in the *Oedipus*, while we can dismiss as merely arbitrary
such dispositions as are laid down in Grillparzer's *Die
Ahnfrau* or other modern tragedies of destiny. And a
factor of this kind is in fact involved in the story of
King Oedipus. His destiny moves us only because it
might have been ours—because the oracle laid the
same curse upon us before our birth as upon him. . . .
Here is one in whom these primaeval wishes of our
childhood have been fulfilled, and we shrink back
from him with the whole force of the repression by
which those wishes have since that time been held
down within us. While the poet, as he unravels the
past, brings to light the guilt of Oedipus, he is at the
same time compelling us to recognize our own inner
minds, in which those same impulses, though suppressed, are still to be found.[3]

The basic assumptions of psychoanalytic criticism are present in this passage: literature contains elements of the repressed unconscious—the "primaeval wishes" of childhood
that are later repressed; the literary work, like a dream,
represents the fulfillment of such forbidden wishes, but in
a way that disguises their true nature so that both the repressing tendency and the wish are satisfied. It is through
its appeal to such repressed interests still active in the unconscious that the work engages our emotions. The formal,
moral, and philosophical aspects of literature are deeply
rooted in unconscious material and are worked out in conjunction with it.

In "Creative Writers and Day-dreaming," Freud traces
the roots of the poet's creative gift back to the common
sources of imagination and fantasy present in all human
beings. The fantasies expressed in children's play, in the
daydreams of adults, and in the night dream are all
rudimentary and natural works of art; they are the universal sources of creative and imaginative activity on which the
poet draws in himself and which he is able to evoke in

others as well. Child's play and daydreams, like night dreams, fulfill wishes; they rearrange the world in a way that gratifies in fantasy desires that must be forgone in real life. These wishes are often selfish and amoral, and thus repugnant to the ego, which must respect the demands of reality. They are a kind of lifelong unconscious rebellion against reality, whether for good or for ill. It is just the power and tenacity of this rebellion, and its appropriation of increasingly complex portions of reality, that make creative activity possible. Of course, the unconscious wish is not a sufficient condition for the creation of literature; there is a considerable difference between the rudimentary art of the dreamer or the child at play and the work of the artist. But it is a strange misunderstanding of Freud to say that he reduces the achievement of the artist by showing its connection with childhood, fantasy, and dream. Literature is not merely an epiphenomenon of high culture, the last adornment of gentility, but a deep human necessity, rooted tenaciously in instinctual life and in its struggle with the repressing and transforming forces of culture. The vitality of the instinctual drives represented in the work, their capacity to elude control, is paradoxically what sustains and invigorates the very culture that tries to suppress them. The recalcitrant wishes rooted in the drives and the repressive tendencies growing out of the demands of culture are both expressed in literature, perhaps more clearly than in any other human activity. It is the intensity of this conflict, never really reconciled but only mediated, that guarantees the endurance of art.

Psychoanalytic method would seem, then, to offer possibilities for a richer understanding of the literary text, and for the exploration of aspects of the literary experience that often elude conventional academic study. The fundamental issue evaded in almost all academic criticism is that of emotional involvement, the fact that the great works endure because of their continuing capacity to engage our feelings profoundly in spite of our remoteness from them in time, space, and social circumstance. It is sometimes hard to account for the intensity of the work's emotional effect in terms of its explicit subject or its beauty of form and language. The emotional experience becomes especially difficult to understand with works that arouse feelings of disgust, anguish, or terror; and yet it is often just those works that one reads with the most intense involvement, as though under a kind of painful compulsion.

The study of background, influences, theme, genre, and so on, ought ideally to break the barriers of time and convention that make a work seem inaccessible. The result would then be the experience of intimate contact with the disturbing, living reality of the text. Often, however, criticism functions to defend against rather than to understand potentially disturbing aspects of the work, imposing on them the familiar labels of literary history and taxonomy. Every fantasy or fear, every representation of aggression or sexuality can be accounted for somewhere in the canons of comedy, tragedy, Gothicism, naturalism, courtly love, or whatever—with the result that literature appears to have no relation to human experience or feeling.[4]

As a method of interpreting expressive texts, psychoanalysis offers us ways of undoing this alienation, of understanding and experiencing more fully the emotional dimension of the work. An approach that integrated psychoanalytic method with other critical techniques might extend the study of themes, form, and language to show how these aspects of the text are implicated in the deep structures of unconscious ideation and feeling.

However, the application of psychoanalytic ideas to literature now arouses a great deal of resistance. This response is part of a general reaction against the rigor and complexity of Freud's thought; the radical implications of his ideas and his relentlessly tragic view of the human situation have been rejected by many people for the commonsensical psychology and hopeful platitudes of such revisionists as Erich

Fromm, Karen Horney, and others. One result of this re-treat is the fad of Laingian anti-psychiatry, which roman-ticizes mental illness and projects the sources of internal conflict outward onto a cruel society, for which evidently none of its oppressed individual members bears any re-sponsibility. Attempts at psychoanalytic interpretation of literary materials arouse the predictable accusation of "re-ductionism": the psychoanalytic critic reduces the work to "nothing but" some banal and obvious theme such as the Oedipus complex, sibling rivalry, or whatever.

Without denying that there are incompetent psycho-analytic studies, or that psychoanalysts often ignore the specifically literary nature of the text and treat it as if it were the experience or the production of a patient, one must still wonder at the special indignation and derision reserved for psychoanalytic studies and withheld from the reams of boring, trivial, and quite unnecessary criticism of more conventional kinds. It is perhaps not the "banality" of psychoanalytic criticism that provokes this wrathful and ir-rational response, but indeed the unfamiliar light it casts on the text and on the literary enterprise itself. Opponents of psychoanalytic criticism maintain that it is not worth-while in any case to uncover the unconscious material in the text, as this material is limited to a few motifs such as the Oedipus complex that are everywhere and always the same. This is, of course, a gross reduction and vulgariza-tion of Freudian theory. A complicated evolution of object relations and a complex process of psychic differentiation precede the oedipal phase, and the Oedipus complex itself is by no means the monolith it appears to be in the popular understanding of Freudian theory; on the contrary, it is a nexus of identifications and object relations that takes a number of forms and is capable of infinite ramifications.

Moreover, simply to say that a work contains traces of the Oedipus complex or some other motif is one thing; to demonstrate convincingly the effects of unconscious mate-rial and the complicated details of its interaction with other

elements of the text is another. In any case, the psychoanalytic critic does not claim that the work of literature has
only an unconscious meaning: Freud tells us that "all
genuinely creative writings are the product of more than a
single motive and more than a single impulse in the poet's
mind, and are open to more than a single interpretation."[5]
That is to say that the work is "overdetermined": it is a
highly condensed precipitate of mental life in which the
complex and shifting forces of unconscious, preconscious,
and conscious processes have come together in a single expression, investing an image of the world with the energies
and wishes of the deepest and oldest layers of mental life.

It is sometimes argued that there can be no unconscious
elements in a successful work, that the measure of the artist's success is his ability to bring every part of the work
under conscious control. This idea of art, however, is excessively rational, and entirely at variance with the richly
irregular texture of some of the greatest works. There are
not many tidy masterpieces.

One of the most convincing theorists of conscious selec-
tion and craft in literary creation is Henry James. In the
preface to *Portrait of a Lady*, James speaks of the "process of
logical accretion" required by his subject: "consciously, that
was what one was in for—for positively organizing an
ado."[6] He emphasizes "technical rigor"; the novel becomes
a "neat and careful and proportioned pile of bricks . . . a
structure reared with an 'architectural' competence."[7] But
these metaphors of organization and accretion, of bricks
and architecture, tell only a part of the story of creation. In
"The Art of Fiction" James writes of the intuitive and irrational capacity that no logic can manufacture and that
evokes an entirely different sort of image. The artist's experience is identified with "sensibility, a kind of huge
spiderweb of the finest silken threads suspended in the
chamber of consciousness"; it "converts the very pulses of
the air into revelations."[8] Those who think of the novel as
"a factitious, artificial form, a product of ingenuity," miss

the point: the novelist must catch "the very note and trick, the strange irregular rhythm of life."[9]

Writers often admit that they do not know the full meaning of their own productions, and that patterns of which they were unaware during the writing have emerged in the work itself. Conscious efforts to evoke and manipulate the unconscious in art have not succeeded very well. The experiments of the Surrealists with free association and automatic writing remind one of Owen Glendower's boast in *Henry IV* that he can "call spirits from the vasty deep." Hotspur replies, "Why, so can I, or so can any man; But will they come when you do call for them?" The self-proclaimed "unconscious" effects of the Surrealists usually seem brittle and contrived, as opposed to the dimly perceived but true and profound unconscious order of works in which spontaneity has been less vigorously courted.

Critics who acknowledge the possibility of unconscious influence in literature are generally more receptive to Jung than to Freud. In the mythic archetypes of the Jungian unconscious, primitive psychic experience has already undergone considerable transformation in the direction of aesthetic beauty; these impressive archetypes do not, therefore, disturb our preconceptions about art with anything like the force of the Freudian unconscious.

In Jung's system, the unconscious is split into two parts— the rather insignificant "personal unconscious," whose content derives from the life experience of the individual, and the "collective unconscious." Significant unconscious imagery, wherever it appears—in dreams, art, or psychic disorders—originates in the "collective unconscious," which contains the archetypes, primordial images that recur in all times and cultures and that are somehow transmitted by inheritance.[10] Jung believes that certain powerful imagery refers to figures of which no one could have had actual personal experience. For instance, in "Psychological Aspects of the Mother Archetype," he writes,

The contents of the child's abnormal fantasies can be referred to the personal mother only in part, since they often contain . . . allusions which could not possibly have reference to human beings . . . as . . . in infantile phobias where the mother may appear as a wild beast, a witch, a specter, an ogre, a hermaphrodite, and so on.[11]

The assertions in this passage show the peculiar literal-mindedness that often accompanies a penchant for the transcendental. It is evidently difficult for Jung to understand the power and agility of fantasy, particularly in childhood, its capacity to make metaphors by attributing to one creature the identity of another on the basis of a shared characteristic, such as cruelty.[12] Jung's treatment of these frightening images serves to remove from the unconscious of Freudian theory much of the pain and shame of childhood, with its terror of rejection and its sexual interests and fears, which in Jung's theory are cut off from their sources in individual experience and projected into a communal store of mythic archetypes.

Dreams, in Jung's system, come from the collective unconscious, or even directly from God. There are *"somnia a Deo missa* (dreams sent by God) . . . which cannot be traced back to any external causes."[13] There is no difference between the manifest dream and the latent dream-thoughts: "The 'manifest' dream-picture is the dream itself and contains the whole meaning of the dream."[14] Thus it is not necessary to interpret the distortions of unconscious content.

Great literature too is an expression of the collective unconscious. The work of the artist evidently bears no relation to his personal experience: "the work of art . . . has its source not in the *personal unconscious* of the poet, but in a sphere of unconscious mythology whose primordial images are the common heritage of mankind."[15]

In all of this, as Edward Glover points out in *Freud or*

Jung?, Jung makes the assumption that the unconscious can be expressed and apprehended directly. But the unconscious is a kind of *Ding an sich* that can never appear in unmodified form once the psychic structure is sufficiently organized to permit even rudimentary verbal expression. In art, dreams, neurosis, and even psychosis, we do not see the unconscious itself, but rather compromise formations between unconscious and conscious processes.[16] Jung abolishes the distinction between consciousness and the unconscious, and with it Freud's complex theories of mental structure and function, while at the same time using and confusing Freudian terminology. Essentially, Jung has backed off from the Freudian conception of the dynamic unconscious and reinstated the earlier view of mental life as coextensive with consciousness. Psychic phenomena whose origins cannot be discovered in consciousness are attributed to divine intervention—for example, the *"somnia a Deo missa"*—or to an autonomous world of spirit that is somehow transmitted by inheritance.

Jung's simplified theory of dreams and art offers little of value to the critic. As there is no distortion or concealment, no complex interaction of conscious and unconscious process nor of external circumstance and internal motive, so no interpretive method is required. All one need do is learn to recognize the archetypes.[17]

But some attention to Jung's views can be instructive, because the nature of his reaction against Freudian theory tells us something of the underlying attitudes that lead many people to reject the application of psychoanalysis to art. In "On the Relation of Analytical Psychology to Poetry," Jung says of Freudian analyses of literature, "we may occasionally be surprised by indiscreet references to things which a rather more delicate touch might have passed over if only for reasons of tact."[18] He refers to the "muddy" tributaries of the personal unconscious, and to the "purgative methods" of Freud;[19] "this kind of analysis . . . strives like a mole to bury itself in the dirt."[20] The im-

agery of dirt recurs incessantly in Jung's attacks on Freud
and the Freudian unconscious. In "The Spiritual Problem
of Modern Man" he writes,

> Freud . . . has taken the greatest pains to throw as glar-
> ing a light as possible on the dirt and darkness and evil
> of the psychic background, and to interpret it in such a
> way as to make us lose all desire to look for anything
> behind it except refuse and smut. He did not succeed,
> and his attempt at deterrence has even brought about
> the exact opposite—an admiration for all this filth.[21]

This conspicuous repetition of scatological images suggests that Jung's wish to spiritualize the unconscious and to
sever it from personal experience comes at least in part
from his dislike of the connection between the "personal
unconscious" and the body, the functions of the body, and
especially the body's dirt. This aversion, usually based in
repression of infantile pleasures, is one of the sources of
the alienation from the self and from the body that is called
neurosis. It implies a failure to accept and understand the
mixed nature of human experience, and to the extent that
we share this failure, it may lead us to turn away as well
from the fullness and complexity of the artistic experience,
because we fear to meet there the very aspects of ourselves
that we have rejected. But in trying to sever the life of the
body from the works of the spirit, we may find that body
and soul are not so easily separated. Like Aylmer in
Hawthorne's "The Birthmark," we may discover that in
removing the stain of animality we have killed the living
being.

In Freud's view, artistic activity is, among other things, a
form of sublimation. In sublimation, a part of the original
energy and pleasure invested by the child in bodily functions such as nutrition and excretion and in sexual and aggressive wishes is gradually modified and rechanneled into
socially valuable activities. The highest achievements of

culture are rooted in this human capacity for sublimation. However, for all that is gained in the process of sublimation, something of the primitive pleasure of the original activity is lost; perhaps no sublimated activity ever entirely gratifies the original impulse from which it derives.[22] Thus the "higher" activities of culture must always retain at least a part of their connection with older and more primitive ones. As a form of sublimation, literature may be particularly volatile, particularly likely to remain in touch with its earliest sources and to reveal at times their nature, because the medium of literature is language, and language involves bringing experience to consciousness in a way that music or painting or sculpture need not. Mnemosyne, goddess of memory, was the mother of the muses, suggesting that the Greeks understood that art is in part an achievement of memory, a recovery of the lost experience of the past. It is just in his intense remembering that the writer may find again those infantile sources of pleasure in which creativity is rooted. Thus the literary sublimation is a perilous one; it strains the long arc that both separates and connects the original activity and its later transformations. For this reason, literature has always a subversive aspect. While creating and affirming the highest values of culture, it is at the same time forever threatening to subvert those values, to overthrow them in favor of the primitive pleasures they have supplanted. Apollo is always about to draw off his Attic mask and reveal the ambiguous smile of Dionysos.

Psychoanalysis helps us to understand the tension of this dialectic within which creation takes place, by reminding us that literature is rooted in the gut and the genitals as well as in the brain, in the infantile and regressive aspects of psychic function as well as in the maturely integrated ego, in delusion and dream as well as in history, reality, and rationality. In refusing to wall off a separate place for art and spirit, psychoanalysis insists on the continuity of all human experience. (Continuity, of course, does not mean equiva-

lence or identity.) In this insistence that nothing human
be regarded as alien, psychoanalytic method is bound to
offend the squeamish. But in tracing the connections
between literary art and primitive physical and psychic
functions, and in suggesting that we may understand the
literary text more fully by studying the expression of
unconscious meaning in dreams, fantasies, and symptoms,
psychoanalytic criticism does not demean the literary work.
On the contrary, psychoanalysis enlarges and enriches the
significance of literature by discovering, scrawled on the
walls of the darkest and inmost caves of the mind, the prehistoric images and scripts that are the rudiments of art,
and that implicate it absolutely in all human life.

III. REPRESSION, THE UNCONSCIOUS, AND THE STRUCTURE OF THE LITERARY WORK

Psychoanalysis begins from the premise that the outward
shape and the explicit content of an expressive "text"—
dream, symptom, or work of literature—do not exhaust its
significance. Most literary criticism is based on the same
assumption—that the text has a meaning that cannot be
communicated directly, that must be evoked obliquely
through imitation, symbol, allusion, and all the devices and
stratagems of literature. Thus the "meaning" or "significance" of a metaphor is not the first term, nor the second
term, nor a simple equivalence between them, but some
third thing that rises out of their conjunction and that cannot quite be named in discursive language. The French
psychoanalyst Jacques Lacan says that literature "stages the
missing object of desire." Like other kinds of textual
analysis, psychoanalytic criticism looks for repeated motifs
of language, character, action, and theme—the whole web
of relations in whose deep internal congruence the "miss-

ing object" is somehow represented. For the psychoanalytic critic, these motifs have, in addition to their other meanings, significant referents in unconscious and infantile experience.

Although the unconscious embodies the most archaic aspects of mental life, it is still a living entity: "These are paths which have been laid down once and for all, which never fall into disuse."[1] The unconscious plays a particularly important part in certain mental formations such as wit, dreams, and neurotic symptoms. In such productions, preconscious ideas associated with recent experience are elaborated in the unconscious, where they undergo the effects of condensation and displacement and attract to themselves wishes originating in childhood. Something similar happens in literary creation:

> A strong experience in the present awakens in the creative writer a memory of an earlier experience (usually belonging to his childhood) from which there now proceeds a wish which finds its fulfilment in the creative work. The work itself exhibits elements of the recent provoking occasion as well as of the old memory.[2]

The path by which the unconscious wish finds its way into literature is fantasy, the mode of mental activity free from reality-testing and thus under the sway of the pleasure principle. Our daydreams, most of them obvious gratifications of erotic and ambitious wishes, are in general a far cry from literary creation, which must at least disguise the egotistical character of the fantasy and appropriate a far larger portion of external reality. However, certain "fantastic" stories are very close to the fantasies of children and adults in their freedom from the strictures of reality or their obviously wish-fulfilling character. But the role of fantasy in literature is not confined to such productions: fantasy is the radical source of all fictional creation, of the most massive and detailed realism as well as of literature

dominated by mythic and romantic elements. We do not
know exactly how fantasy works to accommodate and
transform the real world in either case, but it is imagination
and invention that support, unify, and animate all the
dense social and historical detail of the great realists. The
Petersburg of Dostoevsky, the London of Dickens, the
Paris of Balzac and Zola, and the English villages of Jane
Austen exist for us not only as places experienced in real
time and space but also as dream-landscapes invented by
desire and fantasy.

Conscious fantasies, in life or in literature, do not, of
course, issue straight from the unconscious; they are derivatives whose peculiarities, like those of dreams, put us
on the track of the unconscious. However, there are also
unconscious fantasies, which can never enter consciousness
because they are too deeply implicated in repressed material. Their content must be inferred, as Freud inferred the
nature of the unconscious fantasies represented in hysterical attacks.[3] The influence of such material makes itself felt
in a work of literature through fragments of character,
event, imagery, and idea, all of which seem marked with
the same distinctive sign. No one of these fragments could
be interpreted singly; but together they may form a pattern suggesting a connective tissue of unconscious fantasy.

Unlike Jung, Freud assumed that the unconscious appears only in derivative forms, and that the work of art
contains not only the unconscious wish but its negation or
expiation as well. The expiation or disguise itself, however,
often betrays the forbidden wish. Freud says of the modifi-
cations of dreams by the ego, "They are associatively linked
to the material which they replace, and serve to show us the
way to that material, which may in its turn be a substitute
for something else."[4] Thus there is a kind of continuum of
repressing and repressed material along which conscious
ideas can be traced backward through successive distortions into the unconscious. Moreover, the work of repres-

sion requires energy: the very force with which an idea is repudiated in consciousness suggests the power of the rejected impulse. Repression, then, does not annihilate the influence of the repressed idea, but on the contrary increases it, forcing the idea into manifold derivatives and substitutes and endowing them with the power of repressed instinctual energy. Freud writes, "the instinctual representative develops with less interference and more profusely if it is withdrawn by repression from conscious influence. It proliferates in the dark, as it were, and takes on extreme forms of expression."[5]

The structure and the internal coherence of the literary work take shape out of this "proliferation in the dark" of repressed material, whose drive toward expression creates chains of linked derivatives. The rich ambiguity of the great work, the multiple and overlapping configurations of its meaning, is produced by a network of associations radiating outward from each of its elements to many others, forming a web of internal relationships of immense complexity. The multiple determinants and associations of each element, their protean variety and idiosyncratic form, show the effects of the primary process, of the condensation and displacement that shape and elaborate repressed material. This repressed unconscious dimension is structured not at random, but according to a complex order fundamental to the structure of the work itself.

Psychoanalysis, like structuralism and certain other modern conceptions of language, art, and society, is a holistic theory: that is, it assumes that the object to be interpreted, whether a work of art, a dream, or an analytic session, has an order of which every element, however small, is an integral part. Everything is "determined," nothing is free, in the sense that no element is random or without its place in the configuration that makes up the structure of the whole. Freud writes, "we have accepted it as being just as important to interpret the smallest, least conspicuous and most uncertain constituents of the content of

dreams as those that are most clearly and certainly preserved."[6] This assumption regarding the meaningfulness
of every detail and the unconscious order of the whole is
especially useful in dealing with works that we know to be
great, yet that tend to elude criticism because of their surface irregularities, their apparent discontinuity and disorder.

In writing of Tolstoy and Dostoevsky, Henry James recognized their greatness and yet spoke of their novels as
"baggy monsters" and "fluid puddings," because he could
not find in them the controlled structure and the unified
surface he valued. In Dostoevsky's novels especially, one
tends to be overwhelmed by the unpredictability of the
narrative, the wild vitality of the characters, and the
luxuriant proliferation of subplots; yet somehow the novel
is experienced as a whole, although the principles of unity
may be difficult to identify consciously. It is just in the rich,
bizarre details of subplots and secondary characters, often
somewhat inaccessible to criticism, that the texture and atmosphere of the novel exist. If we can identify in these aspects of the text the derivative forms into which unconscious conflict and fantasy have been forced by repression,
we can begin to discover the unconscious structure of the
whole.[7]

In its emphasis on the organic quality of the literary
work, psychoanalytic method is not unlike James's theories
of organic form; but in his assumptions about the unconscious aspects of creation, the psychoanalytic critic is even
more deeply committed to the idea of the organically determined unity of the whole. In this connection it is interesting to consider James's comments in his prefaces about
his use of a device he called the "ficelle." The ficelle is a
character such as Henrietta Stackpole or Maria Gostrey
who is not an integral part of the original conception of the
novel, but an aid to exposition or general liveliness added
on to that central conception, and only made to appear
part of it by the novelist's skill. The psychoanalytic critic

cannot accept James's utilitarian explanation of these figures. Purely arbitrary creation of this kind is simply not possible: these characters, like others, grow out of the psychic configuration that governs the work, and are inevitably related to it. While James argues that the novel should *appear* to be governed entirely by internal necessity, the psychoanalytic critic would maintain that in fact it *is*.

James introduces here a distinction between content and form: "as certain elements in any work are of the essence, so others are only of the form; . . . as this or that character, this or that disposition of the material, belongs to the subject directly, so to speak, so this or that other belongs to it but indirectly—belongs intimately to the treatment."[8] This process of "treatment"—the elaboration of the central conception, the establishment of coherence in its structure, and the creation of an air of authenticity, or "solidity of specification," in the representation of reality—is analogous to secondary revision in dreams, and is carried out by the same faculty—the preconscious thinking that fulfills the demands of the ego.

> Our waking (preconscious) thinking behaves towards any perceptual material with which it meets in just the same way in which [secondary revision] behaves towards the content of dreams. It is the nature of our waking thought to establish order in material of that kind, to set up relations in it and to make it conform to our expectations of an intelligible whole.[9]

In sleep the influence of the ego is much diminished, and so primary process thinking escapes the control of secondary revision to produce the chaotic and illogical effects of most dreams. In literary creation the preconscious thought of the ego contributes a much larger share, although the balance and relationship of the two modes of thought vary with the individual artist. In a writer of James's type, the ego appears to exercise a high degree of control over unconscious material through secondary elaboration. However, there is finally no real discontinuity between "essence" and "form," "subject" and "treatment"; the treatment derives organically from the subject of the novel as the secondary revision derives from the dream-thoughts.

The form of the dream also represents aspects of the dream-thoughts; the arrangement of images or ideas expresses a logical or syntactical connection between them. "Two thoughts which occur in immediate sequence without any apparent connection are in fact part of a single unity which has to be discovered; in just the same way, if I write an 'a' and a 'b' in succession, they have to be pronounced as a single syllable 'ab'."[10] The form and structure of the literary text, as of the dream text, are part of the language of its unconscious meaning: the juxtaposition of scenes and their internal structure, the arrangement of the narrative, and the rhythm of rising and falling tension in the plot are larger aspects of the unconscious structure also contained in the fine texture of imagery and language.

One significant difference between dream interpretation and the interpretation of literature should be noted: in working with a patient's dream, the psychoanalyst is ultimately interested not in the manifest dream itself, but in the dreamer's associations, the latent thoughts that lead to the unconscious. Thus the dream is only the point of departure for an exploration of mental content that may lead far afield.[11] The critic who interprets a literary text, on the other hand, is interested in the text itself. In the terminology of dream interpretation, the text contains both manifest and latent content; it is both the point of departure and the goal of interpretation. Those skeptical of the psychoanalytic approach argue that the critic cannot arrive at the unconscious meaning of the work because he cannot ask the author for his associations. But even if one could get the author's associations, they would lead mostly to an understanding not of the work, but of its place in the author's life. The best source of knowledge about the text is the text itself. Historical and social background, biographical information, theory and methodology are useful primarily as they help the critic to read the text more accurately, to understand more fully its internal structure. The most significant associations to any part of the text—a dream, a character, a scene—are not in the author's life, but in other parts of the text, which is in this crucial sense a self-enclosed system of relevant associations.

In a novel, a body of psychological material is reworked and elaborated in a variety of contexts. The novel can embody in disguised form the principal elements of a psychological conflict, including its genesis, its elaboration in defenses and secondary derivatives, and its resolution. This conflict is expressed and objectified everywhere in the work. Thus when we speak of an oedipal theme in a novel, or a tendency to passivity or sadism or whatever, we refer to a psychic configuration contained in the work as a whole and expressed in a variety of ways, sometimes in character and plot, but also in other aspects of the text, such as its presentation of social and religious ideas or its structural patterns.

The subject of "character" presents special problems. Characters must sometimes be considered "realistically," as representations of real persons, with all the internal complexity the author has observed in human personality. However, characters also function as symbols, vehicles for the shifting forces of psychic life. Freud writes, "The psychological novel in general no doubt owes its special nature to the inclination of the modern writer to split up his ego, by self-observation, into many part-egos, and in consequence, to personify the conflicting currents of his own mental life in several heroes."[12] A character may embody a single component of a complex psychic conflict; the working out of internal psychological conflict is then represented dramatically in the relationships among characters.

Thus the work itself may be said to have an unconscious,

which influences every aspect of its form and content. The
problem raised by this formulation, a difficulty on which
many attempts at psychoanalytic criticism founder, is the
relationship of the unconscious dimension of the text to
the unconscious mind of the author. The work, after all,
was written by someone, and the conflicts it embodies are
ultimately derived from the psychic life of the writer. The
question here is one of emphasis: what use do we make of
this obvious fact in explicating the text? Most psychoanalytic studies, by relying on the author's life to explain the
text, end up in fact using the text to explain the life.[13] The
work of literature is subordinated to the biography, becoming simply another part of it, like a love affair or an illness.
But whatever personal conflicts the work has come out of,
if it succeeds as art it objectifies those conflicts. And therefore it should, by and large, explain itself; its most important references are internal.

There is no question here of pretending that we know
nothing of the personal and historical setting of the
text. Literature does not grow up in a void. But in literary
criticism, the text has priority over the life. Biographical
material should be used, therefore, not to arrive at an interpretation, but only to support and confirm what is first
discovered in the work itself. And although the configuration of unconscious meaning in the text is derived from the
unconscious psychic life of the author, it is not necessarily
co-extensive or identical with it. The same writer may
dramatize different aspects of his mental life in other
works, or may achieve different resolutions of conflict.
Thus the unconscious dimension of the novel cannot be
entirely identified either with tendencies in a character that
in a real person would be unconscious or with the author's
unconscious.

The unconscious configuration in the work is the form
of the work as it is experienced emotionally—a complex
internal system of correspondences, oppositions, and tensions that operates dynamically through the manipulation

of the reader's attention and feeling. In writing of the contribution psychoanalysis might make to criticism, Kenneth Burke says, "The motive of the work is equated with the structure of interrelationships within the work itself"; and "A statement about the ingredients of the work's motivation would thus be identical with a statement about the work's structure—a statement as to what goes with what in the work itself."[14] Burke argues for a "distributive" or "proportional" as opposed to an "essentializing" strategy. In the proportional strategy, derived from free association, the critic bases interpretations on images as they appear in the multiplicity and complexity of their contexts. The essentializing strategy is the attempt to arrive at a single unconscious essence in the work through the interpretation of symbols. It seems that the ideal strategy might be both proportional and essentializing: proportional insofar as the effects of the unconscious are traced into every corner of the text and their relative pressures assessed; but also essentializing, because in the coherent work the unconscious lines of force tend to converge, not necessarily in a single "essential" meaning, but nonetheless at crucial points that form a pattern of related desires, conflicts, and fantasies associated with significant motifs of unconscious mental life.

Opponents of psychoanalytic criticism argue that it can be used to unearth unconscious materials in inferior productions as well as in great ones, and so provides no criterion of literary value. The same reproach, of course, could be leveled at any critical method, a fact known to anyone who has ever read a meticulous explication in New Critical style of a Tolkien novel or a song by the Beatles, demonstrating that they are as full of themes and symbols, of ambiguity, irony, and paradox, as *Hamlet*. Criticism is ultimately more an art than a science, and no system can replace intelligence and sensitivity in making judgments of value.

Nonetheless, it is possible to suggest in psychoanalytic terms some of the differences between great works and trivial or mediocre ones. All literature probably contains wish-fulfilling fantasies and other evidence of unconscious influence. But these wishes and fantasies are of a different sort, or are treated differently, in the inferior work. The wish for success or love may be of a kind perfectly acceptable to the ego, so that its gratification is achieved after overcoming only enough conflict to create some interest, but no serious guilt. However, in certain kinds of popular literature such as the modern Gothic romance or the crime story, incestuous and sadomasochistic fantasies are the stock in trade. The paradox of these books is that they present forbidden fantasies rather openly, and yet because the material is contained within ritualized literary-cultural conventions, and manipulated in a superficial and mechanical way, without much relation to reality or any sense of the ambiguity of lived experience, the nature of the fantasy is concealed from the naïve reader, and probably provokes little or no anxiety even in the more sophisticated reader. One is permitted to enjoy in fantasy the gratification of forbidden wishes while paying little or nothing in conflict and guilt.[15] In the great works, the forbidden wish is disguised, and yet its threatening reality is deeply felt; the reader is somehow aware of its dubious nature, and of the price its fulfillment would exact.

Much popular writing, or writing that seems to come from a relatively superficial layer of personality, is characterized by a pleasing, willy-nilly wish-fulfillment, a lack of psychological coherence, and the facile resolution of conflict. Great literature, on the other hand, generally seems to come out of intense psychological experience, a descent into the deepest sources of recollection and inspiration. The excitement and suffering usually associated with genuine creation suggest that in this process the writer must encounter repressed material, which threatens to emerge into consciousness in forms that are repellent or frightening. The repressed material comes into conflict again with the repressing tendencies and is then forced into a number of derivative forms that create the psychological density and coherence of the work. To retain its original truth and yet be acceptable in consciousness, dangerous material must be reworked by the unconscious and preconscious ego. It is modified and made to fit into a structural and expressive pattern within which it achieves some degree of moral and aesthetic harmony. The work must meet the id demand for gratification, the ego demand for organization and synthesis, and the superego demand for punishment and expiation of forbidden wishes. In genuine creation the entire personality is powerfully mobilized, and this intrapsychic tension is felt in the work itself. Comic works generally arouse less anxiety, and achieve a positive resolution of conflict without much damage being done; yet even in the comic work of a serious kind, harmony is at least temporarily disrupted by dangerous erotic and aggressive elements.[16] Moreover, in all serious literature the psychological conflict tends to appropriate a broader range of experience than in inferior writing and to be worked out upon materials of greater moral and intellectual interest.

It is difficult to define exactly the grounds for any judgment of aesthetic value, and psychological criteria alone are not sufficient. But it is wrong to suggest that psychoanalytic method can make no discriminations of this kind, or that it must reach the same conclusions about every object to which it is applied.

The most ambitious recent attempt to work out a complete psychoanalytic poetics is Norman Holland's *The Dynamics of Literary Response*. Holland's theory is based on a simple conflict-defense model illustrated with charts and diagrams. The work of literature is seen as originating in a single unconscious fantasy that is equated with "content"; defense against this unconscious fantasy is supplied by form and meaning.

> Defense, in a literary work, takes one of two general
> modes: meaning or form. Typically, the unconscious
> fantasy at the core of a work will combine elements
> that could, if provided full expression, give us pleas-
> ure, but also create anxiety. It is the task of the literary
> "work" to control the anxiety and permit at least par-
> tial gratification of the pleasurable possibilities in the
> fantasy. The literary work, through what we have
> loosely termed "form," acts out defensive maneuvers
> for us. . . . Meaning, whether we find it or supply it,
> acts more like a sublimation: giving the fantasy mate-
> rial a disguised expression which is acceptable to the
> ego, which "makes sense."[17]

While this statement is to some degree accurate, its attractive clarity, with its promise of sudden easy access to the
inner workings of literature, invites oversimplification. All
the critic has to do, it seems, is to run a novel or poem
through this formulation and its mysteries will be revealed.

Unconscious content is seen here as separate from form
and meaning, indeed from virtually everything we ap-
prehend consciously in the work. In fact, Holland carries
this disjunction even further: "We have not one 'content,'
but two. An unconscious content—a wishful or anxious
fantasy—becomes transformed into intellectual content—
an idea that the literary work is 'about.' "[18] Unconscious
content has a logical and chronological priority over conscious meaning in Holland's discussions; it is in some way
the real thing, while form and meaning serve to "manage"
it.

The result of Holland's method can be seen in his interpretations of specific texts. Macbeth's "Tomorrow, and
tomorrow" speech is interpreted as a disguised representation of a sexual scene: " 'Out, out, brief candle,' becomes
ambiguous if we consider possible phallic symbolism: it
may be a command to withdraw the penis concealed in the
sexual act or detumescent after."[19] The fact that the speech
contains none of the excitement associated with such a

scene, but rather a deathly weariness, is attributed to the formal "management" of the fantasy, by which it is transformed into something "reassuringly peaceful." But as neither the explicit meaning nor the emotional effect of these lines shows any sign of the original fantasy, there is no reason to believe it is there at all. Most of Holland's interpretations seem to bear no relation to anyone's actual experience of a text, but are arrived at rather by the purely intellectual attribution of symbolic equivalences, such as that between candle and penis. In Holland's readings, the conscious meaning of the text is simply removed, like a shell. The real meaning is then revealed to be something that has no connection with the explicit content of the work or the interests it arouses in the reader. A good psychoanalytic reading, however, ought to demonstrate a continuity and dialectical tension between what is apparent and what is hidden, to show how the lines of meaning lead back and forth across the frontier of consciousness, so that the explicit meaning of the text is enriched rather than diminished by the understanding of unconscious elements.

Holland's diagrams and formulas seem to guarantee the scientific objectivity of the psychoanalytic study of the text, to protect the critic against the charge that his conclusions may be only the projections of his own psychic conflicts. Unfortunately, this charge cannot be entirely disproved; there is a subjective element in all criticism, and the kinds of experience with which both literature and psychoanalysis deal are simply not susceptible of the scientific verification that produces universally acceptable proofs. No two interpreters will arrive at exactly the same reading of any text. The business of the critic, however, is not proof, but exploration, demonstration, interpretation, persuasion.

Psychoanalysis does provide us with a method: it is based primarily on Freud's approach to the dream, where meaning is explored through both the recurring features of the dreamer's associations and the interpretation of symbols, those representations that occur in dreams, language, and literature so frequently in conjunction with certain meanings that they may reasonably suggest those meanings to the critic. Freud, however, was cautious in his use of the symbolic method:

> many of the symbols are habitually or almost habitually employed to express the same thing. Nevertheless, the peculiar plasticity of the psychical material . . . must never be forgotten. Often enough a symbol has to be interpreted in its proper meaning and not symbolically; while on other occasions a dreamer may derive from his private memories the power to employ as sexual symbols all kinds of things which are not ordinarily employed as such. . . . They [symbols] frequently have more than one or even several meanings, and, as with Chinese script, the correct interpretation can only be arrived at on each occasion from the context.[20]

This is to say that a candle may represent a penis, or a number of other things—even a candle—depending on the context in which it appears.

The fault of interpretations such as Holland's reading of *Macbeth* is to depend on a rather mechanical translation of symbols, without sufficient attention to context. The criterion of validity in interpretation must be redundancy: a single object or action may suggest a meaning, but that meaning can only be confirmed as it is repeated and supported by the entire surrounding configuration.

Criticism cannot be done by formula and chart. Frederick Crews writes,

> literature registers and arouses conflict, and . . . no theoretical preparation can spare a critic the necessity of submitting himself to that conflict. Norman Holland would . . . agree with this statement, yet in practice he empties psychic defenses of their shame and anxiety and treats them much like the formal devices of rhetoric.[21]

Crews goes on to quote Nietzsche: "The charm of knowledge would be small were it not that so much shame has to be overcome on the way to it."[22]

Although theory helps the critic articulate his response to the text, his interpretation derives ultimately from the same source as the response of the common reader: emotional involvement rooted in the unconscious. Freud writes that the artist tries "to awaken in us the same emotional attitude, the same mental constellation as that which in him produced the impetus to create."[23] In the artist the direction of communication is primarily "upward," from the id to the ego, from the unconscious to consciousness. The reader undergoes the same shifts in levels of psychic function, but roughly in reverse order. There is a conscious ego response to the work, with preconscious elaboration and perception of ambiguities, which in turn set up unconscious reverberations in the id.[24] Under the influence of the "suspension of disbelief" induced by the work, the reader is freed to some extent from the reality-testing of the ego. Attention is withdrawn from external reality and the reader is pulled into the work, where he is able to experience even things that in life would seem unlikely or impossible as deeply true, exciting, and moving. In short, the work induces a kind of regression: the secondary process of the ego to some extent gives way to primary process thinking of the sort that predominates in dream and daydream. The work stimulates a stream of images, fantasies, and associations through which it becomes identified with repressed material in the reader's own unconscious.

This identification may be partly determined by some resemblance, perceived or desired, between hero or heroine and reader, so that the protagonist's adventures become a wish-fulfilling fantasy, an extension of one's own life. But this is only the most superficial level of identification, more prominent in casual reading that offers obvious pleasures of escape and vicarious gratification. In the fullest and deepest literary experience, the reader does not simply ride through the work on the back of a favorite character, experiencing the character's problems as if they were his own; rather, he identifies with the work by experiencing the psychic conflicts it objectifies. The characters, although they may resemble real persons, are also elements in those conflicts, embodying the dynamic forces of mental life. The unconscious conflicts represented symbolically in great literature are of such magnitude and depth that they reach a virtually universal layer of the psychic substratum. Fantasies at this level are bisexual and "polymorphous perverse," involving in both sexes erotic and aggressive feelings toward both parents, active and passive wishes, and fears of genital injury. Oedipal feelings shade off into more primitive pre-oedipal fantasies and fears, including those of primary fusion, which involve the wish to incorporate or be incorporated by the mother's body. The protean and primitive quality of the fantasies of this layer of mental life offers the broadest possibilities for identification; thus the conflicts experienced by a male reader can be re-lived through a female protagonist and vice-versa. The specific unconscious memories or fantasies evoked by the work will vary among individuals: what is important is not the exact resemblance of the experience presented in the work to that of the reader, but rather its dynamic effectiveness—its power to stimulate intrapsychic activity and primary process thinking.[25]

In their essay on aesthetic ambiguity, Ernst Kris and Abraham Kaplan write that the literary symbol functions aesthetically only when it evokes the primary process.[26] Thus the "meaning" of a symbol, and by extension of a work of literature, is not a fixed entity but a process, a dynamic tension between unconscious ideation and fantasy and conscious thought. It is the ambiguity of symbols, and ultimately of language itself, that gives to literature its power to mobilize the psychic structure, to engage our conscious, rational, intellectual interests and at the same time the faculties and energies of the dreaming mind. Thus the world evoked in the great work remains, long after its own time and place, the image of our own deepest life.

IV. THE AMBIGUITY
OF LANGUAGE

Freud writes, "Words, since they are the nodal points of numerous ideas, may be regarded as predestined to ambiguity."[1] The ambiguity of words makes possible the richness and density of meanings in literature: it is within that ambiguity that the transformations from image to idea, from primary to secondary process, from unconscious fantasy to conscious meaning take place. The word is a crossroads at which the paths of conscious and unconscious meaning converge. It is also the place where literature and psychoanalysis meet, in their common concern with language as the vehicle of psychic experience. Anna O., Breuer's gifted hysterical patient, called psychoanalysis "the talking cure": while the patient talks the analyst listens, knowing that "words are the nodal points of numerous ideas," and therefore the patient's words must have a meaning of which he is not aware. In their ambiguity, words open channels to the unconscious; and it is through this aspect of language that unconscious meaning is preserved and transformed in literature.

A large part of Freud's writing on all subjects is devoted to linguistic and philological analyses. And the role of language is implicit in Freud's conception of the psychic systems and of the passage of psychic material from the unconscious to consciousness, beginning with his earliest work.[2] Probably the largest amount of material on language is contained in *The Interpretation of Dreams*. Language plays a crucial part in the construction of the dream:

We may suppose that a good part of the intermediate work done during the formation of a dream, which seeks to reduce the dispersed dream-thoughts to the most succinct and unified expression possible, proceeds along the line of finding appropriate verbal transformations for the individual thoughts. Any one thought, whose form of expression may happen to be fixed for other reasons, will operate in a determinant and selective manner on the possible forms of expression allotted to the other thoughts, and it may do so, perhaps, from the very start—as is the case in writing a poem.[3]

The form of the dream is determined in part by the words in which the dream-thoughts may be expressed; these words evoke other words with their associated meanings, and so the dream, like the poem, is to some extent a sort of verbal chain generated by the properties of language. The images of the manifest dream are often the translation into pictures of these verbal ideas. It is not the dream-images themselves but rather the patient's verbal account of them that leads to the meaning of the dream.[4] In the verbal presentation, some of the elements of the original dream-message may re-emerge in the patient's language, particularly in punning or ambiguous words with which the dream has played in an irrational way. The image in the dream may be determined by the sound, the form, or the derivation of the word rather than by its conventional meaning. The dreaming mind is an etymologist and a punster: it creates visual images out of the dead metaphors and the hidden analogies contained in all language, but especially in jokes, slang, and figures of speech. Thus the dream is often like a rebus, as Freud observes in *The Interpretation*, a verbal puzzle in which each syllable or word must be represented by a picture. The combination of images looks quite meaningless until the pictured objects are named aloud; then the sounds combine into words and phrases whose meaning becomes intelligible.

There are many examples of this kind of dream in *The*

Interpretation of Dreams, but the following passage, taken from a female patient's account of a dream, makes the point in a particularly graphic way:

> Her mother sent her little daughter away, so that she had to go by herself. Then she went in a train with her mother and saw her little one walk straight on to the rails so that she was bound to be run over. . . . Then she looked round out of the window of the railway-carriage to see whether the parts could not be seen behind.[5]

The dreamer was in fact the mother of a small child, but the last sentence quoted above revealed to the analyst an unexpected meaning:

> The façade of the dream would of course lead one to think of the parts of her little daughter who had been run over and mangled. But her association led in quite another direction. She recollected having once seen her father naked in the bathroom from behind; she went on to talk of the distinctions between the sexes, and laid stress on the fact that a man's genitals can be seen even from behind but a woman's cannot. In this connection she herself interpreted "the little one" as meaning the genitals and "her little one" . . . as her own genitals.[6]

There seems to be no clue in the visual imagery of this dream to associate it with a memory of the father's genitals. It is only when one thinks, not of the image, but of the words—"Then she looked round . . . to see whether the parts could not be seen behind"—that the sexual meaning becomes comprehensible. The dream has used the verbal form in which the childhood experience might be described as a bridge to an altogether different image, that of the mother looking round at the parts of her child's mangled body.

The dream of another female patient contains a scene in a garden, where workmen are cutting down branches and throwing them into the road; people are taking the branches, and the dreamer asks whether that is all right, whether she too may take or pull one down.[7] The meaning in this dream involves a play on the sense of the German words for "to pull one down" or "out": *sich einen herunter-reissen* or *ausreissen* have also a second vulgar sense referring to masturbation. The crucial words have been used as a sort of "switch-point" or verbal bridge to cross from the track of the repressed sexual thought contained in the obscene meaning of the phrase to an innocuous visual representation in the dream. When the dream is described verbally, however, the sexual meaning is suggested by the double-entendre. Here it seems that the double meaning must have originated in the actual resemblance between pulling off something like a branch and handling the penis in masturbation; this resemblance is then "fixed" in language through the adoption of the innocuous phrase as a slang expression for masturbation, with the result that the apparently innocent words can easily suggest the second, sexual meaning.

Thus language may be the repository of repressed meanings and memories; by virtue of its ambiguity it often serves as the bridge from those unconscious materials to the more acceptable scenes represented in the dream and recalled in consciousness. A large proportion of these memories are sexual, because the sexual discoveries of childhood tend to be fraught with excitement and shame that must be repressed. The sexual ideas and interests remain active in the unconscious, however; they attach themselves to words, where they achieve partial expression through unconsciously perceived analogies and ambiguities. The capacity of language for this sort of ambiguity is particularly well illustrated by the first dream-example: the words "She looked round . . . to see whether the parts could not be seen behind" offer no special possibilities of punning or double meaning, and yet the unconscious has found a way to exploit this apparently straightforward utterance to express a sexual interest. The words change meaning before our eyes as we become aware of the pressure upon them of repressed and infantile ideas.

In the second example, the ambiguity rests on an analogy between the two actions covered by the crucial expression. The dream-image determined by the ambiguous words has a symbolic aspect; because of certain actual similarities, pulling down branches may represent masturbating. In considering the nature of symbolic relations in general, Freud writes, "Things that are symbolically connected today were probably united in the prehistoric times by conceptual and linguistic identity. The symbolic relation seems to be a relic and mark of former identity."[8] Ernest Jones, in his essay "The Theory of Symbolism,"[9] asserts that the unconscious mind does not discriminate between objects that are in some interesting or significant way alike. In the early stages of the development of perception, things that resemble each other are perceived as identical. A branch or a snake, objects that present some similarities to a penis, are seen as identical with it. This primitive identity, lost to the more discriminating conscious perception of the adult, is preserved in the unconscious, and in the unconscious aspects of language.

Thus the very words used by the adult with the intention of communicating conscious ideas also carry the residues of an earlier mode of contact with the world, a pre-verbal mode in which objects are vividly perceived but not sharply differentiated and individualized. The unconscious "remembers" this earlier vision, and so does language, which preserves these primitive analogies and identifications in etymologies, figures of speech, and so on. Thus the ambiguity of language keeps open the channel to primordial and unconscious meaning even in our most rational and deliberate utterances. The structure and meaning of lan-

guage are in part unconscious, and in speaking and writing
we are often relating a story rather different from the one
in the conscious mind.

The central role of language in psychoanalysis also has to
do with its importance in the development of the ego.
Freud saw the ego as a largely preconscious structure
whose critical features are determined by language and its
derivatives, and which develops in conjunction with language.[10] In the early phases of this development, the child
uses and interprets sounds in primitive ways that are retained as unconscious residues in the complex and highly
differentiated language of the adult. Victor Rosen tries to
reconstruct the stages of the child's acquisition of language
by dividing communicative phenomena into three cate-
gories: signals, signs, and symbols.[11] The earliest infantile
communication is in signals: the cry of hunger is the signal
for the mother's breast. Signs, the next addition to the
communicative repertoire, are based not on spatial or temporal relationship to the referent, but on similarity between the sign and the thing signified. As the child's babbling and gestures become imitative of the parent's speech
and action, signs are added to the signal system. Only when
the sounds the child makes become phonemically organized and when he is able to separate them from the imitative stimulus and attach them consistently to the same referent do words achieve true symbolic status.[12]
In the early stages of psychic organization, visual elements predominate over auditory stimuli, accounting in
part for the sense of greater concreteness and immediacy
in memories of childhood experience and for the preva-
lence of visual imagery in regressive states such as dreaming.[13] As the child masters language, however, the audi-
tory-linguistic mode becomes dominant in the structuring
of psychic experience. Verbal sounds are assigned to referents to which they bear no mimetic or "iconic" relationship: these sounds are symbols, in the linguistic sense, in

that their relationship to the referent is arbitrary and conventional; they do not generally sound or look like the thing they represent. Thus for the sensuous and emotional mode of signals and signs, the child learns to substitute the abstract and arbitrary mode of symbols. The system of communication becomes less immediate, but capable of infinitely greater flexibility and complexity.

As he learns language, the child goes through an idiosyncratic process whereby particular sensations, experiences, and fantasies—phenomena of the signal-sign type—become associated with the word and help him assign to it its conventional meaning.[14] These early associations are retained in the preconscious, giving to the word—the arbitrary symbol—the power to evoke the matrix of infantile sensory and emotional experience in which it was first learned. Freud's theory of consciousness and repression is based in part on the relation of such preconscious memory traces to words. In *The Ego and the Id*, he writes:

> the real difference between a *Ucs.* and a *Pcs.* idea (thought) consists in this: that the former is carried out on some material which remains unknown, whereas the latter (the *Pcs.*) is in addition brought into connection with word-presentations. . . .
>
> These word-presentations are residues of memories; they were at one time perceptions, and like all mnemic residues they can become conscious again.[15]

Repressed ideas have lost their connection with words. The words themselves, however, continue to exist in the preconscious language system, containing memories that can again become conscious. What is necessary, evidently, is that words regain the full meaning they once had, a meaning lost to repression.

Language is a crucial area of differentiation within the psyche: the passage from the unconscious to the preconscious is accomplished through language, and its function is implicit in the transitions from primary to secondary process and from pleasure principle to reality principle.[16] Thus language is a system of mediation and transformation: it is a kind of filter or permeable barrier, with one side facing inward toward the unconscious and the other turned outward toward consciousness. Because of this doubleness—because it is the very medium within which unconscious material is transformed into the verbal symbols of preconscious thought—all language has an unconscious aspect. Words are indeed "predestined to ambiguity."

In literature the double nature of language is the source of the richest expressive possibilities. On one level, the secondary process aspect of language as a system of abstract symbols is made to yield the maximum articulation of conscious meaning under the control of a complex and highly developed ego. The arbitrariness and discreteness of the word permit the "encoding" and the re-presentation of every object, every emotion, virtually every relationship of which thought or feeling is capable, so that the world is transubstantiated and recreated in a symbolic universe of language.[17]

Yet at the same time, because of its special relationship to fantasy, dream, and childhood memory, literature also uses language in a more primitive way, restoring to words the ambiguity, the suggestiveness, the evocative quality of the infantile language of signs and signals. The word is no longer merely the denotative symbol of a fixed referent; in literature we are given back words that sound and feel like the things they stand for, words that evoke sensations, images, and fantasies. Literature returns to language its sensuous and "iconic" qualities; and with this language we are restored to an earlier mode of experience, in which there was no barrier between the word and the thing, between consciousness and the unconscious, between the self and the object. Literature gives us back some sense of the world as we knew it before it was transformed by the development of the ego and the acquisition of language.

In the primary fusion of the oral phase, the mother who appears in answer to the infant's cry of hunger is experienced as a part of himself. In the later imitative babbling, the child also feels a kind of at-oneness, a primitive identification with the parent whose signs he copies. But with the development of symbolic language, the child must perceive the object as separate from himself: the word, the mediatory symbol, comes to stand as both barrier and bridge between himself and the world of objects. With the development of the ego and of language, the child gains more control over external reality: the experience of absence or separation is less total and terrifying. He can believe that things exist—his mother, food, other objects—even when they are not physically present, because he has words for them, and as long as he can manipulate the word, in some sense he retains the object: it will come back. Yet with language, which gives us this mastery over the world, we also lose the world: the brilliant joy and terror of the first unmediated relationships is muffled and diminished.

Art recreates at least the illusion of a fluid and unmediated experience. In the aesthetic response, we relax the ego controls that usually distance and organize reality, and in this partial dissolution of boundaries, we are drawn into the work, or draw it into ourselves.[18] This fusion is perhaps achieved more fully in literature than in any other art. Music may arouse the emotions more directly because of its independence of the mediation of language. But the emotional experience of literature may be even more complete: language, just because of its mediational capacity, can evoke not only undifferentiated emotion but also an almost infinitely wide range of imagery and experience through which emotion is not only expressed but specified and articulated.

Literature is able to accomplish this mediation, paradox-

ically, just because of the abstractness of its medium. In
transmitting factual information, words can seem as hard
and discrete and colorless as little gray pebbles. And yet it is
because of their very neutrality and arbitrariness, their
meaninglessness-in-themselves, that words attract and retain the primary experiences through which they are mastered. In literature, language is saturated with this kind of
experience: the neutral symbols become once again iconic
and mimetic, as they are for the child for whom language is
still rooted in sensation and desire. In literature we have
the impression of seeing through the words to the sensations and images they evoke. Thus language, the organ of
the controlling ego, the most rational, highly articulated,
and explicit medium for the apprehension of experience,
also gives us back the pre-rational world of sensuous images, the brilliant world of childhood. It bridges the gap
between the mind and the world with the very symbols that
created that gap, that first gave us a secondary and abstract
linguistic world for the primary world of objects and sensations. In great literature, language functions to heal the division between ourselves and the world, as well as the division within ourselves between the articulated consciousness
of reason and logic and the unformed but vivid sense of
things and persons as we once knew them, the brilliant archaic world that still lives in dreams and in fragmentary
memories of childhood.

V. LITERATURE AND
PSYCHOPATHOLOGY

In re-creating through language a direct and unmediated
sense of experience, the writer must undergo a kind of
temporary regression, a return to certain primitive modes
of function associated with childhood. This regressive aspect of artistic creation links it with other regressive phe-

nomena such as dreams and symptoms, and brings us back again to fundamental issues on which the psychoanalytic treatment of art has encountered resistance. Two principal questions must finally be considered. One concerns the psychology of the artist and the relationship between creativity and psychopathology. The other involves the nature of the repressed material uncovered in the work itself by psychoanalytic method, material that in the life of a real person would often appear pathological.

Perhaps the first thing to be said with regard to both of these questions is that psychoanalysis provides no fixed norm by which the psychology of the artist or the materials of art may be stigmatized as "abnormal." The whole tendency of Freud's thought is to break down rigid distinctions between the normal and the pathological and to show the basic continuity of all mental processes. In his study of Jensen's *Gradiva* he writes, "the frontier between states of mind described as normal and pathological is in part a conventional one and in part so fluctuating that each of us probably crosses it many times in the course of a day."[1]

However, what we know of the lives of artists suggests that the artist is exposed to special dangers of breakdown of personality. It would be difficult to arrive at any statistics on this subject, and in any case the statistics would not tell us much about the difference between the mental health of the artist and that of the rest of humanity. Deep psychopathology may exist in lives that appear quiet and are lived in relative conformity with prevailing cultural standards. However that may be, it would seem particularly difficult for the artist, especially the literary artist, to deal with internal conflict by means of repression, because his attention during creativity is turned deeply inward and must inevitably revive those conflicts that other persons may be able to keep out of consciousness.

Freud characterizes the specific psychological endowment of the artist as "a strong capacity for sublimation and a certain degree of laxity in the repressions."[2] He suggests the ambiguous nature of the artistic gift, with its risks and compensations, when he writes, "a not inconsiderable increase in psychic efficiency results from a disposition which in itself is perilous."[3] The gift of the artist, and also perhaps his curse, is in part this "laxity," or flexibility, in the repressions. That is, the barrier that in other persons serves to keep unacceptable material out of consciousness functions differently in the artist: repression is in some way incomplete or intermittent, so that repressed material or rather direct derivatives can break through into consciousness. Thus the writer has access, to an unusual degree, to the unconscious aspects of language, to childhood memories and fantasies, and to the brilliant images and the rapid and highly condensed prelogical thinking of the primary process. Another way of putting this is to say that the artist has the capacity for creative regression.

Since ancient times, the experience of inspiration has been likened to regressive mental states such as dreams and madness. Plato speaks of the state of "creative madness," and Aristotle tells us that "poetry implies either a happy gift of nature or a strain of madness." In inspirational states, there is often a breakthrough into an area of experience that is normally inaccessible, a rush of ideas, associations, and images so rapid and exciting that ordinary thought processes can scarcely transcribe them. Inspiration is often felt as coming from some source so entirely alien to ordinary life that it can only be represented as a supernatural being—a god, a muse, an angel, or a demon. The unconscious sources of inspiration *are*, of course, alien to consciousness, and so the ego experiences them as something—a voice or vision—coming from outside itself. In her diary, Virginia Woolf describes her state immediately after completing *The Waves*: "having reeled across the last ten pages with some moments of such intensity and intoxication that I seemed only to stumble after my own voice or, almost, after some sort of speaker (as when I was mad): I was almost afraid, remembering the voices that used to fly ahead."[4] The image of stumbling after that voice suggests the relative slowness and awkwardness of conscious thought in comparison with the speed and energy of the unconscious mental process released during creation.

Ernst Kris believes that the creative process involves some alternation between id and ego levels of mental function and between primary and secondary process.[5] The inspirational phase of creation shows many regressive features, with the emergence of repressed impulses and energies. The regression that takes place during creation resembles the regressive phenomena of neurosis and particularly psychosis in that the barriers of repression break down, permitting an influx of unconscious material into the ego. However, in psychosis this loss of ego control, which may at first produce a euphoric heightening of consciousness, leads to panic, progressive deterioration of ego functions, and loss of contact with external reality. The ego is overwhelmed by an often terrifying fantasy content and regresses to an entirely private mode of symbolism unintelligible to the outsider; as the ego has no control over the unconscious material, it can perform no secondary elaboration upon it. There is a crucial distinction between this regressive breakdown of the ego and what takes place in creation: in the creative process the regression is only partial, and the ego can regain control. In fact, "it can be considered a sign of the ego's strength if, occasionally and for a specific purpose, it is capable of tolerating the mechanisms of the id." The psychological endowment of the artist includes "the capacity of gaining easy access to id material without being overwhelmed by it, of retaining control over the primary process, and perhaps specifically, the capability of making rapid shifts in levels of psychic function." Kris characterizes this aspect of creation as "regression in service of the ego."[6]

The concept of controlled regression should not, however, reassure us overly as to the safety of the creative experience. It is, of course, extremely difficult to generalize about the psychology of the writer, to make any statement that will apply equally to Jane Austen and Emily Brontë, to Henry James and Dostoevsky. If a capacity for regression is an important component of creativity, the depth of the regression, the degree of ego control, and the nature of the repressed material all vary with the individual writer. However, in some of the greatest works, we sense the presence of rather thinly disguised and extremely threatening unconscious content; works of this kind have a quality of primitive excitement and danger that suggests regression into deeply repressed material. In creation of this sort, the danger to the integrity of personality must be extremely great, and in fact the ego may lose control at least temporarily, giving way to pathological symptoms that become inextricably bound up with the creative process.

While Kris emphasizes the health of the ego and its capacity for control, Kurt Eissler, in his studies of the psychology of creativity, does not hesitate to associate genius with psychopathology: "the greater the artistic genius, the more he is in danger of psychosis." Eissler writes further: "In moments of high inspiration, the artist is in a state of excitement and reduced reality-testing . . . so immersed in the onrush of internal imagery as to be, in effect, immune to the reality that surrounds him—very much as though he were in the grip of an acute psychosis."[7] In his study of Goethe, Eissler finds a crucial period during Goethe's adolescence when a disruption and realignment of the psychic structure occurred. The effect of such an episode on the artist is not necessarily destructive: "a partial psychosis may, by the dissolution of ego structure, remove inhibitions and enable the ego to achieve performances theretofore inaccessible."[8]

Eissler speculates that the ego of the genius may be distinctively different from that of the ordinary person. This difference would consist in a weakness of defense mechanisms because of unusual innate abilities, which during childhood pre-empt energy from the development of ego defenses.[9] If this is indeed the case, the ego is left vulnerable to unconscious images and energies, a condition that could invite psychosis. But "what would constitute a disease . . . in the non-creative or moderately creative mind is to be seen as a prerequisite of outstanding creations on the part of the genius."[10]

Eissler's approach applies best to those artists whose creative activity has an obviously compulsive aspect, and whose lives show evidence of rather severe psychopathology; the work of such artists often bears the signs of deep regression. But we often value most highly just those works where ego control appears most perilous, most threatened by the introduction of potentially terrifying or disgusting material, because the tension between order and disorder produces effects of extraordinary emotional and aesthetic intensity. The ability to assimilate this kind of material and render it intelligible, to integrate it into meaningful structure, places the greatest strain on the ego and demonstrates, paradoxically, the strength of its capacity to organize and execute. The flexibility of repression that results in an increase in psychic capacity may well constitute a defect in ego defenses against unconscious material; but such a defect evidently does not preclude enormous compensatory strength in other aspects of ego function.

Strangely enough, the great wild geniuses whose lives and work appear continually threatened by a maelstrom of internal conflict and fantasy are often those who have managed to assimilate most fully the social and historical reality of their times and to reconstruct and transform it in their own image. One thinks here particularly of the great novelists of the nineteenth and early twentieth centuries, gigantic figures such as Dickens, Balzac, Proust, and of course Dostoevsky and Tolstoy. In their works, the reality of the external world is depicted in such accurate detail and with such brilliant vitality that real life seems by comparison a pallid imitation. It is as if the ego, threatened by the loss of contact with external reality and by regression to a private world of unconscious fantasy, must "hyper-cathect" the real world, maintaining contact by endowing it with all the energy at its disposal. Thus the world, which threatens constantly to disappear, is recreated again and again and infused with a reality that cannot be doubted—that of the inner life. In this way art is akin to the restitutive phenomena of psychosis—for example, the fantastic cosmologies of the paranoid schizophrenic—pseudo-creative acts whereby the psychotic tries to restore the lost world of objects. But the artist succeeds where the psychotic fails: he makes of external reality an objective correlative of his internal world, and in endowing it with the energy and imagery of the unconscious he creates a sort of transitional object that mediates between inner and outer reality, between the unconscious and consciousness, between the pleasure principle and the reality principle.

In a passage often misunderstood as a denigration of the artist, Freud writes:

> *Art* brings about a reconciliation between the two principles in a peculiar way. An artist is originally a man who turns away from reality because he cannot come to terms with the renunciation of instinctual satisfaction which it at first demands, and who allows his erotic and ambitious wishes full play in the life of phantasy. He finds the way back to reality, however, from this world of phantasy by making use of special gifts to mould his phantasies into truths of a new kind, which are valued by men as precious reflections of reality. Thus in a certain fashion he actually becomes the hero, the king, the creator, or the favourite he desired to be, without following the long roundabout path of making real alterations in the external world. But he can only achieve this because other men feel the same dissatisfaction as he does with the renunciation demanded by reality, and because that dissatisfaction, which results from the replacement of the pleasure

principle by the reality principle, is itself a part of reality.[11]

We all share with the artist a disappointment at the frustration of infantile wishes and instinctual demands by the inevitable requirements of the real world, and a desire for another world in which those wishes would be gratified. However, it is only the artist who is both enabled and compelled by the structure of his personality to act upon this dissatisfaction. He creates in the work of art a transitional reality in which elements of the world available to the ego and secondary process are made to gratify unconscious desire, and unconscious wishes are given intelligible objective form. Thus art, which may begin in a flight from the real world, ends by transforming that world, by finding in it the images of human pain and desire, and by imposing on it the values and meanings that make of it a human place.

There remains the question of the "pathological" elements in the content of the work of art itself, the incestuous and aggressive wishes of childhood with their attendant conflict and guilt that psychoanalytic method may uncover. In the great tragic works, primitive wishes that in life are normally repressed are acted out in some way, and then punished. The unabated persistence of such desires into adult life is a pre-condition of illness, and so it might appear that works in which they play so important a part would seem alien and repellent to most readers. But in fact, this is not the case: it is just these works that have the most enduring and universal appeal.

One of the unconscious forces that drive the artist in the creation of the literary work is guilt: through the exposure in disguised form of his guilty wishes he shares them with an audience, which in a sense absolves him by participating in the work and thereby acknowledging such wishes in themselves.[12] Thus one aspect of the reader's experience of literature is a kind of regression, with the writer, to the

archaic psychic strata where infantile wishes and conflicts
lie buried. The potentiality for such regression must be
universal: the unconscious, as Freud points out again and
again, never really relinquishes anything. But the writer
differs from the rest of mankind in that he actually recreates the exciting and painful crises of childhood in his
work, as though compelled to relive them in a much fuller
and more explicit way than other persons. In addition to
and intermingled with the peculiarities of structure in the
artist's personality, there must also be idiosyncrasies of individual life history, traumatic events or situations that
keep infantile conflicts alive with special vigor and that
compel the artist to re-create them again and again in the
effort to resolve them.[13] In most persons, those old wishes
and fears and the vivid and immediate modes of experience associated with them are in some way forgotten—
modified, repressed, buried in the overall experience of
our lives, whose deepest patterns they may shape without
our knowledge. They emerge only in the chaotic and unintelligible imagery of dreams or symptoms, in fantasies, in
mistakes, in all the aspects of experience that seem margi-
nal and without meaning to the conscious mind.

It is at once the gift and the curse of the artist that he
does not "forget" the past in this way. For him, words and
images and stories reverberate with their earliest meanings, and his work becomes for us, too, the way back to that
archaic world whose desires and energies are the well-
springs of life. In his descent into those deepest sources,
the artist risks destruction by exposing himself to the
power of unmodified drives. The oldest and darkest places
of the mind hold images of radiant beauty, but also nightmare revelations of horror, filth, and pain. In the greatest
works, the energy and the violent clarity of this primordial
experience is somehow brought back from the depths
alive, so that the world available to consciousness and the
ego is invested with a brilliant sense of authentic life and
power. To achieve this, the artist must submit to a vision of

the savage energies at the heart of existence. We recognize that vision in the almost unbearable intensity of truth in the great works. Their beauty is terrible, like agony.

Rilke, who had lived in this vision, and who knew that "each single angel is terrible," wrote in the first of the *Duino Elegies*,

> For Beauty's nothing
> but beginning of Terror we're still just able to bear,
> and why we adore it so is because it serenely
> disdains to destroy us.

2
DEMONSTRATION

Dostoevsky's
The Idiot

I. "A KIND OF UNNATURAL FEAR . . ."

Dostoevsky wrote of himself in a well-known passage from his notebooks, "They call me a psychologist: this is not true. I am merely a realist in a higher sense, i.e., I depict all the depths of the human soul."

Dostoevsky was not a psychologist in the scientific, systematic way; but no great writer has ever had a more powerful understanding of the "depths," the irrational, contradictory, and perverse aspects of human life that are alien to conscious understanding. And no writer provides richer material for the study of the unconscious in literature. Indeed, Dostoevsky not only "depicts" the depths; there is in his work a sort of fascinated compulsion toward them. Each novel is a spiritual and psychological experiment with the most destructive forces in the human soul. In *The Diary of a Writer*, in a passage dealing with the Russian character, Dostoevsky speaks of "an urge for the extreme, for the fainting sensation of approaching an abyss, and half-leaning over it—to peep into the bottomless pit, and, in some very rare cases, to throw oneself into it head-forward as in a frenzy."[1] In all of Dostoevsky's work there is this perilous flirtation with the abyss. More than any other writer, he makes cruelly seductive those aspects of experience most fraught with moral danger; and yet, in the same works, the dark forces are juxtaposed with images of great moral beauty. Out of the equivocal relationship between these opposed aspects of experience comes the extraordinary psychological excitement and aesthetic tension of Dostoevsky's fiction. Nowhere in his work are these extremes juxtaposed more dramatically than in *The Idiot*, and nowhere are the hidden connections between them so strongly suggested.

The Idiot is perhaps the strangest of the world's great novels. Here, even more than in Dostoevsky's other major works, one is struck with a sense of mystery, of something alien to ordinary understanding. The protagonist is one of

the most attractive and lovable characters in all of literature, a good and charming young man who comes to the
city to seek his fortune—like the typical protagonist of the
nineteenth-century novel, the provincial outsider who
conquers the sophisticated society and the desirable
women of the capital. Myshkin also resembles an older
figure of legend and fairy tale: the prince who comes to the
rescue of the beautiful captive maiden. Yet in this case, the
patterns are all strangely inverted: the prince is an epileptic, the maiden is no maiden and more than half-mad. The
hero's progress through society ends not in a triumphant
assertion of selfhood, but rather in a collapse of the self.
And Myshkin is destroyed not by the evil designs of rivals
and enemies, but paradoxically by himself and his own
goodness.

At the simplest level of description, the plot of *The Idiot*
might be called a love triangle, although of a very strange
kind. Nastasya Filippovna, a fabulous beauty corrupted in
her girlhood by an older man, is pursued by the Idiot,
Prince Myshkin, who offers her Christ-like love and redemption, and by Rogozhin, a passionate and crudely
powerful young merchant, who desires her with lust and
hatred. Tormented by guilt and unable to accept the
Prince's vision of her innocence, Nastasya vacillates between the two men and finally elopes with Rogozhin, who
murders her. In the novel's last great scene, Myshkin and
Rogozhin lie side by side near the dead body of Nastasya,
their faces pressed together so closely that Myshkin's tears
run down Rogozhin's cheeks.

The principal action of the novel is surrounded by a rich
proliferation of secondary intrigues and characters, all of
them related in some degree to the primary plot. The central dynamic of the novel, however, is in the Myshkin-
Nastasya-Rogozhin relationship. These three are "characters" in the usual literary sense—they are memorable and
convincing personalities. But they are also, even more than
Dostoevsky's other major figures, great dramatic embodi-

ments of impulse and idea; indeed, their behavior often has less to do with the claims of the plot upon them than with the movement toward expression of the forces they embody. In the shifting patterns of action and feeling among them are represented the dynamic tensions that animate Dostoevsky's vision of existence, the contradictions between faith and reason, submission and rebellion, charity and lust, Eros and Thanatos.

At the center of the novel is the extraordinary figure of the Idiot, the epileptic Prince Myshkin. The dialectic of the novel is played out around him, but within him too; in his character and his fate the other characters and their passions are included and transformed. His Christ-like will to absorb and redeem the world's hatred and evil through the total gift of himself represents the culmination of the dialectical oppositions, not in synthesis, but in transcendence of the dialectic itself. Yet this great embodiment of Dostoevsky's most powerful vision of the good is strangely flawed. Although Myshkin is moved by compassion and tenderness for everyone, the lives he touches deeply are ruined. Epileptic and apparently impotent, an "idiot" who is imposed upon by everyone, a disturbingly contradictory mixture of incapacity and saintliness, Myshkin is one of the most mysterious characters in all of literature. He is like a core of unearthly light at the center of the novel; when his personality and motives are examined they seem to dissolve in indecipherable ambiguity, a kind of negative radiance that defies analysis.

The structure of the novel itself also presents problems and ambiguities. Although *The Idiot* finally makes an effect of powerful coherence, there are obvious flaws in the progress of the narrative, gaps in the action that are never fully accounted for, unexplained comings and goings of the characters and apparently inconsistent images of their personalities, bursts of spectacular dramatic action followed by sudden lapses of tension and continuity in the narrative sequence. Mysterious holes open up in the novelistic texture, through which the entire conception threatens to disappear.

The novel occupied a crucial and troubling place in Dostoevsky's own life. He wrote to his niece Sofia Alexandrovna Ivanova:

> The idea of the novel is an old one that is dear to me, but so difficult that for a long time I didn't dare try it; if I've committed myself to it now, it's only because I was in a desperate situation. The principal idea of the novel is to portray a positively beautiful man. There is nothing more difficult in the world—especially now. All writers, not only ours, but even all the European writers, who but undertook this depiction of the *positively* beautiful man always had to give it up. Because this problem is immeasurable. The beautiful is an ideal, but the nature of that ideal—whether it be ours or that of civilized Europe—is far from having been worked out. There exists in the world only one positively beautiful person—Christ, so that the appearance of this immeasurably, infinitely beautiful person is, of course, an infinite miracle. (The whole Gospel of Saint John was conceived in this spirit; he finds the whole miracle in the one Incarnation, in the one appearance of the beautiful.) [. . .] Of the beautiful characters in Christian literature, the most fully achieved is Don Quixote; but he is beautiful simply because he is also comic. Dickens' Pickwick (an infinitely weaker conception, but nevertheless immense) is also comic, and only for that reason convinces us. Compassion is felt towards the beautiful that is mocked and does not recognize its own worth, and consequently, the readers experience sympathy. [. . .] Jean Valjean is also a powerful attempt, but he arouses sympathy through his terrible misfortune and the injustice done him by society. I have nothing similar, absolutely nothing, and that's why I'm terribly afraid it will be a failure.[2]

The reception of *The Idiot* in Russia was somewhat disappointing, and Dostoevsky himself felt that the novel was flawed. In another letter to his niece he wrote, "I'm dissatisfied with the book, for I haven't expressed even a tenth part of what I wanted to express. Nevertheless, I don't repudiate it, and to this day I love my idea that did not succeed."[3] And to his friend Strakhov, "In the novel much was written in haste, much is too drawn-out, much has not succeeded, but something did succeed. I am not defending the novel, but I do defend my idea."[4]

This "idea," which was nothing less than the representation of "a positively beautiful man," a sort of Russian Christ living in the world, would continue to haunt Dostoevsky and to elude him. He tried again to deal with it in an unrealized project for a novel to be called "Atheism," and again later in a plan for a trilogy entitled "The Life of a Great Sinner," which also remained unwritten, although the plan was the source of many elements in the later works.[5]

Criticism of *The Idiot* for the most part takes the author's intention for the deed. Whatever misgivings are aroused by the effects of Myshkin's actions on those around him, he is seen as the ultimate literary representation of the good man. Ernest Simmons writes:

> The enduring quality of *The Idiot* rests squarely upon the treatment of its idea and the great character that embodies it. . . . His failure in an intensely pragmatic world, where things of the spirit are consumed in the flame of reality, does not lessen the appeal of his Christlike nature or the rightness of his moral principles. Myshkin is one of the supremely great "good" characters in fiction. . . .[6]

In a more recent interpretation, Edward Wasiolek takes essentially the same attitude toward the novel and its central character. Wasiolek writes:

> Never is the Prince's helplessness more pathetic and
> more appealing than in the scene in which he stands
> between the hot tongues of Nastasya and Aglaya, and
> never is it more beautiful than in the final scene when
> he lies by the body of Nastasya and consoles the bro-
> ken spirit of Rogozhin.[7]

In that grotesque and terrifying last scene, the Prince's
"helplessness" has become not only "pathetic" but "beautiful." Before the deeply disturbing implications of
Myshkin's character, the critic retreats into unanalytic piety. There is, in fact, less interesting and vigorous criticism
of *The Idiot* than of many of Dostoevsky's other works.
Perhaps because the novel involves a religious and even
mystical conception of experience, the novel itself is regarded as if it were a religious revelation rather than a
work of literature, the product after all of a human mind.
The enigma of Myshkin's character is generally treated as
something not given to the human intellect to comprehend, a mystery like the Trinity or the Incarnation.[8]
    In view of this reverential attitude on the part of the
majority of critics, it is startling to find several writers who
advance a counter-interpretation, which takes an entirely
opposed view of Myshkin and of the novel. According to
Murray Krieger, Myshkin suffers from a "psychosis of
humility"; in his Christ-like transcendence of ethical judgment, he presents a moral provocation and burden that destroys the other characters.[9] In his book on Dostoevsky,
Robert Lord goes even farther toward standing the usual
reading of the novel on its head, and with it the character
of the Prince. He gives us Myshkin as a "princely humbug,"
"an open sore, a paranoiac introvert." "Beneath a cloak of
simulated innocence he makes the most of his talent for
scheming, playing off the various characters one against
the other, and never failing to exploit his charm and in-
genuousness to the full."[10] Lord's version is, of course, a
grotesque misinterpretation. But the very possibility of ex-

plaining the action and the principal character in such a perverse way points to a strange doubleness in the novel. It is like one of those trick pictures in which one image has been superimposed upon another: looked at *en face*, *The Idiot* presents an image of sublime beauty and charity, but from an oblique angle a meaning quite different from the apparent one is suggested. It is as if the novel contains within it in some mysterious way the negation of its own central conception. The character of Myshkin himself is somehow an absence or negation: his personality is defined in large part by what he does *not* do, by what he is *not*, and thus not only evokes a vision of its opposite, a shadowy double embodying all that is missing and yet somehow contained by its absence in Myshkin, but also suggests in him a sort of gulf or abyss, the possibility of a terrifying fall into a negative realm of being where the very forms of personality might be annihilated.

The more usual interpretation of *The Idiot* as a story of the failure of innocence and Christ-like goodness in the world does not quite accord with what actually happens in the novel. Myshkin's relations with the other characters end in chaos and horror: Nastasya is murdered; the murderer, Rogozhin, is sentenced to prison in Siberia; Aglaia, the innocent and beautiful girl who loves Myshkin, makes a ruinous marriage; and Myshkin himself reverts to idiocy and presumably passes the rest of his days in an institution. The paradoxical results of Myshkin's charity are sometimes explained by referring to Dostoevsky's comment in the notebooks for the novel: "The prince has had only the slightest effect on their lives. [. . .] But wherever he even made an appearance—everywhere he left a permanent trace."[11] Christ himself, after all, did not prevent men from continuing to do and suffer evil. But in fact Myshkin does leave more than a trace of himself in the world—his gentle passage through the lives of the other characters has laid waste to them with a kind of apocalyptic destructiveness. To explain this, one must move beyond the facile idea of

the good Prince in a bad world that perverts his actions to
evil ends; there must be an organic connection between
what the Prince is and what he does, between the character
and the novelistic world he inhabits.

Moreover, the notion of the book as simply recording
the fate of the Russian Christ does not account for what
one actually feels when reading the novel. *The Idiot* presents itself first of all as an emotional experience of an extraordinarily concentrated kind; it arouses in many readers
an almost unbearable excitement and intensity of feeling.
Perhaps more consistently in *The Idiot* than anywhere else
in Dostoevsky's work, our emotions are forced again and
again to the breaking point. The action of the novel seems
headed constantly toward hysteria and frenzy. The characters themselves lose control of their emotions frequently, as
in the wild behavior of Nastasya, the hysterical laughter of
Aglaia, Mme Epanchin's comic outbursts of indignation
and rage, the compulsive lying of General Ivolgin,
Lebedyev's orgies of self-abasement, Ganya's fainting fit,
the feverish raving of Ippolit. Myshkin's epileptic seizures
are the culmination of this pervasive tendency toward loss
of control. To understand the novel, it is necessary to take
account of these phenomena within the book itself and of
their effects on the emotions of the reader.

The Idiot was written during a period of intense turmoil
in the author's life. Dostoevsky had gone to Europe with
his new wife under threat of arrest from his creditors; he
left Russia, as he wrote his friend Maikov, "to save not only
my health but even my life." Epileptic seizures were occur-
ring once a week: "it was unbearable to be fully *conscious* of
the disorder of my nerves and *brain*. My reason was really
falling apart,—that's the truth. I felt it; and the disorder of
my nerves sometimes drove me to moments of furious
madness."[12] He went to Dresden, to Hamburg, and finally
to Baden, where he and his pregnant wife installed themselves in miserable quarters above a blacksmith's forge.

During these months Dostoevsky suffered an intense recurrence of his gambling mania. Every day was a dizzying succession of wins and losses; he could not leave the roulette tables until he had won brilliantly or, more often, gambled away his last farthing. At one time or another he pawned his wife's fur pelisse, her lace shawl, earrings, brooch, wedding ring, flannel petticoat, his own underdrawers. He borrowed from the novelist Goncharov, from his editor, from his wife's mother.[13] Finally his wife managed to get him out of Baden. They went to Geneva, where in a state of great mental agitation Dostoevsky began work on *The Idiot*.

He was to find this novel harder to write than anything he had yet done, perhaps the most difficult of all his books. For months he struggled without success to subdue and organize the material that poured into his mind. In a letter to Maikov, he wrote, "I must have worked out six plans a day (not less) on the average. My head was turned into a mill. I don't understand how I didn't lose my mind."[14] Dostoevsky had received and spent a number of advances from his publisher, and the novel was scheduled to begin serial publication in January 1868. By December 1867 he had prepared eight different outlines without arriving at a satisfactory plan. Finally in disgust he threw out everything he had done, and after two weeks of agonizing mental effort he began writing at a furious pace an entirely "new novel," producing the first seven chapters in twenty-three days.

The whole novel was created under these conditions, with each section being published before the author knew how, or indeed whether, the plot would develop. Dostoevsky was distressed afterwards at the effects of this mode of composition, but perhaps the novel could have been written only against these gambler's odds, and in fact he spoke of the book in the desperate metaphors of the gaming table: "The novel is my only salvation. . . . I must take the novel *by storm*, fling myself into it head first, I've staked everything on a single card, come what may!"[15] And later:

"Only my desperate situation compelled me to take up this premature thought. I took the kind of risk one takes at roulette: 'perhaps it will develop under my pen!' "[16]

Something about the book evidently had quite special significance for its author. As the story of the epileptic prince took shape in the following months, Dostoevsky's own epileptic condition worsened: "the disorder of my nerves has increased, as well as the number and violence of my fits."[17] He complained of being in "the most terrible depression. . . . The day before yesterday I had a very serious attack [of epilepsy]. Nevertheless I wrote yesterday, in a state close to madness."[18] In another letter to Maikov, he wrote, "As for the Idiot, I'm so afraid, so afraid—you can't imagine. Even a kind of unnatural fear such as I've never felt before."[19] It seems that only the extremity of his circumstances, his decision to "stake everything on a single card," could have forced out of Dostoevsky this great, fearful, imperfect novel, as if it contained almost too clearly the deepest thought of his mind.

II. PRINCE CHRIST

Myshkin comes into the dark, hectic world of *The Idiot* on the Warsaw train to Petersburg, a tall, fair young man whose dreaming blue eyes have the strange look of epilepsy. With him in the same third-class compartment are Rogozhin, the sinister young merchant-millionaire, and a fat, nosy, servile person who turns out to be Lebedyev. In the company of these two dark souls, ridiculously dressed in Swiss cloak and gaiters with his belongings tied up in a kerchief, Myshkin has something of the archetypal traveler about him, like the youngest son in a fairy tale, walking with an air of dreaming abstraction into the deep wood where some awful fate awaits him. Yet, like the youngest son, Myshkin turns out to be alert and courageous as well as ingenuous, and in fact his very ingenuous-

ness disarms the ogres. To the sneering and impertinent
questions of Rogozhin and Lebedyev, Myshkin responds
with perfect good humor, telling them about his childhood, his illness, and his stay in the Swiss sanitarium; when
they laugh at him, he laughs too. Rogozhin ends by inviting
the Prince to come and see him, offering to outfit him with
new clothes and cash. "Thank you very much for liking
me," says the Prince. "Thank you, too, for the clothes and
the fur coat you promise me, for I certainly shall need
clothes and a fur coat directly. As for money, I have
scarcely a farthing at the moment" (I.1).[1]

In each of his encounters on that extraordinary first day
in Petersburg, the Prince behaves with the same sweet and
friendly simplicity, the same lack of pretense, the same expectation of loving and being loved. He also manifests an
alarming readiness to lead everyone he meets immediately
into the depths of emotional and spiritual experience. He
disconcerts the Epanchins' footman terribly by chatting
with him as an equal, then moves the man's heart with an
extraordinary description of a condemned criminal going
to the guillotine; a few minutes later he again evokes in
agonizing detail the last thoughts of the condemned man,
this time during his first meeting with the wife and
daughters of General Epanchin. The Prince simply assumes that the conventions associated with social rank and
social manner are a veneer, beneath which the sentiments
of human brotherhood and compassion lie ready to be
touched.

The Prince's goodness is given a kind of scriptural authority by a story he tells the Epanchins of an episode that
took place in the Swiss village where he lived for four years.
A village girl, Marie, was seduced by a commercial traveler
and then forced to return alone, sick and ashamed, to the
village. The villagers persecute Marie, particularly the
children, who follow her in the street, taunting her and
throwing clods of earth at her. But then the Prince be-
friends her, and one day the children see him kiss Marie.

The Prince is their great friend and hero, and they are so enchanted by this "romance" with Marie that they follow the Prince's example and begin to love and care for her, bringing her cast-off clothing and bits of food. Marie dies finally from consumption, but according to Myshkin, "she died almost happy" (I.6).

In this story Myshkin is clearly the "Prince Christ" that Dostoevsky conceived of in the letters and in several entries in the notebooks for the novel. There are two obvious Gospel parallels: the story of the woman taken in adultery— "He that is without sin among you, let him first cast a stone at her"—and Christ's redemption of the prostitute Mary Magdalen. Myshkin's association with children in this episode, and throughout the novel, also evokes the figure of Christ—the Christ of "Suffer the little children to come unto me."

The theme of the child and the childlike is in fact extremely important in this novel, as it is throughout Dostoevsky's work. At the end of the story of Marie and the children, Myshkin tells the Epanchins of a conversation with his doctor in Switzerland:

> At last Schneider expressed a very strange thought to me[. . .] . He told me that he had come to the conclusion that I was a complete child myself, altogether a child; that it was only in face and figure that I was like a grown-up person, but that in development, in soul, in character, and perhaps even in intelligence, I was not grown up, and that so I should remain, if I lived to be sixty. I laughed very much, of course. He was wrong, for what kind of child am I? But in one thing he is right, in fact, I don't like being with adults, with grown-up people. I've known that a long time. I don't like it because I don't know how to get on with them. Whatever they say to me, however kind they are to me, I always feel somehow oppressed with them, and I am awfully glad when I can get away the sooner to my

companions; and my companions have always been
children. (I.6)

It is to the child in everyone that the Prince addresses himself; he is happy only when he has found, beneath the crust
of social convention and adult self-importance, the spontaneity of childlike feeling. To Madam Epanchin, who in
her eccentric and abrupt way acts always from the heart, he
says "I feel positively certain that you are a perfect child in
everything, everything, in good and bad alike, in spite of
your age" (I.6). Aglaia, Nastasya, Rogozhin, the pathetic
and boorish boxer Keller, are all told by the Prince at some
point that they are like children. Even Ganya, whose personality seems almost entirely corrupt and masklike, can be
caught off guard by the Prince: "I am surprised at your
laughing so genuinely. You still have the laugh of a child"
(I.11). Myshkin believes with Christ that "Except ye be converted, and become as little children, ye shall not enter into
the kingdom of heaven."

Although he denies it, the personality of Myshkin himself is obviously childlike in many respects. It is in part his
childlike simplicity and innocence that people refer to as
his "idiocy." This conception of the hero as fool or idiot is
based in part upon the archetypal figure of the "holy fool,"
in Russian the *yurodivyi*, the radically innocent or even
mentally defective person who sees the truths hidden from
the corrupted vision of the worldly-wise. And although this
childishness or "idiocy" of Myshkin's is intensely attractive,
it does raise questions about Myshkin's idealization of the
child, about the nature of the moral ideal proposed by the
book, and about Myshkin's own nature. Myshkin's childlike
qualities have another side, a cutting edge that begins to
suggest the ambiguity and the dangers of his goodness.
This other side first shows itself when he meets the Epanchins. Myshkin enters the household at a moment of family
crisis. General Epanchin is trying to arrange the marriage
of his eldest daughter, Alexandra, to the wealthy Count

Totsky; first, however, Totsky's former mistress, Nastasya Filippovna, must be got rid of. Totsky settles a dowry of seventy-five thousand roubles on her, and the two older men are trying to induce General Epanchin's secretary, Ganya Ivolgin, to marry her. At the same time General Epanchin himself is fascinated by Nastasya and has purchased an expensive pearl necklace for her birthday, with the plan of paying court to her after she is safely married off to his secretary. To further complicate matters, Ganya is in love, not with Nastasya, but with the General's youngest daughter, Aglaia.

In this intensely confused situation, the Prince's innocence is devastating. He tells the Epanchin women that he has seen the General and Ganya with a portrait of Nastasya and compares her with Aglaia, saying that Aglaia is nearly as beautiful. Then he carries a note from Ganya to Aglaia; Ganya orders him not to read the note, but at the behest of Aglaia he does read it. Aglaia tells him freely of her scorn for Ganya, and Myshkin in turn repeats what she has said in full detail to Ganya. "You must excuse me if I've forgotten her exact expression and only repeat it as I understood it," says Myshkin conscientiously (I.7). Although the onus in this matter rests on the hypocrisy and corruption of Totsky, General Epanchin, and Ganya himself, and we can properly enjoy Ganya's discomfiture, we cannot help but understand why Ganya finally sputters at Myshkin, "Oh, da-damned idiot!" Myshkin has found himself in the midst of what is clearly a complicated tangle of sexual and financial intrigue. His idiocy here consists in his refusal to recognize the nature of the situation in which he has consented to play a part. He behaves rather like a child who has overheard an adult conversation and later blurts it out at the most compromising moment, as though to reject the adult world in which he feels so uncomfortable, especially its greed and sexuality. In his refusal to lie or at least to conceal the truth, Myshkin rejects one of the ways in which the adult learns to protect himself and others, to navigate

in a world of conflicting egos and passions. Myshkin's
straightforwardness cuts like a solvent through the tissue
of nuance and half-truth in which the Epanchins are living.[2]

Like his childishness, Myshkin's humility also associates
him clearly with Christ and the moral order of the Gospels,
expecially the Sermon on the Mount, with its inversion of
the values of this world: "Blessed are the meek: for they
shall inherit the earth." Myshkin arrives on the scene without family, social connections, or money. He comes from
outside the world of the novel, and his social status remains
ambiguous throughout; although he is a prince, his kingdom is not of this world. At the simplest level, Myshkin's
humility functions as social criticism. His plainness and his
indifference to rank constitute a measure against which the
inflated self-importance and false values of the other characters may be judged.[3] However, the real question posed
by Myshkin's humility to the life around him is far more
radical than this: it involves not only the conventions of a
particular social milieu but the structure of life in any society, and indeed the fundamental structure of personality
itself. What is at stake is ultimately the legitimacy of self-
assertion and desire, the meaning of guilt, and the nature
of the ego in its transactions with reality.

In the first section of the novel, which coincides with
Myshkin's first day in Petersburg, a consistent pattern can
be discerned in his encounters with others. Each scene begins by his being humiliated or treated contemptuously in
some way, and ends with his emergence as the dominant
figure in the transaction in question. This is true of the first
scene on the train with Rogozhin and Lebedyev, and of the
meetings that follow with the various members of the
Epanchin and Ivolgin households and finally with Nastasya
and her guests at the birthday party that ends Part I. By the
end of each of these episodes, Myshkin has become the
center of the action and the touchstone of moral authentic-

ity. It seems that the initial humiliation is necessary for this reversal, that in some way Myshkin finds in it the source of his uncanny power. In the notebooks for the novel, Dostoevsky wrote, "Humility is the most terrible force that can ever exist in the world."[4] The virtue of humility and the experience of humiliation are not, of course, the same thing; but in this novel they are very close indeed.[5]

The clearest example of Myshkin's peculiar force at work is the episode in which Nastasya comes to the Ivolgin flat, followed by Rogozhin and his noisy crew, and provokes a scandalous scene before Ganya's family. The episode begins with Myshkin by chance opening the door to Nastasya, who mistakes him for the footman, tosses him her coat, and berates him for dropping it. "What an idiot!" she cries (I.8). In the action that follows, Myshkin intervenes only twice. The first time he merely says to Ganya, "Drink some water [. . .] and don't look like that." This mild remark has an extraordinary effect. "All Ganya's spite seemed suddenly turned against the prince. He seized him by the shoulder and looked at him in silence with resentment and hatred, as though unable to utter a word" (I.9). In some peculiar way, the Prince's gentleness magnetizes Ganya's fury, drawing it away from its original object onto himself. The second intervention is far more decisive. Rogozhin has burst into the flat with his friends and begun to bargain for Nastasya, offering Ganya "cash down" to give her up. Ganya's sister, Varya, demands that he get Nastasya out of the flat, and then she spits in her brother's face; in a fury, Ganya raises his arm to strike her, but Myshkin holds him back.

> "Are you always going to get in my way?" roared Ganya, flinging away Varya's arm, and with his free hand, in the most extreme rage, he slapped the prince across the face with all his might.
> "Ah!" cried Kolya, clasping his hands, "My God!"
> Exclamations were heard on all sides. Myshkin

turned pale. With a strange and reproachful expression he looked Ganya straight in the face; his lips quivered, trying to articulate something; a kind of strange and utterly incongruous smile twisted them.

"Well, you may . . . but her . . . I won't let you," he said softly at last.

But suddenly he broke down, left Ganya, hid his face in his hands, moved away to a corner, stood with his face to the wall, and in a breaking voice said:

"Oh, how ashamed you will be of what you've done!"

Ganya did, indeed, stand looking utterly crushed. Kolya rushed to hug and kiss Myshkin. He was followed by Rogozhin, Varya, Ptitsyn, Nina Alexandrovna—all the party, even the old man Ardalion Aleksandrovich, who all crowded about Myshkin. (I.10)

The usual reversal of the Prince's role has taken place: the episode begins with Myshkin's humiliation and ends with the establishment of his moral ascendancy over everyone else, particularly over Ganya and Nastasya, the two who have insulted him; and the Prince has behaved in a peculiarly characteristic and revealing fashion. That is, he has not prevented evil, nor even actively opposed it. He seems powerless or unwilling to do that. Rather, his behavior has an essentially passive character. He observes and waits, as though to allow the evil immanent in the situation to work itself out. At the moment of its violent eruption he intervenes, but even his intervention, although it is an action, is characterized by a passivity that turns the actor into an object for another to act upon. Myshkin offers himself to receive Ganya's slap: he presents himself as a victim, a sort of magnet or lightning rod to evil, as though to absorb and neutralize it in his own person.

The central position or dominance of the Prince in this scene might seem to be due, paradoxically, to his having no personal motive in it, to his being peripheral to the drama played out among the others. This absence of personal desire makes the Prince a neutral or receptive element, a conductor through which the currents of feeling at large among the others may be grounded. And yet this description of the Prince's neutrality and passivity does not account for what actually takes place. The Prince's curious silence and passivity in the face of the aggression and evil of others is itself a mode of action and encourages these tendencies to express themselves fully, drawing them out with a purgative violence. There is a small example of this in the conversation between Myshkin and Ganya about the business of Nastasya's picture and the letter to Aglaia: Ganya becomes more and more furious with Myshkin until "Ganya, having once begun to be abusive and meeting no resistance, little by little lost all restraint, as is always the case with certain sorts of people" (I.7).

The same principle is illustrated later in an extremely funny episode with General Ivolgin. The General, a compulsive liar, is usually somewhat restrained by the disbelief of his listeners; Myshkin, however, allows him to embroil himself further and further in an obviously fantastic story of his childhood in which he figures as an adviser to Napoleon. Afterwards the General evidently blames Myshkin for indulging his folly and sends him an indignant note saying that "he could not accept 'proofs of compassion which were humiliating to the dignity of a man who was unhappy enough without that' " (IV.4).

Myshkin's nonresistance to evil is far more disturbing in the scene of Ippolit's suicide attempt. Ippolit, a seventeen-year-old boy who has been told he has only three weeks to live, has read a long document to Myshkin and the other characters assembled for Myshkin's birthday in which he announces his intention to shoot himself at sunrise. Suddenly he leaps up and cries out to Myshkin, "The sun has risen." Myshkin remains silent. Kolya cries, "Only look at him. Prince, prince, what are you thinking of?" The others begin to laugh, accusing Ippolit of trying to frighten them, while Ippolit becomes increasingly frenzied. At last he goes up to the Prince and embraces him, saying "I want to look you in the eyes. . . . Stand like that and let me look. I am saying good-bye to Man" (III.7). A moment later Ippolit puts a pistol to his head. Later the Prince wonders, "Perhaps I really did egg him on by . . . not saying anything. He may have thought I didn't believe he would shoot himself? What do you think, Yevgeny Pavlovitch?" (III.7). Yevgeny Pavlovitch absolves the Prince, but it is not easy for the reader to do so. Ippolit's entire performance is clearly addressed primarily to the Prince; when the Prince fails to respond, Ippolit must prove his seriousness. It is not the Prince, but Ippolit's own carelessness in preparing the pistol that thwarts the suicide.

The Prince's passivity acts as a sort of goad; it eggs others on to more and more outrageous behavior. This abyss of meekness that accepts everything and resists nothing is a seduction to loss of control. But the escalating fury it excites in the other characters seems also, paradoxically, an attempt on their parts to provoke at last some resistance from him, to find in the frighteningly undifferentiated personality of the Prince a structure that will control and limit aggression. But the attempt is futile: in Myshkin's presence every character is reduced to the last truth of his nature, every situation is forced to tragic extremity. The Prince's humility is like a firebrand.

Myshkin is unique as a tragic figure. We ordinarily think of the tragic hero as defined by the arrogance of hubris; but another fundamental principle of tragic character is its identification with the absolute, with the truth that kills. The absolute at the bottom of the Prince's unresisting goodness is humility, that "most terrible force that can ever exist in the world." Myshkin's hubris is a kind of hubris of submission; in it we see that the passive will is as dangerous as the active will, and makes its own assertions. Myshkin's "I won't hinder" is as closely bound up in the ultimate evil of the novel as Rogozhin's "I shall murder." In the death of

Nastasya, submission and aggression meet and reveal themselves as the two faces of the same dark truth.

Some quality in Myshkin clearly invites the cruelty and aggression of others, and that quality is involved in the final catastrophe. It is worthwhile looking again at the scene in which Myshkin is slapped by Ganya; that incident shows clearly how Myshkin deals with aggression, and gives some clue to the structure of this extraordinary personality. Even stranger than the slap itself is Myshkin's response to it: Myshkin looks reproachfully at Ganya, then "suddenly he broke down, left Ganya, hid his face in his hands, moved away to a corner, stood with his face to the wall, and in a breaking voice said: 'Oh, how ashamed you will be of what you've done!' " (I.10). What is obviously missing here is anger, the urge to retaliate. Instead, Myshkin seems to suffer not only the slap but the guilt for the slap. He acts out a little pantomime of remorse, hiding his face as though he and not Ganya were the guilty one. Thus the drama of aggression becomes a purely internal one played out in Myshkin's own personality, with Myshkin punished as both victim and aggressor.

Something similar happens later in the novel in the episode with Antip Burdovsky, the "son of Pavlishtchev." Burdovsky is a rather stupid young man whom a group of nihilists have put up to swindling the Prince out of his inheritance. Burdovsky claims to be the illegitimate son of Myshkin's benefactor, Pavlishtchev, who paid for his treatment in Switzerland. The nihilists claim that Myshkin should pay back to Burdovsky the money spent on the Swiss cure by Pavlishtchev. Burdovsky turns out to be no relation at all to Pavlishtchev, but Myshkin announces that he will give him 10,000 roubles anyway, "for though Mr. Burdovsky is not the 'son of Pavlishtchev,' he is almost as good as a 'son of Pavlishtchev' because he has been so wickedly deceived." When Burdovsky refuses, Myshkin is in a "paroxysm of shame and extreme distress" because he thinks he has made the offer "coarsely"; " 'Yes, I am an

idiot, a real idiot!' he decided [. . .]" (II.8). Here again,
Myshkin offers himself as a victim to the rapacious demands of others, and responds to those demands with
guilt.

These instances of Myshkin's willingness to suffer are
somewhat easier to consider in detail than the more significant experiences of victimization and suffering in relation to Nastasya and Rogozhin. To both Nastasya and
Rogozhin, Myshkin offers himself as a sacrifice: this is quite
explicit in the case of Nastasya. In speaking with Aglaia of
his plan to marry Nastasya, Myshkin says at one point, "I
can't sacrifice myself like that, though I did want to at one
time . . . and perhaps I want to still" (III.8). And of course
he does "want to still": in the later scene of confrontation
between the two women, Myshkin gives up Aglaia, who offers him happiness, and chooses Nastasya, who represents
the more potent attractions and possibilities of suffering,
both her own suffering and the misery and destruction in
which she inevitably involves Myshkin. Myshkin's attraction to suffering is accompanied by a pervasive sense of
guilt, which becomes even more explicit in the larger actions of the novel than in such incidents as those with
Ganya and Burdovsky. On the day Rogozhin tries to murder him, Myshkin feels overcome with guilt. Speaking of
the murder attempt afterwards with Rogozhin, Myshkin
says, "Our sin was the same" (III.3). It is evidently as much
a sin to be murdered as to murder! This remark demonstrates Myshkin's irrational tendency to self-reproach, but
it also shows that he (as well as his creator) has some sense
that such an event does not simply "happen," that it is not
an accidental visitation from outside; its victim must in
some way will it and collaborate with it.

The consistent way in which Myshkin finds suffering
suggests that he seeks it, and the attraction to suffering calls
for the kind of understanding that psychoanalysis offers.
The role of suffering and guilt in *The Idiot*, and specifically

in the life and personality of Myshkin, suggests the work-ings of what Freud calls "moral masochism." In "The Eco-nomic Problem of Masochism," Freud writes:

> moral masochism . . . is chiefly remarkable for having loosened its connection with what we recognize as sex-uality. All other masochistic sufferings carry with them the condition that they shall emanate from the loved person and shall be endured at his command. This re-striction has been dropped in moral masochism. The suffering itself is what matters; whether it is decreed by someone who is loved or by someone who is in-different is of no importance. It may even be caused by impersonal powers or by circumstances; the true masochist always turns his cheek whenever he has a chance of receiving a blow.[6]

The ego of this type of character is dominated by the need for punishment; to provoke it he must "do what is inexpe-dient, must act against his own interests, must ruin the prospects which open out to him in the real world and must, perhaps, destroy his own real existence."[7] The con-science of the moral masochist is excessively strict and sen-sitive; it adds to the real punishments that the ego brings down upon itself in the external world the internal suffer-ings inflicted by a domineering superego. Thus the sadistic superego and the masochistic ego collaborate. In noting one especially peculiar feature of this type of character, Freud makes an observation that might account for the ir-rational guilt Myshkin so often manifests, as in his strange behavior in the episodes with Ganya and the "son of Pav-lishtchev," and especially in response to Rogozhin's attack on him: "the suppression of an instinct can—frequently or quite generally—result in a sense of guilt . . . a person's conscience becomes more severe and more sensitive the more he refrains from aggression against others."[8]

This paradox can be illuminated through some consid-eration of the formation and function of the superego.

The superego originates through introjection into the ego of the first objects of the libidinal impulses in the id, the two parents; through this process the relation to them is desexualized, the Oedipus complex is overcome, and the prohibitions and ideals associated with the parents are internalized. The superego is able to enforce these prohibitions by means of aggressive energies deflected from sadistic expression in the outside world and turned inward against the ego. The superego then has the possibility of becoming harsh and cruel. Thus, paradoxically, the more the aggressive instincts are restrained in their expression in the outside world, the more aggressive energy becomes available to the sadistic superego to direct against the ego in the form of the reproaches of conscience.

Freud explains the process at work in moral masochism in this way: "Conscience and morality have arisen through the overcoming, the desexualization, of the Oedipus complex; but through moral masochism morality becomes sexualized once more, the Oedipus complex is revived and the way is opened for a regression from morality back to the Oedipus complex."[9] That is, the moral masochist is making use of opportunities in the external world to re-enact the relationship with a loved and punishing parent. He may seek a parent substitute in other persons, in circumstances, or even in Fate itself.

Freud's views on moral masochism are sometimes misunderstood as reducing conscience or morality to nothing but the precipitate of pathological guilt. But the particular kind of moral development outlined in this essay is not that of the normal moral sense; on the contrary, it is a regression from morality back to the Oedipus complex, which is "to the advantage neither of morality nor of the person concerned."[10] The superego is part of the ego, the psychic system that deals with external reality. Thus its primary function should be not to inflict suffering on the ego, but to protect the ego by helping to modify and control destructive expressions of unconscious impulse.

The charm and sweetness of Myshkin's personality cannot be fully comprehended under the rubric of moral
masochism; but neither can the terrible effects of this personality be understood without it. Myshkin's goodness is
obviously problematic; it has a dark underside of which
Myshkin himself is aware in the form of what he calls
"double thoughts." Myshkin's conscience seems to have lost
contact with the realities of the external situation, to be
functioning instead in the service of some more obscure
inner purpose; thus instead of preventing harm and doing
good, it wreaks havoc.[11]

At the end of the essay on masochism, Freud links moral
masochism with the darkest and most destructive forces in
human personality, suggesting its ultimate dangers and the
questionable nature of the instinctual renunciation, the
purity and goodness, it seems to achieve:

> Its danger lies in the fact that it originates from the
> death instinct and corresponds to the part of that in-
> stinct which has escaped being turned outwards as an
> instinct of destruction. But since, on the other hand, it
> has the significance of an erotic component, even the
> subject's destruction of himself cannot take place
> without libidinal satisfaction.[12]

If aggression does not appear at all in the Prince, except
as it is directed inward in the form of conscience and the
need to suffer, the other great drive, the sexual instinct, is
also apparently absent in him. Like almost all of Dostoevsky's meek and Christlike characters, the Prince is asexual.
He is evidently impotent: when Rogozhin asks him
whether he is keen on women, the Prince answers, "I, n-no!
You see. . . . Perhaps you don't know that, owing to my illness, I know nothing of women" (I.1). Later Myshkin says
to Ganya, "I can't marry any one, I am an invalid" (I.3). He
is even apparently without sexual feelings; desire for either
of the two women he loves is inconceivable to him. He cannot associate his feelings for Nastasya with desire: "for him,

Myshkin, to love that woman with passion was almost unthinkable" (II.5). And toward Aglaia his behavior is maddeningly innocent. Yevgeny Pavlovitch, Aglaia's other suitor, rebukes Myshkin for this, saying "Aglaia Ivanovna loved you like a woman, like a human being, not like . . . an abstract spirit" (IV.9). This unearthly absence of physical passion associates Myshkin again with the Christlike, childlike nature that is proposed as a moral ideal in the novel—with the child, of course, necessarily conceived of as totally free of sexual feeling. When the Prince tells Rogozhin that he knows nothing of women, Rogozhin replies, "Well, if that's how it is [. . .] you are a regular blessed innocent, and God loves such as you!" (I.1).

The overt picture presented by Myshkin is that of a personality of ideal purity in which instinctual drives are totally absent. But the lust and aggression forced out of Myshkin's character find expression elsewhere in the novel. They erupt in the character of Myshkin's polar opposite, Rogozhin. Myshkin and Rogozhin stand along with Stavrogin and Verkhovensky, Raskolnikov and Svidrigailov, and the two Golyadkins in the long series of Dostoevsky's doubles. If the personality of Myshkin is dominated by superego, that of Rogozhin is all id, a grisly other self that corresponds exactly to the elements denied and repressed in Myshkin.

As an imaginative creation, Rogozhin is quite different from the other characters in the novel; he seems to stand on another plane of reality. The others are more or less in the realistic tradition of character, given a kind of three-dimensional solidity by their involvement in the dramatic action and by description of the details of their appearance, speech, and manner. In comparison even with a relatively peripheral character such as Lebedyev, Rogozhin is not fully fleshed out with this sort of idiosyncratic detail that makes for the illusion of reality. In the first section, his appearance and dress are described, giving him a physical body, and he is treated as a real person. When he enters on the scene, however, it is characteristically a kind of violent break-in from outside amid noise and confusion, as at Nastasya's birthday party, like the eruption of some elemental force. After the end of the first part, Rogozhin becomes strikingly unreal. He appears most often simply as a pair of "strange glowing eyes," or as an indistinct figure half-glimpsed in darkness and often not even identified as Rogozhin, or named only later. In the hotel in Petersburg before Rogozhin's attack on him, Myshkin "suddenly saw in the half dark under the gateway close to the stairs a man. [. . .] but he vanished at once. Myshkin had caught only a glimpse of him and could not see him distinctly and could not have told for certain who he was (II.5)." In the park at Pavlovsk, "A man whose face was difficult to distinguish in the dark came up to the seat and sat down beside him" (III.3). Ippolit tells of seeing Rogozhin walk into his room in the middle of the night and sit for a long time without speaking; Ippolit, half-delirious, cannot decide whether it is an apparition or the real Rogozhin, until the next morning, when he discovers that his door was locked all night. The point is that it does not matter, because Rogozhin himself is a kind of hallucinatory figure, an internal force projected outward and perceived in consciousness as a physical image. But always he retains the fantastic power and mobility and the eerie flatness of a figure in a dream; like the dream-figure, he is an element of the mind itself.

Of course, every character in a work of literature embodies elements of mind in some way; characters are, after all, not real persons, but linguistic artifacts created out of the author's own mental life. But to the extent that a character is represented as looking and behaving like a person in the real world, his quality as a projection of mental life is modified and disguised. The modification and disguise are relatively thin in the case of Rogozhin. One could not subject Rogozhin to the kind of psychological analysis that can be done with Myshkin because he does not have the inter-

nal psychological complexity that would make it possible to
discuss him almost as if he were a real person. Myshkin is
more realistically conceived, not necessarily with regard to
the type of his character, but in the mode of its representation. That is, if such a person as Myshkin existed, his
speech, dress, and behavior could well appear to us as
Myshkin's are presented in the novel. But if such a character as Rogozhin were met with in the real world, he would
not be perceived as he is represented in the novel, as a pair
of eyes or an indistinct face materializing out of nowhere.
This is simply not the way the ego perceives external reality. Rogozhin, however, is not an external reality to be perceived by the ego in the outside world; he is an internal reality, an embodiment of the instinctual forces that threaten
the control of the ego. The impulses represented by
Rogozhin cannot be acknowledged consciously; they must
be projected and perceived by the ego as existing outside
itself. Rogozhin's sudden appearances in the action, as
when he breaks in on Nastasya's birthday party or materializes in the park at Pavlovsk, are like sudden eruptions
into consciousness of the repressed forces he represents.
Rogozhin lacks the density of the more realistic characters,
the discrepancy between what they appear to be and what
they are. He is all of a piece, The internal motives ascribed
to him are extremely simple; he has the self-explanatory
force of lust and hatred, which are not really motives but
the energies that animate motives.

The relationship of Rogozhin to Myshkin is quite different from that between Dostoevsky's other doubles, for instance Piotr Verkhovensky and Stavrogin in *The Possessed*
and Svidrigailov and Raskolnikov in *Crime and Punishment*.
In these novels the secondary figures, Verkhovensky and
Svidrigailov, bear obvious resemblances to the heroes: they
embody in debased or exaggerated form certain tendencies already present in the primary figures. But the relationship of Myshkin and Rogozhin is one of total opposition. Even physically, one is the negative of the other:

Myshkin is tall, slender, and fair, a Nordic type, while Rogozhin is short and dark with a flat nose and high cheek-bones, something of a Tartar. The contrast between them evokes a more primitive mode of thought and appeals to a deeper and more archaic layer of the mind than that suggested by the other pairs. Myshkin and Rogozhin are related as a thing may be represented by its contrary in a dream, as primal words have antithetical meanings, as the masochist is also a sadist. Their relationship suggests that even tendencies that are perceived in consciousness as entirely opposed—such as lust and purity, or aggression and passivity—may be only different aspects of a single entity in the unconscious.

III. THE SAINTLY WHORE

It seems important to discover why the double relationship assumes this particular character in *The Idiot*, why the energies represented by Rogozhin have been split off in so dramatic a form and kept so entirely isolated from the personality of Myshkin. The answer must be sought in the third part of the triad on which the novel is built, the figure of Nastasya, and in Myshkin's feelings for her. From the moment when he first sees her face in a photograph, Nastasya arouses feelings of extraordinary intensity in Myshkin.

> There was a look of unbounded pride and contempt, almost of hatred, in that face, and at the same time something confiding, something wonderfully simple-hearted. These two contrasting qualities roused a feeling almost of compassion. This dazzling beauty was even unbearable—the beauty of a pale face, almost sunken cheeks and burning eyes—a strange beauty! The prince gazed at it for a minute, then started suddenly, looked round him, hurriedly raised the portrait to his lips and kissed it. (I.7)

When he first sees Nastasya herself at Ganya Ivolgin's flat, he responds with the same intensity, staring at her speechless, "like a statue" (I.8). A few moments later, he explains this reaction by saying, "I felt I'd seen you somewhere [. . . .] I seem to have seen your eyes somewhere . . . but that's impossible. That's nonsense. . . . I've never been here before. Perhaps in a dream" (I.9).

Myshkin has with Nastasya an experience that is evoked a number of times in the novel at moments of deep and rather inexplicable emotion, the sensation of *déjà vu*. That sensation has a special psychological significance, to which in fact the Prince is very close when he says that perhaps he has seen Nastasya's eyes in a dream. For in *déjà vu* the subjective impression that something has been seen or experienced before is, in a way, accurate: the uncanny sense of familiarity is evoked by the "return of the repressed." That is, an experience that causes this peculiar alteration of consciousness has touched on an unconscious fantasy, or on the memory of a dream or of an actual experience that has undergone repression.[1] It is not yet clear exactly what unconscious memory or fantasy is disturbed in Myshkin by the face of Nastasya.

In any case, Myshkin sees in her something that other men do not. To the others, Nastasya is an object for sale to the highest bidder. To Myshkin she is an honest woman, she has "come pure out of [. . .] hell" (I.15). In fact, the actual sexual character of Nastasya is never really established in the novel. Contradictory reports are made of her. Lebedyev, who is an incorrigible gossip and knows everything about everybody, says of her,

> "No, she is not an Armance [a courtesan in the novel of that title by Stendhal]. There is only Totsky. And of an evening she sits in her own box at the Bolshoi or the French Theatre. The officers there may talk a lot about her among themselves, but even they can't prove a thing. 'That's the famous Nastasya Filippovna,' they say, and that's all; as to anything

further—nothing. Because there isn't anything more."
(I.1)

Technically Nastasya is a kept woman. But Totsky, who
keeps her, has been getting nothing for his money for five
years, since Nastasya came to Petersburg. And for the time
before that, the four years he kept her in the country, no
one considers her to blame: Totsky made her his mistress
when she was a girl of sixteen, an orphan and his legal
ward. Since coming to Petersburg to avenge herself on
Totsky for her shame, she has lived virtuously, even gaining a reputation for austerity.

Yet after the end of Part I, when Rogozhin takes Nastasya off to Ekaterinof Vauxhall for a "terrible orgy" and
then follows her to Moscow, matters become more ambiguous. Presumably Nastasya lives with Rogozhin in Moscow as his mistress; yet she still manages to seem virtuous.
Later she challenges Myshkin: "Ask Rogozhin whether I'm
a loose woman, he'll tell you!" (IV.8). This period in Moscow is part of the mysterious six-month gap between Parts
I and II that is one of the most conspicuous flaws in the
novel's structure. Dostoevsky plainly had no idea how to
proceed after the brilliant climax of Part I, and created a
sort of pause in order to reorganize his ideas. As the plot
began to develop again, he tried to fill in this period ret-
rospectively, alluding back to events that supposedly occurred then. During this time Myshkin went to Moscow to
claim his inheritance; Nastasya ran away several times from
Rogozhin to Myshkin; and Myshkin and Nastasya evidently
lived for a month in the same flat, on terms that are never
clear. In fact, all of these events remain confused and
shadowy. This gap in the novel seems rather like one of the
indistinct areas left by the censorship in a dream, in which
only fragments of repressed material can be glimpsed. Significantly, the principal action of this obscure section concerns the extremely conflicted subject of Nastasya's sexuality. If in fact Dostoevsky had clarified the events of this

period, it might have been impossible to maintain the ambiguity that is crucial to the portrayal of Nastasya.

Rogozhin tells Myshkin that Nastasya shamed him with other men.

> "I know it for a fact," Rogozhin persisted with conviction. "She is not that sort of woman, you say? It's no good telling me she is not that sort of woman, brother. That's nonsense. With you she won't be that sort of woman, and will be horrified herself, maybe, at such doings. But with me she's just like that. That's the way it is. She looks on me as the worst refuse. I know for certain that she got up that affair with Keller, that officer—the man who boxes—just to make a laughingstock of me." (II.3)

Although Rogozhin speaks convincingly, we still do not know quite what to believe. Is this story the truth, or only his jealous fantasy?

At Pavlovsk, the summer retreat where most of the latter part of the novel takes place, Nastasya becomes the center of a crowd of officers and attracts attention and gossip, and again nothing specific can be said against her. But although Myshkin says to her, "It wasn't your doing that you were with Totsky," and "you have suffered and have come pure out of that hell," yet he seems to see her increasingly surrounded by an aura of shame and guilt. Twice in Pavlovsk he has an agonizing dream of her: "At last a woman came to him; he knew her, and knowing her was torture [. . .]. There was such remorse and horror in this face that it seemed as though she must be a fearful criminal, and had just committed some awful crime" (III.7).

The ambiguity surrounding Nastasya is never really resolved; the figure of this woman seems to evoke ideas and images so contradictory that they cannot be reconciled in a single unified vision. It is never clear whether Nastasya is pure or debased, a saint or a whore. The opposing images simply coexist in her, and in the thoughts of the other characters about her, both equally powerful.

There is, of course, a large element of literary and cultural convention in Dostoevsky's conception of Nastasya's character. It is based on one of the stereotypes of nineteenth-century fiction, the type of "La Dame aux Camélias," the fallen woman or *grande cocotte* whom the hero wishes to redeem. In the essay entitled "A Special Type of Choice of Object Made by Men,"[2] Freud discusses the prototype in life of this literary figure, in the person of a certain kind of woman. This woman, who has a powerful hold on the erotic life of some men, always presents several specific features: she is in the possession of another man, a third person who plays the role of injured party; she is sexually discredited in some way; and she arouses in the man the desire to rescue her. In Freud's essay the peculiar fascination with this type of woman and the mixture of ideas in which she appears to the young man is traced back to the painful experience of the little boy on discovering the nature of his mother's relationship with his father. Freud points out that the almost invariable reaction of the child is to deny the facts of sexual life as they relate to his own parents: other children's parents may do these things, but his own certainly do not. The mother has been seen hitherto as an idealized, desexualized figure for whom the boy's own sexual feelings have had to be repressed; it suddenly becomes clear that she engages in a kind of activity forbidden to the child, and with someone else, the father. The mother's sexual relations with the father seem to the child an act of infidelity to himself, and earlier oedipal feelings of desire for her and hatred of the father are revived. But this crisis has a further ramification: the child is also likely to find out that there are women who will do with any man for money what his mother does with his father, and who are despised for this. "When after this he can no longer maintain the doubt which makes his parents an exception to the universal and odious norms of sexual activity, he tells himself with cynical logic that the difference between his mother and a whore is not after all so very great, since basically they do the same thing."[3]

Because of this fear of the unequal competition with the father, the child cannot afford to maintain consciously this disillusioned vision of the mother and the sexual feelings for her that it reawakens. The earlier idea of the mother as a spotless figure must be reinstated in consciousness, but thoughts of the mother's sexuality and resentment of her relationship with the father persist in the unconscious. The exclusive fascination with the fallen woman who is the property of another man derives from this repressed aspect of the feeling for the mother. It seems also that the more totally and energetically thoughts of the mother's sexuality have to be repressed and her purity insisted on, because of fear of rivalry with the father, the more likely it is that the female image will be split into the antithetical types of the saint and the whore. The figure of the "good" woman, who does not feel or arouse desire, is the desexualized image of the mother consciously preserved in the child's mind; that of the whore, who is sexually exciting and available, represents the child's repressed knowledge of the mother's sexuality. Many works of literature present us with the result of this splitting of the maternal image in the persons of two female characters, one sexless and "good," the other sexual and "bad." In *The Idiot*, the innocent and respectable Aglaia plays the part of the good girl in contrast to Nastasya. What is more striking, however, is that the split in the female archetype appears again *within* each of the two women, as though the centripetal tendency were extremely powerful. Although Aglaia is overshadowed by the far more commanding figure of Nastasya, she too exhibits some of the wildness, instability, and self-destructiveness of the bad woman.

In Freud's essay on the special type of object choice, the response of the young man to the fallen woman who be-

longs to another man is the desire to rescue her. This wish
has the meaning, according to Freud, of wanting to give
the mother a child. Myshkin certainly wishes to rescue Nastasya through his offer of marriage. But the sexual aim of
the wish seems to be entirely absent or displaced. First,
Myshkin has made it clear that he is incapable of sexual relations. Moreover, he feels a special horror at the idea of
Nastasya as a sexual object: "And for him, Myshkin, to love
that woman with passion was almost unthinkable, would
have been almost cruelty, inhumanity" (II.5). Although to
everyone else Nastasya is the supremely desirable woman,
in Myshkin her sexual availability arouses not lust but
compassion. The quality in her that appeals most strongly
to him is her suffering. When Mme Epanchin asks him apropos of Nastasya's photograph whether that is the sort of
beauty he appreciates, he says yes, just that sort, because
"In that face . . . there is so much suffering" (I.7). This vision of Nastasya could, of course, rationalize a sexual interest in her by making it appear altruistic. But the emphasis
on the suffering of the sexually debased mother figure may
serve the more significant purpose of desexualizing and
purifying her. The transformation reassures the son by
telling him that the mother is not a sexual creature who
betrays him willingly with the father, but a helpless victim
of the father's lust; and it wards off the son's own consciousness of his incestuous desire for her. Myshkin even
sees Nastasya as insane—"that broken, insane woman"—as
though to make still more powerful the taboo on her as a
sexual object.

Behind Nastasya, as the final determinant of the feeling
for her, looms the disturbing figure of Rogozhin and the
Prince's equivocal relationship with him. Although
Myshkin tries to take Nastasya away from Rogozhin, he
wants the other man to understand that his love for her is
not sexual, that he and Rogozhin can be friends rather
than rivals:

"I explained to you before that I don't love *her* 'with love, but with pity.' I believe I define it exactly. You said at the time that you understood what I said. Was that true? Did you understand? Here you are looking at me with hatred! I've come to reassure you, for you are dear to me too. I am very fond of you, Parfyon." (II.3)

Finally, of course, the purity of Myshkin's love for Nastasya, his refusal to see her as a sexual being, is the guarantee against the dreaded anger of the oedipal rival and the punishment of castration.

The episode of Marie, the girl in the Swiss village who was seduced and abandoned by the commercial traveler, is a kind of emblematic reduction of the story of Nastasya: motifs that are to some extent disguised and concealed in the larger plot are revealed here with a naïve iconographic clarity. Here the story of the fallen woman is placed explicitly in the context of childhood experience. Myshkin himself establishes the subject of the story as the child's understanding of adult sexuality when he says,

"Later on, when everybody blamed me [. . .] for talking to them [the children] like grown-up people and concealing nothing from them, I said that it was a shame to deceive them; that they understood everything anyway, however much things were concealed from them, and that they learnt it perhaps in a bad way; but not so from me. One need only remember one's own childhood." (I.6)

When Marie first returns to the village after her escapade with the man, the children treat her harshly—they taunt her and throw dirt at her, like the child who responds to the discovery of his mother's sexual activity with hostility and contempt. But this disillusioned vision of the mother

as soiled and contemptible cannot be maintained; the feelings for her reawakened in the boy by the discovery of her
sexual accessibility carry with them the danger of castration. Thus the image of the mother must be re-established
as pure and respectable. Myshkin accomplishes this transformation for the children when he arranges to meet
Marie in secret outside the village and gives her a redeem-
ing kiss. The children are spying on this scene unbe-
knownst to Marie and the Prince. As the Prince describes
the encounter to the Epanchins, "Then I kissed her and
said that she mustn't think that I had any evil intent, and
that I kissed her not because I was in love with her, but because I was very sorry for her, and that I had never, from
the very beginning, thought of her as guilty but only as unhappy" (I.6). The children betray their presence by breaking into jeers at the moment of the kiss—for them it has the
usual sexual meaning, which arouses their hostility and derision. But when Myshkin explains to them how unhappy
Marie is, they understand, and they come to love her. In
the watching children and the man and woman who think
themselves alone together, we have what is clearly a primal
scene fantasy, a representation of the child's wish to see the
parents in the sexual act. By replacing the act of intercourse with the Christlike kiss of peace, the Prince gives to
the children, and to the child in himself, a kind of desexualized primal scene that makes it possible to love and
respect the mother again.

Myshkin's sense of *déjà vu* when he meets Nastasya represents the recognition, in the tragic face of the fallen
woman, of the mother debased by the sexual relation with
the father and purified by suffering. It is this fixation on
the mother that determines the form of the relationship
between Myshkin and his double. Like all products of unconscious mental processes, the figure of Rogozhin is
over-determined: as Myshkin's rival for Nastasya, he represents the oedipal father and the threat of castration; as
the shadowy counterpart of Myshkin, he embodies the

dangerous lust and aggression repressed in Myshkin's own character because of this very threat. In "On the Universal Tendency to Debasement in the Sphere of Love," Freud writes that the fixation of erotic feeling on the mother causes either total impotence or the familiar split in the feeling for women into tenderness and sensuality. "The whole sphere of love in such people remains divided in the two directions personified in art as sacred and profane (or animal) love. Where they love they do not desire and where they desire they cannot love."[4] The impotent Myshkin, under the influence of the incestuous fixation, can only love without desire, thus preserving in consciousness the pure asexual mother; Rogozhin's lust, however, pays tribute to the unconscious perception of the mother as a whore and also, by withholding tenderness or respect, isolates that perception from the pure image in consciousness. The two sides of this division in erotic feeling embodied in Myshkin and Rogozhin are also projected outward onto the object and represented in the radical polarities of Nastasya's character. In the notebooks, Dostoevsky wrote that Myshkin stood for "Christian love" and Rogozhin "passionate and spontaneous love";[5] the split between them indicates that both are equally under the sway of the fixation on the mother and the incest taboo.

IV. "WHOM I LOVE I CHASTISE"

"Spontaneous and passionate love" has a special quality in the novel. It is something archaic and violent, like the appearance of Rogozhin himself at Nastasya's birthday party; dirty and coarsely dressed but with a massive diamond on his grubby hand and carrying a hundred thousand roubles wrapped in newspaper, he is like some fabulous underworld king, Pluto come to carry off Proserpine. Rogozhin defines the character of his love for Nastasya when he says to Myshkin,

"You see, we love in different ways too. There's a difference in everything," he went on softly after a pause.
"You say you love her with pity. There's no sort of pity
for her in me. And she hates me too, more than anything. I dream of her every night now, always that she
is laughing at me with another man. Because that's the
way it is, brother." (II.3)

In its savage extremity and its urge toward total possession
and domination, Rogozhin's love seems indistinguishable
from hatred.

In one way, however, it is like Myshkin's love: it defines
itself against the recurring image of the beloved with
another man, a continual nightmare of betrayal. Rogozhin
keeps watch outside Nastasya's house in the fear or the
hope of catching her with someone else. When in Moscow
he accuses her of infidelity, she mocks him, and he tells
Myshkin: "I threw myself at her and beat her till she was
black and blue" (II.3). Afterward, he abases himself, going
on his knees before her and begging forgiveness. But all
the time the desire to avenge himself for this new humiliation is mounting in him again. Nastasya compares him to
Henry IV doing penance barefoot in the snow before the
palace of the Pope at Canossa: "What do you suppose that
emperor thought about for those three days, and what
vows did he make while he was kneeling there? [. . .] Then
perhaps you are making vows: 'When she is married to me
I'll make her remember it all! I'll humble her to my heart's
content' " (II.3). The sexual passion in Rogozhin is a per-
petual cycle of self-abasement and revenge.

Curiously, there is no explicitly sexual action in the
novel, not even an embrace or a kiss, except for that of
Myshkin and Marie. Instead, the forms toward which
Rogozhin's passion tends constantly are cruelty and violence; its final apotheosis is the total lustful domination of
murder. Rogozhin knows this. He says to Myshkin, "To be
drowned or knifed! [. . .] Ha! Why that's just why she is

marrying me, because she knows my knife awaits her. Do you mean to say, prince, you've never yet had a notion of what's at the root of it all?" (II.3).[1]

Rogozhin's love is a sadistic passion that expresses itself in the infliction of pain, a desire for total domination that can only be satisfied by the destruction of the object. But as Myshkin says, "I've heard there are women who seek just that sort of love" (II.3). And indeed Nastasya knows what her fate will be, just as Rogozhin says, and despite her attempts to escape, is drawn to it inexorably. She even foretells almost exactly the details of her own death in a letter to Aglaia:

> "His house is gloomy, dreary, and there is a secret in it. I'm sure that he has, hidden in his box, a razor, wrapped in silk like that murderer in Moscow; he too lived in the same house with his mother, and kept a razor wrapped in silk to cut a throat with. All the time I was in their house, I kept fancying that somewhere under the floor there might be a corpse hidden there by the father perhaps, wrapped in oilcloth, like the corpse in the Moscow case, and surrounded in the same way with jars of Zhdanov's fluid. I could show you the corner. He is always silent: but I know he loves me so much that he can't help hating me. [. . .] I would kill him from terror. But he will kill me first." (III.10)

The relationship of Rogozhin, the man who inflicts pain and ultimately destroys, with Nastasya, the woman who offers herself for destruction, is the most dramatic instance of a configuration that appears throughout the novel, a fundamental pattern of sadistic feeling that shapes all the principal erotic relationships and that provides the last key to the character and fate of the chaste and gentle Prince.

The pattern is repeated most clearly in the Ganya-Nastasya relationship, which is to some extent a subform of that between Rogozhin and Nastasya, as Ganya himself is a

sort of minor Rogozhin, with the savagery of his passions
modified and embodied in a more conventional form.
Ganya's feelings for Nastasya are exactly like Rogozhin's,
but scaled down to fit the smaller proportions of his nature:

> Passion and hatred were strangely mingled in his soul,
> and although he did after painful hesitation give his
> consent to marry the "disreputable hussy," he swore in
> his heart to revenge himself cruelly upon her for it
> and "to take it out of her" afterwards. (I.4)

Beneath their apparent opposition, sadism and masochism are reciprocal manifestations of the same phenomenon: the erotic excitement associated with cruelty and suffering. Thus the roles of the sadist and the masochist are
easily reversed. With both Rogozhin and Ganya, Nastasya
often plays the tormentor's part. Ganya says of this, "it's
her character. She is a very Russian woman, I tell you"
(I.11). And Myshkin tells Rogozhin, "the more she torments you, the more she loves you" (III.3). And of course
this provocative torment also invites suffering in the form
of retaliation; she knows the man will "take it out of her"
afterward.

As Ganya is related to Rogozhin, Aglaia is derived in
somewhat the same way from Nastasya. Beneath the charm
of Aglaia's pranks and caprices is the same perversity that
appears in Nastasya's more dangerous behavior. Aglaia
imagines having Ganya prove his love for her by holding
his finger in a candle flame for half an hour; she shows her
love for Myshkin by calling him at various times a freak
and an idiot, telling him she never wants to see him again,
and sending him a hedgehog in a basket. But her mother
says, "Don't be angry. She's a wilful, mad, spoiled girl—if
she cares for any one she'll be sure to rail at him aloud and
abuse him to his face" (II.12). This "abuse to his face," only
a figure of speech in Aglaia's case, is acted out quite literally

by Nastasya in the scene in the park at Pavlovsk, where she cuts the officer across the face with a riding whip.

The pattern appears even at the level of Lebedyev, who has a kind of grotesque lovers' quarrel with General Ivolgin over a stolen wallet and ends by persecuting him literally to death. It is Lebedyev who describes as clearly as anyone the bond between lovers when he invites Rogozhin to beat him, saying "And if you beat me, it means that you don't reject me! Beat me! By beating me you'll have put your seal on me" (I.1). The motto of the entire book could be the Biblical "Whom I love I chastise," which Ganya quotes apropos of Nastasya.

Behind this pervasive conception of the erotic relationship is the fantasy that dominates the novel, and that appears in shadowy but evocative form in an image that occurs to Myshkin just before Nastasya whips the officer:

> If, loving a woman more than anything in the world, or foreseeing the possibility of loving her thus, one were suddenly to see her in chains behind an iron grating and beneath the rod of a prison warder, one would feel something like what Myshkin felt at that moment. (III.2)

This vignette is entirely consistent with the character of the love relationships around which the plot is constructed; it presents in economical form the conception of the sexual relationship that is at the core of them: the idea that in the sexual act one partner is punished or injured by the other.

The "primal scene," the imagined or actual experience of seeing or hearing the parents in the sexual act, is extremely significant in the fantasy life of the child, providing a focal point for his sexual curiosity, particularly his scoptophilia, or wish to gaze at sexual things, and for oedipal feelings. The child who is exposed to the act of intercourse usually understands the sounds and the activity as a fight or a beating in which the mother is getting the worst of it.

Thus the sexual act is transformed in the child's mind into a sadistic scene of punishment: a woman loved "more than anything in the world" is being beaten. In Myshkin's fantasy the chains and the iron bars represent the belief, or wish to believe, that the mother submits to the sexual act only unwillingly, and the warder's rod is the father's penis seen under the familiar aspect of a weapon. The child's feelings in the primal scene situation must be a mixture of excitement and terror. Myshkin characterizes his response to this image of Nastasya as horror.[2]

The primal scene derives much of its meaning for the child from the feelings associated with the Oedipus complex, and may also affect the evolution of those feelings. The more or less "normal" oedipal pattern in the son is the feeling of tenderness and desire for the mother and an ambivalent attitude toward the father composed of a mixture of love and rivalry. Normally both components of this ambivalent attitude lead the boy toward identification with the father: he admires his father and wants to be like him; but this being like the father also implies taking the father's place with the mother, which might provoke the father to retaliate with castration. The fear of castration then redoubles the wish to get rid of the father as a rival and, again, to take his place.

If, however, the father is in fact a brutal or frightening person, the Oedipus complex takes another turn: the fear of castration inherent in the boy's normally ambivalent attitude is reinforced, and the identification with the father is inhibited insofar as it implies taking the father's place with the mother, because the threat of castration is too real. In this case, the boy may abandon his rivalry with the father and adopt instead a passive, "feminine" attitude in the attempt to be loved by the father as a woman and to avoid rivalry and the threat of castration.[3]

Under the influence of the normal Oedipus complex the son might be expected to identify in the primal scene with

the father and to wish to take his place. However, if the
scene is interpreted sadistically, the father appears as a
brutal and overpowering figure who might actually cas-
trate the son who tried to replace him. Particularly if the
father is in reality such a person, toward whom the son has
adopted the passive, "feminine" attitude, the son will tend
to respond to the instinctual excitement aroused by the
scene by identifying with the mother and experiencing vicarious gratification in the masochistic form of pain and
terror, as he thinks the mother does.[4] In this event, the
Oedipus complex takes the "negative" form, which implies
a homosexual resolution.

In *The Idiot*, all the life of the novel is deeply imprinted
with the sadistic conception of the primal scene. There is
also evidence of a negative or homosexual resolution of the
Oedipus complex, with deflection of the feeling for the
father in the direction of passivity and masochism. This
development is most clearly represented in the character
and history of Nastasya. One aspect of Nastasya's role in
the novel has already been discussed—the part she plays in
Myshkin's thoughts as a mother-figure whom he wishes to
rescue from the brutal Rogozhin. However, Nastasya also
has a history and a mental and moral life of her own, aside
from the part she plays in Myshkin's thoughts of her. Nastasya has been a child, a daughter, and the mistress of
Totsky before her meeting with Myshkin. This aspect of
Nastasya is an important part of the overall psychological
dynamic of the novel. It is one representation of the resolution of the Oedipus complex in attitudes that identify the
role of the child with a passivity and masochism perceived
as feminine. And although the past and the inner life given
to Nastasya by the novel are apparently independent of
Myshkin, they can be shown finally to converge in a significant way with Myshkin's conception of her and to represent important aspects of his own mental life. Guilt and
suffering exist everywhere in the novel, manifesting themselves at times in one character, at times in another. But all

these manifestations are related: they flow from a specific conception of suffering that animates the entire novel. In Nastasya, guilt and suffering drop the disguise they wear in Myshkin's personality and show their origins in sexuality. "Even the subject's destruction of himself cannot take place without libidinal satisfaction."[5]

Nastasya is almost entirely defined by suffering; it seems that she has only awaited the arrival in her life of Myshkin and Rogozhin to find her consummation in total destruction. The masochistic quality of Nastasya's suffering is made quite explicit in the novel. Aglaia says to her, "You can love nothing but your shame and the continual thought that you've been brought to shame and humiliated. If your shame were less or you were free of it altogether, you'd be more unhappy" (IV.8).

Nastasya feels guilty of a crime that everyone assures her she did not commit: her past life with Totsky was not of her own choosing. And yet to herself and to others, including even Myshkin, who wants to marry her and tries to convince her of her innocence, Nastasya also seems mysteriously stained by the guilt of forbidden sexuality. The ambiguity about her appears to go beyond the actual facts of her experience. If she was violated by Totsky at the age of sixteen and later lived virtuously, there would seem to be no question of guilt on her part. The logic of this formulation is for some reason unsatisfying, however, both to Nastasya and to others. In view of the youth and defenselessness of Nastasya at the time of her seduction, how could she be held guilty for her unwilling part in the relationship? The answer lies in the very nature of that relationship. Nastasya was left an orphan at the age of seven. The responsibility for her upbringing was assumed by Count Totsky, an old friend of her father, who took Nastasya to his own estate and became her guardian. Thus Totsky assumed the role of father, and the later sexual relationship had the significance for the girl of a fulfillment in reality of the unconscious wish for incest. The punishment for such fulfillment is, of course, guilt.

Nastasya lives in the country as Totsky's mistress for four years. Then she hears that he plans to be married, and she comes to Petersburg with the intention of punishing him by preventing the marriage. She does manage to spoil that project and the later engagement to Alexandra Epanchin. But her real revenge on Totsky is the spectacle she presents of her own degradation, her deliberate refusal to save herself from ruin. After Nastasya has refused Ganya and Myshkin and run off with Rogozhin "to the gutter," as she says, one of the guests at her birthday party characterizes this strange mode of revenge:

> "they say something of the sort is done among the Japanese," observed Ivan Petrovitch Ptitsyn. "They say any one who has received an insult goes to the offender and says, 'you have wronged me, and in revenge I've come to cut open my stomach before you,' and with these words he actually does rip open his stomach before his enemy, and probably feels great satisfaction in doing so, as if he had really avenged himself." (I.16)

The abuse Nastasya heaps on herself, her insistence on being seen as a "low creature" and finally on being destroyed, are in some way meant as reproaches to Totsky. This is exactly the mechanism of suffering described by Freud in "Mourning and Melancholia": "the self-reproaches are reproaches against a loved object which have been shifted away from it on to the patient's own ego."[6]

In her thirst for suffering and her delusional self-hatred, Nastasya behaves like someone in a melancholiac depression. Melancholia, like the mourning that follows a death, is occasioned by the loss of a love object; however, in melancholia the love object is not necessarily dead in reality, but only dead to the ego. The lost object is not given up, but introjected—that is, the ego identifies itself with the object. Thus reproaches originally directed against the loved person are now turned round upon the self. This punishment of the introjected object may go as far as suicide, which is always in part a reproach to someone else.

> If the love for the object . . . takes refuge in narcissistic identification, then the hate comes into operation on this substitutive object, abusing it, debasing it, making it suffer and deriving sadistic satisfaction from its suffering. The self-tormenting in melancholia, which is without doubt enjoyable, signifies . . . a satisfaction of trends of sadism and hate which relate to an object, and which have been turned round upon the subject's own self. . . . the patients usually still succeed, by the circuitous path of self-punishment, in taking revenge on the original object and in tormenting their loved one through their illness.[7]

The vengefulness and sadism in the melancholiac's depreciation of himself suggest one of the preconditions of this type of response to the loss of love: a strong original ambivalence toward the object, a conflict of love and hatred from which the only escape is to turn the hatred against oneself.[8]

It may seem wrong to conceive of Nastasya's suicidal self-hatred as occasioned by loss of love, since she professes never to have felt for Totsky anything but contempt— "nauseating contempt, which had come upon her immediately after her first surprise" (I.4). Yet even in this description of her emotions by Nastasya herself, there is some suggestion of a more positive feeling for Totsky: her "contempt" was not in fact immediate, but developed only after an earlier reaction, which she characterizes here as "surprise." It was only when she heard of Totsky's plans to marry that Nastasya descended on him in Petersburg with the fury of an avenging angel. Her feeling for Totsky must certainly be ambivalent: such a relationship could only arouse a mixture of excitement and fear, love and hatred.

Nastasya came to Petersburg with the idea of punishing Totsky; but then this desire for punishment is turned round on herself. What is most revealing here is the way in which the self-punishment is carried out: strangely enough, it takes the form of sexual debasement, which is clearly a *repetition* of the original relationship with Totsky. Myshkin casts some light on the paradoxes of Nastasya's behavior and their hidden meaning in speaking of her to Aglaia:

> "Oh, she's crying out every minute in her frenzy that she doesn't admit going wrong, that she was the victim of others, the victim of a depraved and wicked man. But whatever she may say to you, believe me, she's the first to disbelieve it, and to believe with her whole conscience that she is . . . to blame. When I tried to dispel that darkness, it threw her into such misery that my heart will always ache when I remember that awful time. It's as though my heart had been stabbed once for all. She ran away from me. Do you know what for? Simply to show me that she was a degraded creature. But the most awful thing is that perhaps she didn't even know herself that she only wanted to prove that to me, but ran away because she had an irresistible inner craving to do something shameful, so as to say to herself at once, 'There, you've done something shameful again, so you're a degraded creature!' Oh, perhaps you won't understand this, Aglaia. Do you know that in that continual consciousness of shame there is perhaps a sort of awful, unnatural enjoyment for her, a sort of revenge on some one." (III.8)

The "awful, unnatural enjoyment" is the recapitulation of the erotic and aggressive pleasures of the original relationship, the gratification through shame and self-punishment of the love and hatred for Totsky.

The suffering and the disguised pleasure of the melancholiac depression are, of course, masochistic in nature. The same division of the ego against itself takes place here as that described by Freud in the essay on masochism, and

with the same result: the turning of sadistic energies
against the self to the end of recreating within the ego an
ambivalent relationship with a love object. Both in the reproaches of conscience she directs against herself and in offering herself for sexual debasement, Nastasya experiences
again the masochistic pleasure of the relationship with
Totsky: the very punishment for the illicit gratification becomes its re-enactment. She does indeed, as Aglaia puts it,
love her own shame.[9]

The figure of Nastasya is overdetermined: that is, she is
the vehicle for the expression of more than one unconscious idea, although the ideas are closely related. Most obviously, she represents the mother, the forbidden incestuous object whom the son unconsciously desires and wishes
to rescue from the father. However, she must also be identified with a part of Myshkin himself. If Rogozhin represents one split-off part of Myshkin's identity—the lustful
and aggressive masculine strivings that are repressed because of fear of castration—Nastasya is the other, the
objectification in the novel of the passive, masochistic
"feminine" strivings in relation to the father.[10] These strivings are represented in Nastasya in two forms, corresponding to the two situations in which she is placed by the plot.
In relation to Rogozhin, she offers an opportunity for identification with the abused mother in the sadistic primal
scene, interpreted by the child as a scene of beating or
punishment. But in relation to Totsky, she is also the child
feminized and seduced by the father, as the boy watching
or imagining the primal scene might both wish and fear to
be.

The masochism of Nastasya and that of Myshkin are in
essence the same. Both present clearly an irrational guilt
and a need to suffer. Freud explains the final meaning of
this need, and the link between the sadistic conscience and
the repressed sexual impulses of masochism, in the following passage:

We were able to translate the expression "unconscious sense of guilt" as meaning a need for punishment at the hands of a parental power. We now know that the wish, which so frequently appears in phantasies, to be beaten by the father stands very close to the other wish, to have a passive (feminine) sexual relation to him and is only a regressive distortion of it. If we insert this explanation into the content of moral masochism, its hidden meaning becomes clear to us.[11]

In both Nastasya and Myshkin, guilt and the need to suffer represent the wish to experience masochistic pleasure in relation to the father. In Myshkin, this aim is achieved primarily in the disguised form of moral suffering. But in the character of Nastasya and through Myshkin's intense interest in and identification with her, moral suffering shows its roots in the desire for sexual debasement. At the level of literal meaning, of course, Nastasya and Myshkin are separate and distinct characters, fully achieved in realistic terms. But at the unconscious level they are rooted in the same tendency to identify the dreadful pleasures of guilt and suffering with a feminine attitude toward the father.

V. THE SCENE ON THE STAIRCASE: "A WEAPON MADE TO A SPECIAL PATTERN"

The need for suffering is imposed on all the significant life of the novel by the sadomasochistic conception of the sexual act. This unconscious fantasy is most fully embodied in a single coherent sequence that represents the primal scene and the wishes and fears associated with it in powerful and unmistakable symbolic language. This is the stunning scene of Rogozhin's attack on Myshkin in the hotel, ending with Myshkin's epileptic seizure, which is the fullest dramatic revelation of the unconscious motifs at work in the book.

The scene takes place near the beginning of Part II; Myshkin has just returned to Petersburg from Moscow after the break in the action following Nastasya's birthday party and her elopement with Rogozhin, which ends Part I. The episode of the attack is preceded by a long day in which Myshkin wanders about Petersburg in a pre-epileptic state of increasing anxiety and disorientation. During most of this haunting sequence, Myshkin is distracted and confused; his attention is fixed on peculiar details or odd impressions that appear to be unrelated, but that have strong unconscious connections which form the psychological context of the climactic scene.

The first of these details is Myshkin's vision of "the strange, burning gaze of someone's two eyes" fixed on him as he gets out of the train (II.2); these eyes will reappear throughout the day. Myshkin goes first to Lebedyev's house, where he complains of feeling unwell, then to Rogozhin's, where he recognizes in the "strange and heavy gaze" of Rogozhin the same eyes he glimpsed at the train station (II.3). The second curious detail that attracts Myshkin's attention at Rogozhin's house is a shop on the ground floor owned by Skoptsy, members of a sect who practice self-castration.

At this meeting, Myshkin and Rogozhin compare the different kinds of love Nastasya inspires in each of them, and Rogozhin tells Myshkin of his experiences with Nastasya in Moscow. During that time, Nastasya ran away from Rogozhin almost on their wedding day and came to Myshkin, begging him to save her from Rogozhin. Now she has come back to Rogozhin. "And . . . and you are marrying her now? What will you do afterwards?" Myshkin asks. "Rogozhin bent a lowering, terrible gaze on Myshkin and made no answer." Myshkin is horrified by the implication of this silence. But then, shortly afterward, he does something very strange: he stands up suddenly as if to leave, saying "I won't hinder you anyway." He says this "softly, almost dreamily, as though replying to some secret inner thought of his own" (II.3).

Following this dreamlike moment in which Myshkin's horror turns to acquiescence, he finds himself toying absently with a knife on Rogozhin's table. Myshkin is somehow fascinated by it, although it is an ordinary garden knife, with "a blade seven inches long and of about the usual breadth" (II.3). Rogozhin snatches the knife away from Myshkin and begins to show him out, but again Myshkin's attention is fixed in a peculiar way, this time on a picture, Holbein's painting of the body of Christ just taken from the cross. The picture provokes a discussion of religion and atheism. Myshkin tells a story, which for him defines the essence of Russian religious feeling, about two peasants preparing to go to bed in an inn, one of whom is suddenly seized with a desire for the other's silver watch. Praying "God, forgive me for Christ's sake!" he cuts his friend's throat. After hearing the story, Rogozhin takes Myshkin to receive the blessing of his old mother, and exchanges crosses with him. Myshkin wishes to embrace Rogozhin in parting, but Rogozhin turns away:

"Don't be afraid! Though I've taken your cross, I won't murder you for your watch!" he muttered indistinctly, and suddenly began to laugh strangely. But suddenly his whole face changed; he turned horribly pale, his lips trembled, his eyes blazed. He raised his arms, embraced Myshkin warmly, and said breathlessly: "Well, take her then, since it's fated! She is yours—I give in to you! . . . Remember Rogozhin!" (II.4)

In the chapter that follows this renunciation by Rogozhin in favor of his rival, Myshkin wanders the streets in a state of growing confusion and anxiety. His loss of conscious control is accompanied by an increasing disorientation of the narrative sequence; it is extremely difficult to follow Myshkin's movements through the city and to distinguish what actually happens from what he imagines. The peculiar fixation of attention or sense of *déjà vu* experienced earlier with Rogozhin's eyes, the knife, and the Holbein painting now manifests itself in Myshkin's impression of being followed. He is dimly aware of an unknown idea pressing for consciousness, something he cannot or will not remember; but "he did not want to think anything out, and he did not." He buys a ticket for Pavlovsk, gets on the train, gets back off, finds himself before a shop window staring at an "article worth sixty kopecks." He begins musing on the famous Zhemarin murder case, in which the murderer used a special weapon: "Had Rogozhin a weapon made to a special pattern?" He finds himself standing before Nastasya's house, where again he sees "those eyes," and experiences a crushing sense of guilt (II.5).

At last he returns to his hotel. There, suddenly, just before the gate, he thinks of Rogozhin's knife and remembers that the window in which he saw the "article worth sixty kopecks" was a cutler's. At that moment the storm that has been building up all day breaks, there is a downpour, and the tension that has accumulated throughout this long hallucinatory sequence comes to a climax.

As Myshkin nears the hotel gateway, he sees a man standing in the half-darkness under the arch; he tries to overtake him, but the man vanishes.

> The staircase up which Myshkin ran from the gateway led to the corridors of the first and second floors, on which were the rooms of the hotel. As in all old houses, the staircase was of stone, dark and narrow, and it turned round a thick stone column. On the first half-landing there was a hollow like a niche in the column, not more than half a yard wide and nine inches deep. Yet there was room for a man to stand there. Dark as it was, Myshkin, on reaching the half-landing, at once discovered that a man was hiding in the niche.

Myshkin suddenly wanted to pass by without looking
to the right. He had taken one step already, but he
could not resist turning round.

Those two eyes, *the same two eyes*, met his own. The
man hidden in the niche had already moved one step
from it. For one second they stood facing one another
and almost touching. Suddenly Myshkin seized him by
the shoulders and turned him back towards the staircase, nearer to the light; he wanted to see his face
more clearly.

Rogozhin's eyes flashed and a smile of fury contorted his face. He raised his right hand and something gleamed in it; the prince did not think of stop-
ping it. He only remembered that he thought he cried
out, "Parfyon, I don't believe it!" Then suddenly
something seemed to have opened wide before him;
an extraordinary *inner* light illuminated his soul. The
moment lasted perhaps half a second, yet he clearly
and consciously remembered the beginning, the very
first sound of the fearful cry which broke of itself from
his breast and which he could not have checked by any
effort. Then his consciousness was instantly extin-
guished and complete darkness followed. (II.5)

The confusion and mounting panic of the day, the tormenting sensation of a frightful thought hovering at the
back of consciousness, the peculiar attention to the eyes,
the knife, and the painting of the dead Christ, all gather
and burst here in a violent revelation of instinctual fury. In
the conversation earlier in the day between Myshkin and
Rogozhin, the two men have, as it were, verbally passed
Nastasya back and forth between them. Myshkin, imagining
what Rogozhin will do to Nastasya, has said, "I won't hinder
you"; however, at parting Rogozhin has said, "Take her
then . . . I give in to you!" with the disquieting postscript,
"Remember Rogozhin!" It is as if this strange transaction,
in which each man has somehow given the other permis-
sion to do as he will, provokes in Myshkin a fantasy of in-

tercourse in which the act takes the peculiar form dictated
by the repressed sexual wishes embodied in his personality
throughout the novel. At the literal level, of course, the
scene "really happens." But in the pattern of unconscious
meaning in the text, the sequence embodies a fantasy of
parental intercourse in which the childish wishes to see and
to participate are both gratified for Myshkin. The primal
scene here takes the sadomasochistic form of a violent attack, in which Myshkin's identification is not with the sadistic father, but with the sadistically violated mother.

The topographical details of the scene, presented with
unusual clarity, suggest familiar symbolic meanings; they
are dream-language for the body, and for the gratification
and punishment of desire. By itself or in another context,
no one of these images would necessarily have the meaning
here ascribed to it; the elements of such a sequence,
whether in a dream or in a work of art, do not have fixed
meanings that can be read like a code, in a predetermined
and mechanical fashion. Rather, the images take on meaning, not only from the analogues they suggest in human
anatomy and function but from the pattern of internal relationships among them and from the surrounding context
in which they appear. Given both the larger context of the
novel with its typical pattern of sexual relationship, and the
narrower context of the preceding action, which arouses
specific fears and emphasizes repeatedly certain significant
details, a strikingly coherent and suggestive pattern
emerges in the staircase scene. The intense emotion and
hallucinatory vividness of the sequence and the peculiar
emphasis on topography are signals of an unusually direct
and concentrated expression of the unconscious comparable to that in a dream.

In dreams, gateways and doors often represent the
opening of the female genitals: the hotel gateway is a sort
of covered arch, and within it is a man. The gateway leads
to a staircase, which is dark and narrow, like the ascending
passages of the body. Moreover, the stairs wind around a

"thick stone column": the staircase enclosing the column is a strikingly graphic representation of the vagina enclosing the penis. But within this representation is a second one: on the landing is a niche in the column; like the staircase itself, the niche is very narrow, "yet there was room for a man to stand there." This peculiarly detailed topography emphasizes again the apparent smallness of the opening within which there is nonetheless "room for a man to stand"; the emphasis seems to express the child's amazement and fascination at the mysterious idea of the hidden space inside the female body, and at the impressive phenomenon of erection.

This sort of repetition is characteristic of the primary process thinking that goes on in dreams and in states of diminished ego control. Just as a single dream image may be the condensation of several unconscious ideas, so a single pressing unconscious thought may be expressed in several images in the manifest dream. However, the repetitions, particularly the last two, also create an effect of ambiguity. That is, the male figure inside the niche, which is in turn inside a column enclosed in a winding staircase, introduces an effect of sexual confusion, corresponding to the child's confusion about what actually happens during intercourse, and about the difference between the genitals of the two sexes. The small child who sees or imagines the primal scene does not know for certain who has a penis and who does not, nor what becomes of it during intercourse; whatever intellectual understanding may exist is likely to be weakened by the fear and excitement of the actual scene. The sight of the mother's genitals suggests to the boy the disturbing idea that some people have no penis or have lost it, perhaps during the very act he is witnessing, when the father's penis seems to disappear.

The confusion is increased by darkness and by the difficulty of seeing anything clearly. It is dark under the gateway, the sky is dark, the stairway is dark: the persistent emphasis on darkness and indistinct vision suggests that this is a scene that takes place at night, and that at once arouses and frustrates the desire to see. The primal scene presents itself primarily as a visual experience, in which the child discovers, by looking, something that has been concealed from him. "Dark as it was, Myshkin, on reaching the half-landing, at once discovered that a man was hiding in the niche. Myshkin suddenly wanted to pass by without looking to the right. He had taken one step already, but he could not resist turning round." The wish not to look is clearly a defense against the wish to look, which finally triumphs.

This essentially visual aspect of the primal scene explains the recurring apparition throughout the day of the eyes of Rogozhin. Through a mechanism of reversal, the one who wishes to spy projects onto others the wish to spy on him.[1] Moreover, such a reversal seems only just: the child fears being found out in his own sexual activities and even in his thoughts, which he believes are in some mysterious way transparent to adults. Rogozhin's eyes represent at once the visual aspect of the child's sexual wishes and the threat of discovery and of punishment for those wishes, which is castration.

When Myshkin looks round, the eyes meet his own, and the man moves toward him until they are almost touching. Myshkin tries to see the other more clearly; and at this crucial moment, when the wish to see and the wish to touch are both about to be gratified, "Rogozhin's eyes flashed and a smile of fury contorted his face. His right hand was raised and something gleamed in it." The undefined fear that has pursued Myshkin all day suddenly materializes in this terrifying image: Rogozhin does indeed have a "weapon made to a special pattern," this knife that so obsessed Myshkin and that will later be used on Nastasya. The knife represents at once the instrument that penetrates—the sadistic penis itself—and the instrument of castration. And castration is the punishment for all the wishes expressed in this scene. It is the penalty for looking at forbidden things and for wishing to replace the father, to compete with him for the mother in an aggressive way; but it is also the punishment for the wish that emerges most clearly here, the wish to avoid the competition with the father and to submit in a passive feminine way. The alternative of being loved by the father as a woman also seems possible only at the terrible price of loss of the penis.

All the events of the day that have attracted Myshkin's attention in a fixed way or evoked the sense of *déjà vu*, of a repressed idea struggling to consciousness, suggest the emergence of the feared homosexual wish and the penalty for submission: the significance of Rogozhin's eyes and his knife is clear; the Skoptsy, the tenants of Rogozhin's house, practice self-castration; the Holbein painting of Christ, his body so bruised and so thoroughly dead that, as Myshkin says, "that picture might make some people lose their faith," depicts the terrible fate of the Son who submits to the Father: "not my will, but thine, be done." Even the story of the peasant who slits his friend's throat and steals his watch as they prepare for bed together suggests the submerged homosexual wish and the accompanying fear.

The wish and the fear are perilously close to realization in the image of Rogozhin with his knife raised. At this point the excitement aroused by the desire to submit sexually to the father and by the terror of castration becomes unbearably intense, and the ego is overwhelmed in the epileptic attack; the barriers of the ego are broken, and it is flooded with instinctual excitement. The cry, the convulsive movements, and the loss of consciousness of the fit are at once a sort of exaggerated representation and a substitute for the release of orgasm, the logical culmination of this symbolic coitus in which Myshkin is both spectator and participant. The scene ends with Myshkin falling downstairs and striking his head. The fit has saved him from Rogozhin's knife, but through a familiar equation by which the head stands for the penis, the feared injury to the genital is represented symbolically in the bloodied head.[2]

Moreover, the head is perhaps punished as the organ of evil impulses, the representation of the mind in which the whole fantastic episode has originated.

One curious aspect of this sequence is the guilt Myshkin feels throughout the day whenever he becomes momentarily aware of his suspicions of Rogozhin:

> (Oh, how the prince was tortured by the hideousness, the "degradation" of this conviction, of "that base foreboding," and how he had reproached himself!) "Say of what if you dare," he kept telling himself continually with reproach and challenge. "Formulate all your thought, dare to express it clearly, precisely, without faltering! Oh, I am ignoble!" he repeated with indignation and a flush on his face. "With what eyes shall I look upon that man for the rest of my life! Oh, what a day! Oh, God, what a nightmare!" (II.5)

Myshkin assumes that his suspicions of Rogozhin, his loss of confidence in him, are in some way responsible for Rogozhin's attack on him. In the deepest sense, this is true, for the attack is in fact a representation of Myshkin's thoughts and desires. The chaste and gentle Prince, "a regular blessed innocent" such as God loves, has the same passions as other men, the same energies of lust and hatred. What distinguishes him from the violent souls around him is that Myshkin can only experience these forces passively; they must appear to overwhelm him from outside, through the agency of Rogozhin, who represents both the violation from outside that is the destiny of the meek soul, and the violence that it fears within itself and projects outward onto the figure of the aggressor. The form in which instinctual forces are expressed in the scene of the attack, the primitive lust and aggression of Rogozhin, unmodified by the influence of the ego, suggests the reason for the terror these forces inspire in Myshkin and explains the purity of his personality: the expression of instinct is conceived of as leading to mutilation and even death.

VI. FATHERS AND CHILDREN

If a person such as Myshkin were to appear in real life, one would be curious about his childhood, particularly about the character of his father and the relationship between his parents, expecting to find in them circumstances that had shaped his personality and his response to instinctual drives. A character in a novel is not a real person; but it is in the power of the great writer to create the illusion of reality, and in fact to create through illusion a reality more vivid than that of life because more consistent and lucid. In looking for confirmation of the psychological patterns of Myshkin's adult experience in his childhood, we must avoid the familiar mistake, not peculiar to psychoanalytic criticism, of confusing literature with life, of assuming that because certain things happen to the character in the book, other events *must* have occurred in his life before the story began. Myshkin exists only on the page; he has no childhood, nor any other experience, except what is given to him by the words of the text. Nor is there any causal relationship between the past and the present of a character in literature, as there is in life: Myshkin's childhood experiences do not *determine* his adult personality; they are neither logically nor chronologically prior to it, but exist on the same logical and temporal plane with it. But if, as seems reasonable, we assume in a great work a high degree of psychological coherence and of fidelity to the dynamic of mental life, we should expect to find the hero's childhood *consistent* with his adult personality. Literature often reveals even more clearly than life the connections between past and present and the essential timelessness of the unconscious.

The text does give Myshkin a childhood and parentage, although this material is so scattered and off-hand as to be easily overlooked. Moreover, a striking pattern can be composed from the relationships of the three principal characters with their fathers and father-figures. Nastasya and Rogozhin are brilliantly individualized and differentiated from Myshkin as characters, but they also objectify in the action certain aspects of Myshkin himself and of the attitude toward the father that is at the heart of the book.

Myshkin casts an air of ambiguity over his childhood in his recollections of it, as though it contained mysteries he cannot or will not fathom: "although he remembered everything, there was little he could explain satisfactorily because there was so much he could not account for. Frequent attacks of his illness had made him almost an idiot (the prince himself said 'idiot')" (I.3). The attacks and the "idiocy" have evidently served the purpose here of preventing understanding; like neurotic symptoms, they represent interrupted mental processes.

One certain fact is that Myshkin was orphaned at the age of six or seven. His mother died of a "chill"—whatever that means. The death of the father, an army officer, is more interesting. "My father died while he was awaiting trial," Myshkin tells General Ivolgin, "though I've never been able to find out what he was accused of." Ivolgin, who pretends to have known the father, tells Myshkin, "Oh, that was about the case of the private Kolpakov, and there's no doubt that the prince would have been acquitted." He then tells the following story: private Kolpakov stole, and Myshkin's father threatened to have him flogged. Kolpakov went back to the barracks, lay down on his bed, and died a quarter of an hour afterward. He was buried, but six months later at brigade review "Kolpakov turns up, as though nothing had happened" (I.8). Ivolgin's story is, of course, another of his fantastic lies. But a similar story appears later, in the slanderous article written about Myshkin by Antip Burdovsky and the nihilists. The article says of Myshkin's father,

"he was a lieutenant, who died while on his trial for a sudden disappearance at cards of all the company's money, or possibly for an excessive use of the rod on some subordinate [. . .]." (II.8)

The two stories have in common the idea of the flogging of subordinates. Both Ivolgin's and Burdovsky's stories are "false"—that is, if the novel itself is taken to be a "true" story, Ivolgin and Burdovsky are telling lies, stories whose truth is denied by the main character, who is represented as a truthful person. However, these stories form part of the text, like any of its other pages, and are drawn from the same imaginative sources. The stories are in fact the only accounts of the character of Myshkin's father in the text; no other explanation of the offense for which he was awaiting trial is ever advanced.

The relationship of officer to subordinate resembles in significant ways that of father to son. Private Kolpakov, threatened publicly with flogging, lies down on his bed and dies quite by coincidence, thus exposing Myshkin's father to the suspicion of having been too enthusiastic a disciplinarian; however, six months after his death and burial, Kolpakov reappears unharmed. Thus General Ivolgin's story at once confirms and denies in a fantastic way the idea of a man who brutalizes those under his authority, sons or subordinates.[1]

Kolpakov's death and return to life also parallel the losing and regaining of consciousness in epilepsy, and suggest a further meaning in Myshkin's seizures. The child, wishing for the death of the brutal father, fears that he will be punished by the same fate he has wished for another. Thus in the deathlike seizure, the child is killed by the father for having desired the father's death; he punishes himself for the guilty wish by identifying with the father and inflicting it on himself, as though to say, "I wished my father dead, so as to replace him; now I am the father, but the *dead* father."[2]

Threatened by the officer, Kolpakov undergoes a fate like that feared by the child full of hatred and guilty wishes: he goes to bed and dies. But he also miraculously comes back to life, as the child hoped to survive the frightening deathlike loss of consciousness. And while Kolpakov was *apparently* dead, the officer, Myshkin's father, has *really*

died, meanwhile having been put on trial for a serious offense. This wish-fulfilling aspect of the fantasy appears in
all versions, both "true" and "false," of the story of
Myshkin's father.

After the father's death in these ambiguous circumstances, a friend of the father, Pavlishtchev, takes charge of
Myshkin, putting him in the care of two maiden ladies who
raise him in the country. The elder lady was evidently very
harsh; a relative who visited when Myshkin was a child recalls "how severe his elder cousin, Marfa Nikitishna, had
been with her little pupil, 'so that on one occasion I stood
up for you and attacked her system of education. For the
rod, and nothing but the rod with an invalid child . . . you'll
admit . . .' and how tender, on the contrary, the younger
sister, Natalya Nikitishna, was to the poor child" (IV.7). In
this new parent-child situation can be recognized once
more the father who flogs, here seen in the person of the
harsh elder sister, who is paired with a gentle, loving
mother figure, the younger sister.

Myshkin's benefactor, Pavlishtchev, is a third father
figure, and he too appears in the rumors about Myshkin's
past. In his article about Myshkin, Antip Burdovsky claims
to be an illegitimate son of Pavlishtchev, unfairly displaced
by Myshkin. According to this story, "the licentious P. had
in his youth seduced a virtuous poor girl, a houseserf, but
of European education (taking advantage no doubt of his
seignorial rights in the old serf days)" (II.8), and Burdovsky is the result of that union. Myshkin denies this
slander, and later proves that it is false, that Pavlishtchev
had made the ten-year-old serf girl his ward from altruistic
motives. But what is striking in Burdovsky's story is the
reappearance of the motif of the child seduced by the
adoptive father, as in the case of Nastasya and Totsky.[3]

Thus the stories about Myshkin's own father, his lady
guardian, and his benefactor suggest again the image of a
sadistic father, and a father who abuses the child sexually:
the sadistic part of the pattern appears in the accounts of

flogging connected with Myshkin's real father and his harsh lady guardian; the sexual abuse figures in the slander against Pavlishtchev, which corresponds to the story of Nastasya's childhood.[4]

The brutal father emerges openly in the history of Rogozhin; not surprisingly, the parricidal wishes aroused secondarily by fear of castration are most openly admitted there too. At the beginning of the novel, Rogozhin's father has just died. "He kicked the bucket," Rogozhin tells Myshkin. "Eternal memory to the deceased, but he almost killed me!" The quarrel with the father had been over Nastasya, who here appears explicitly as the bone of contention between a father and a son: Rogozhin, entrusted with ten thousand roubles by his father, had spent the money on a pair of earrings for her. "He found it all out at once," says Rogozhin. "My father took me and locked me up upstairs and was at me for a whole hour. 'This is only a preface,' he said, 'but I'll come in to say good night to you' " (I.1).

Rogozhin runs away from his father to his aunt's house, and there falls ill; during his absence his father dies, at a time when Rogozhin is lying unconscious. Here, as in the story of private Kolpakov, the unconsciousness of the young man following an encounter with the sadistic father-figure and the death of the father are simultaneous, suggesting again the son's self-punishment for parricidal wishes through identification with the dead father. A further meaning is suggested by Rogozhin's unconsciousness: like Smerdyakov's pretended epileptic fit at the time of Fyodor Karamazov's murder, it functions as a sort of alibi, as if to say, "You see, I had nothing to do with my father's death. I was even unconscious when it happened."

Rogozhin's frank hostility toward his dead father is carried further by his brother Semyon: "At night my brother cut off the solid gold tassels from the brocaded pall on my father's coffin. [. . .] For that alone he can be sent to Siberia if I like, for it's sacrilege" (I.1). Here disrespect for the dead father is expressed in an action perhaps symbolic of a retaliatory castration, and is punishable by imprisonment in Siberia.[5]

Thus in a cluster of facts and fantasies concerning the fathers and substitute fathers of the Myshkin-Nastasya-Rogozhin triad are found again the principal elements of the sadomasochistic primal scene and the son's response to it: the theme of beating and physical abuse appears in the stories of Myshkin's real father; with the two maiden ladies, the powerful and sadistic parent is coupled with a gentle and timid one; in the slander against Pavlishtchev and the true story of Nastasya and her guardian, the father-figure seduces a female child; and in the story of Rogozhin and his father, the parricidal wishes aroused by the fear of a castrated "feminine" role in relation to the sadistic father are expressed.

There is another interesting fantasy invented by General Ivolgin, in which he imagines himself in a relationship with Myshkin's father. The story is a kind of scenario of the negative or homosexual resolution of the Oedipus complex. It also presents in miniature a repeated pattern of action in the novel and forecasts the outcome of the Myshkin-Nastasya-Rogozhin situation. Ivolgin tells Myshkin that he was passionately in love with Myshkin's mother when she was betrothed to Myshkin's father. One morning Myshkin's father roused Ivolgin from his bed, took out two pistols, and the two men stretched a handkerchief between them and aimed at each other's hearts. Gazing into each other's faces, suddenly both began to weep. "Then naturally followed embraces and a conflict of mutual generosity. The prince cried, 'She is yours.' I cried 'No, yours' " (I.8).

Here a man in competition with another man for a woman and faced with the prospect of a duel to the death abandons his aggressive attitude toward his rival, gives up the woman, and instead embraces the other man. In the same way the son, fearing the consequences of rivalry with an overwhelming father, may give up the masculine competition for the mother and instead adopt a passive attitude toward the father, hoping to be loved by him as a woman. This configuration can be discerned in the scene in which Myshkin protects Varya from Ganya's slap: Ganya hits Myshkin, who has intervened on the woman's behalf, but the episode ends with a reconciliation and later an embrace between the two men. In the principal action of the novel, the pattern appears in the interview between Myshkin and Rogozhin at Rogozhin's house in Petersburg. When the two rivals for Nastasya meet, each resigns in favor of the other in "a conflict of mutual generosity": Myshkin says "I won't hinder you anyway," and Rogozhin replies "Take her then . . . I give in to you!" The meeting ends with an embrace. And the last great scene of the novel brings that pattern of feeling to its logical conclusion: there Myshkin and Rogozhin are united, lying side by side near the dead body of Nastasya, who in life had been the obstacle between them.

VII. THE EPILEPTIC MODE OF BEING[1]

One has the sense in reading *The Idiot* that the action of the novel is balanced quite perilously, that just beyond or beneath its precarious coherence is a kind of maelstrom or abyss in which emotion might lose its connection with intelligible form and manifest itself in some unimaginably direct, "raw" state; here ordinary coherent speech and gesture might give way to frenzy or blankness. And indeed the novel does present us with the image of this extremity in the epileptic seizure. In fact, the seizure is a sort of paradigm of the emotional progression in the book's great scenes. In most of these scenes there is a pattern of rising excitement focused upon one central figure whose consciousness becomes more and more strained or exalted, until a moment of unbearable tension, when there is a loss of control, followed by physical and mental collapse.[2]

This is the emotional pattern of the climactic episode at

Nastasya's birthday party, when Nastasya throws the hundred thousand roubles into the fire and Ganya, torn between greed and pride, falls in a faint. It is also the pattern
of Ippolit's confession, read to the guests at Myshkin's
party at Pavlovsk in a state of growing delirium that
reaches a climax in Ippolit's suicide attempt. This sequence
also appears, of course, in the two episodes that end with
Myshkin's epileptic attacks, the first on the hotel staircase
and the second at the Epanchins' party; moreover, the second attack is preceded by a separate incident in which
Myshkin, after a long and increasingly euphoric tirade
about the greatness of Russia, swings his arm in an uncontrolled gesture and breaks Mme Epanchin's precious
Chinese vase. The last scene of the novel, in which
Rogozhin leads Myshkin to the body of Nastasya, ends with
a total loss of control, the collapse of Myshkin into idiocy
and blankness. In lesser forms, the same phenomenon appears throughout the novel, in the constant tendency to
frenzied and uncontrolled behavior and in many scenes of
wild emotion.

The novel also shows this "epileptic" pattern in its larger
structure: the action seems to progress unevenly, in waves
of tension that gather and burst in climactic scenes of spectacular emotional violence, leaving the narrative energy of
the novel depleted and for a time directionless, until a new
wave of tension begins to accumulate. The first break of
this kind occurs after Nastasya's birthday party, which ends
Part I; the opening of Part II is almost like the beginning of
a new novel. The next episode is Myshkin's long day in
Petersburg, ending in the climactic scene on the staircase.
Once again there is a sort of break in the narrative, and
then a new action begins at Lebedyev's villa at Pavlovsk,
with the gathering at which Antip Burdovsky and the
"nihilists" confront Myshkin. The narrative connection
from one of these climactic scenes to the next is rather
tenuous. In the intervals between them there is a kind of
"forgetting"; the action wanders, the novel appears not to

remember what it is about. Highly charged material crucial to the plot seems submerged under the effects of repression, as in the six-month lacuna between Parts I and II, in which significant episodes in Nastasya's relationships with both Rogozhin and Myshkin are presented so sketchily as to be virtually lost. *The Idiot* does not have the tightly integrated plot structure of *Crime and Punishment* or of *The Brothers Karamazov*, with their relentless forward motion and evenly calibrated tension, nor the complex intrigue of *The Possessed*. Its dramatic scenes are not strongly connected by the thread of continuous narrative. Each scene, instead of being generated by the preceding one on the horizontal plane of the plot, seems to be derived directly from the explosive emotional experience at the center of the novel.

We know from the notebooks that Dostoevsky had great difficulty in projecting the plot of *The Idiot*. And because of his commitment to his editor and his terrible financial plight, each section had to be submitted for publication before the next had been written or even sketched out. In these desperate circumstances, it would seem that Dostoevsky was forced back upon the spontaneous images and rhythms of his mental life to a greater extent than in any other work. It is perhaps because the novel reveals so openly the nature of that life that its author's feelings about it were peculiarly intense. The progress of the novel was intimately linked in Dostoevsky's mind to the course of his epilepsy. The excitement that informs the climactic scenes with their fury and brilliance expressed itself in life in the epileptic seizures, and Dostoevsky reckoned the cost of the great scenes in fits: "I wrote this finale [Nastasya's birthday party] in a state of inspiration, and it cost me two fits in a row."[3] Dostoevsky expressed parts of himself in all of his characters, but to Myshkin alone among his principal heroes he gave the ambiguous gift of his illness. The novel is in some sense Dostoevsky's exploration of the meaning of his epilepsy, a study in the epileptic mode of being.

Myshkin's disease appears so much a condition of the soul that one almost forgets its connection with the body. Medically, epilepsy remains a complex and little understood disorder; the term itself designates a configuration of symptoms rather than a single clinical entity. The symptoms may come from a number of quite different sources, including a physiological alteration of the central nervous system such as a lesion or chemical imbalance, a psychological cause such as a traumatic incident or hysteria, or some combination of physical and psychological elements. The facts of Dostoevsky's illness are unclear and difficult to interpret; however, even if his epileptic pattern of response was based on an organic predisposition, as seems likely, the disease certainly assumed a psychological meaning for him in the context of his experience and personality, as it must for anyone who suffers from such a condition. Whatever the organic basis of his epilepsy, he seemed always to conceive of it primarily as a psychological and moral phenomenon. In his presentation of Myshkin's epilepsy, there is virtually no interest in it as an organic disorder; it is treated almost entirely as a mental and spiritual condition.

In "Dostoevsky and Parricide,"[4] Freud argues that Dostoevsky's epilepsy was probably "affective" and hysterical in character. The epileptic reaction, whatever its organic basis, was available for the expression of his neurosis; thus the psychological function of the seizure was to get rid, by somatic means, of masses of stimuli that could not be dealt with psychically. From information about Dostoevsky's later life and personality, Freud concludes that the Oedipus complex was resolved in the negative form, and that there was a strong bisexual predisposition and an element of latent homosexuality in his character. Thus the hatred of the father and the fear of castration implicit in the normal Oedipus complex received a pathogenic reinforcement from the fear of being made to play the castrated "feminine" role in relation to the father, leading to the intensification of parricidal wishes. The guilt attendant upon such wishes was disastrously reinforced in Dostoevsky's case by their fulfillment in reality; the death of his father, whom Dostoevsky and the rest of the family always believed to have been murdered by his serfs, could have been construed as a kind of parricide.[5] Freud sees Dostoevsky's epileptic attacks as self-punishment for the parricidal wishes; in the seizure he became temporarily dead, like the murdered father, for whose death he unconsciously held his own guilty wishes responsible. Accounts of Dostoevsky's illness suggest that the attacks did not assume a definitely epileptic character until some time after his father's death.[6]

In *The Idiot* the epileptic seizure is overdetermined in an extremely complex way; it is a sort of nodal point at which all the strands of sexual and aggressive feeling are tied into a single expression. It has a clearly sexual meaning as a substitute for and symbolic representation of erotic contact with the father, which implies the terrifying corollary of castration. But the suffering or deathlike aspect of the attack also serves as a punishment for the parricidal wishes aroused by the fear of castration, here reinforced by the homosexual wish. Thus pleasure and pain are united, the pleasurable fantasy supplying its own pain and punishment, and the punishment taking an erotically gratifying form. The suffering and humiliation of the epileptic attack is thus a somatic version of the internal drama of self-punishment played out in the novel on the moral plane, the vengeance of the sadistic superego upon the masochistic ego, which keeps alive within the personality the erotically gratifying suffering of the old relationship with the punishing father.

As it is represented in the novel, then, the epileptic personality is one in which sexual and aggressive drives have assumed a particularly dangerous character, involving homosexual and parricidal wishes so threatening to the ego

that they must be entirely repressed. In the epileptic seizure these energies erupt periodically in the form of a violent attack in which the ego does indeed lose all control.

But Myshkin's epilepsy also has another dimension, a
powerfully positive aspect that makes it the fundamental
enigma of his being, the point of transformation at which
disease may become sanctity. Epilepsy is what sets Myshkin
apart from other men in every way: it is weakness, idiocy,
illness. But if it is illness, it is the *morbus sacer*, the sacred
disease of shamans and prophets who are torn by the
rough hand of God, who see through this rent in the fabric
of their beings into another world, a luminous reality free
of the limitations and ambiguities of ordinary experience.
This mystical aspect of Myshkin's epilepsy is concentrated
in the aura, the momentary alteration of consciousness that
precedes the fit, which is described in the following passage:

> He remembered among other things that he always
> had one minute just before the epileptic fit (if it came
> on while he was awake), when suddenly in the midst of
> sadness, spiritual darkness and oppression, there were
> moments when it seemed as if his brain had caught
> fire, and with extraordinary impetus all his vital forces
> would be intensified. The sense of life, the conscious-
> ness of self, were multiplied almost ten times at these
> moments, which passed like a flash of lightning. His
> mind and heart were illuminated with extraordinary
> light; all his uneasiness, all his doubts, all his anxieties
> were relieved at once; they were resolved into a kind
> of lofty calm, full of serene, harmonious joy and hope,
> full of understanding and the knowledge of the ulti-
> mate cause of things. But these moments, these flashes,
> were only the presage of that final second (it was never
> more than a second) with which the fit itself began.
> That second was, of course, unendurable. Thinking of

that moment later, when he was all right again, he often said to himself that all these gleams and flashes of a higher self-awareness, and therefore also of "a higher form of existence," were nothing but disease, the violation of the normal conditions; and if so, it was not at all a higher form of existence, but on the contrary must be reckoned the lowest. And yet he came at last to an extremely paradoxical conclusion. "What if it is disease?" he decided at last. "What does it matter that it is an abnormal intensity, if the result, if the minute of sensation, remembered and analysed afterwards in health, turns out to be the acme of harmony and beauty, and gives a feeling, unknown and undivined till then, of completeness, of proportion, of reconciliation, and of ecstatic devotional merging in the highest synthesis of life?" These cloudy expressions seemed to him very comprehensible, though too weak. That it really was "beauty and prayer," that it really was the "highest synthesis of life" he could not doubt, and could not admit the possibility of doubt. It was not as though he saw abnormal and unreal visions of some sort at that moment, as from hashish, opium, or wine, destroying the reason and distorting the soul. He was quite capable of judging of that when the attack was over. These moments were precisely an extraordinary quickening of self-consciousness—if the condition was to be expressed in one word—and at the same time of the direct sensation of existence in the most intense degree. (II.5)

The features repeatedly stressed in this account of the aura are the flashes of light, the heightened intensity and directness of the sensation of self and of existence, and above all the ecstatic sense of harmony in which qualities of reconciliation, synthesis, and merging are emphasized. In this "ecstatic devotional merging" Myshkin, like others who have had the mystical revelation, experiences a sudden resolution of doubts and conflicts and a sense of oneness with something outside of himself, with "the highest synthesis of life." This sense of oneness with the universe seems to be the "oceanic feeling" described by Freud in *Civilization and Its Discontents*, where he explains it as a dissolution of the boundaries of the ego, a regression to the primordial state of the infant at the breast, who "does not as yet distinguish his ego from the external world as the source of sensations flowing in upon him."[7]

The "extraordinary quickening of self-consciousness" in the aura may seem inconsistent with the *loss* of a sense of self suggested by the oceanic feeling and by Myshkin's sense of ecstatic merging. However, the "self" in this passage is not Myshkin's everyday self, which is often beset by doubt and guilt, but a quite different self free of any sense of limitation, open to "the direct sensation of existence in the most intense degree." This euphoric sense of self is quite compatible with the oceanic feeling. Freud writes,

> originally the ego includes everything, later it separates off an external world from itself. Our present ego-feeling is, therefore, only a shrunken residue of a much more inclusive—indeed an all-embracing—feeling which corresponded to a more intimate bond between the ego and the world about it. . . . There are many people in whose mental life this primary ego-feeling has persisted . . . side by side with the narrower and more sharply demarcated ego-feeling of maturity. . . . . The ideational contents appropriate to it would be precisely those of limitlessness and of a bond with the universe. . . .[8]

Myshkin's quickened consciousness of self in the aura is not the "sharply demarcated ego-feeling of maturity," but rather a return to the all-embracing "primary ego-feeling." The effect of this regression is to restore the boundless narcissism of the infant; thus the often painful and alienating feeling of separation between the self and the external world is overcome in the mystical ecstasy.[9]

This dissolution of boundaries affects the ego's relationship not only with the external world but also with the other parts of the mind. With the decrease in repression comes increased access to the contents of the id. Freud writes, "certain mystical practices may succeed in upsetting the normal relations between the different regions of the mind, so that, for instance, perception may be able to grasp happenings in the depths of the ego and in the id which were otherwise inaccessible to it."[10]

This change in the functions and relations of the different parts of the mind in mystical experience can also be understood through a comparison with manic-depressive illness. Although the behavior and the personality of the mystic and the manic-depressive are different in obvious ways, interesting resemblances suggest that the underlying pattern of sudden changes in the distribution of energy within the mental systems may be similar. In manic-depressive illness, the personality is dominated for long periods by a severe superego, which prohibits instinctual expression. At the onset of the manic phase, the dammed-up instinctual energy erupts explosively, overthrowing the superego and producing a feeling of elation and fantasies of omnipotence. The ego, no longer obliged to repress, is flooded with the instinctual energy of the id; this collapse of the structures of personality is experienced as a narcissistic triumph, producing a brilliant sense of euphoria.[11]

The personality of the mystic, at least that typical of the great Catholic mystics of Europe, is also dominated by superego: the mystic lives under a severe regime of mortification of the flesh, fasting, and chastity. But this instinctual deprivation is apparently compensated by the joy of the mystical experience, for which denial of the senses is the preparation. The mystical vision is often preceded by a terrible period of intellectual and sexual temptation, doubts and obscene visions, not unlike the ordeal of Myshkin's long day in Petersburg before the first fit. After enduring this torment, the mystic is rewarded by the mystical revelation. This revelation may include the apparition of Christ, the saints, or the Virgin, often described in intensely sexual language. Or it may be a more generalized experience—an ineffable sense of beatitude or absorption into the radiance of the divine being such as Myshkin has during the aura. As in mania, there is an eruption of long-repressed instinctual energy, the superego is overthrown, and the ego is free to experience the gratification of id impulses, although in a form disguised by and consonant with religious beliefs.

Thus the sense of merging, reconciliation, and synthesis in the mystical experience refers not only to the ego's feeling of oneness with the external world but also to the annihilation of internal conflict and the merging of psychic structures as the repressive superego is overthrown and id energy rushes into the ego. The "extraordinary light" that floods the mind and heart of Myshkin appears to be an image of this surge of energy. The successful rebellion against the superego represents a narcissistic victory for the ego, producing the intensely heightened feeling of self-consciousness and of "the direct sensation of existence." The infantile oral union with the world, in which the infant at the breast feels as though he incorporates everything into himself, is restored. The reality principle is deposed by the pleasure principle of the primitive ego, which seeks immediate gratification. The sense of time, a function of the mature ego associated with the delay of gratification, is suspended during the mystical experience, which is always described as somehow outside of time. Myshkin understands during the ecstatic moment the saying "there shall be no more time"; it is this moment, he says, "which was not long enough for the water to be spilt out of Mahomet's pitcher, though the epileptic prophet had time to gaze at all the habitations of Allah" (II.5).

Thus the brilliant, unlimited, harmonious vision that comes to Myshkin during the pre-epileptic aura is a regression to the timeless world of the primitive ego, buried in the oldest layers of the mind and illuminated during the instant of the aura like a dark landscape in a flash of lightning. The vision occurs during the moment when the structures of the differentiated personality collapse under the pressure of unconscious instinctual impulses and the mind regresses to an earlier and simpler mode of function, which is remembered after the experience as a sort of radiant pre-lapsarian paradise in contrast to the fallen world of the reality principle and the adult ego.

The moment of the aura is virtually the only point in *The Idiot* at which instinctual impulses break through the barriers of repression with sufficient force to be felt in direct, unmodified form as pleasurable and gratifying. At this point the sexual and aggressive feelings usually experienced by Myshkin in the disguised masochistic form of suffering rush into the ego with an effect of ecstatic and joyful release. But the ego cannot tolerate the force of these energies in their original unmodified form, nor can it allow their meaning to rise into conscious awareness. The moment of orgiastic release is followed by the total eclipse of the ego in the epileptic seizure. The fit is also the revenge of the superego, which can be deposed only temporarily; for the uninhibited release of sexual and aggressive energy it exacts the talion penalty of symbolic castration and death. The instinctual drives are once more experienced under the negative sign of superego, in the form of asceticism and suffering.

There is another kind of episode in *The Idiot*—related in form and meaning to the scenes of epilepsy—in which this negative form of instinctual excitement is most fully expressed, and in which mental experience and the sense of existence reach the same unbearable intensity as in the epileptic seizure. Myshkin describes several times the thoughts of a condemned man on the scaffold; these passages present a kind of inversion and counterpart of the epileptic seizure, and complete its meaning. There are two such descriptions, which are really two versions of the same scene. In one version, Myshkin relates a story based on Dostoevsky's own mock-execution: a friend of Myshkin, sentenced to be shot for a political offense, is led out to the scaffold fully convinced that he is about to die, and then at the last moment is given a reprieve.[12] When Myshkin's friend believed that only five more minutes remained to him before his execution,

> "those five minutes seemed to him an infinite time, a vast wealth; he felt that in those five minutes he could live through so many lifetimes that there was no need yet to think about himself for the last time, so much so that he divided his time up. He set aside time to take leave of his comrades, two minutes for that; then he kept another two minutes to think for the last time; and then a minute to look about him for the last time. [. . .] Then [. . .] the two minutes came that he had set apart for *thinking about himself*. He knew beforehand what he would think about. He wanted to realise as quickly and clearly as possible how it could be that now he existed and was living and in three minutes he would be *something*—someone or something. But what? Where? He meant to decide all that in those two minutes! Not far off there was a church, and the gilt roof was glittering in the bright sunshine. He remembered that he stared very persistently at that roof and at the rays of light flashing from it; he could not tear himself away from the light. It seemed to him that those rays were his new nature and that in three minutes he would somehow melt into them. . . . The un-

certainty and feeling of aversion for that new thing which would be and was just coming was awful. But he said that nothing was so dreadful at that time as the continual thought, 'What if I were not to die! What if I could go back to life—what eternity! And it would all be mine! I would turn every minute into an age; I would lose nothing, I would count every minute as it passed, I would not waste one!' He said that this idea turned to such fury at last that he longed to be shot quickly." (I.5)

In the second version, a man condemned to the guillotine experiences a similar intensification of perception and self-consciousness:

"It's strange that people rarely faint at these last moments. On the contrary, the brain is extraordinarily lively and must be racing, racing, racing, like a machine at full speed. I fancy that there is a continual throbbing of ideas of all sorts, always unfinished and perhaps absurd too, quite irrelevant ideas: 'That man is looking at me. He has a wart on his forehead. One of the executioner's buttons is rusty.' . . . and yet all the while one knows and remembers everything. There is one point which can never be forgotten, and one can't faint, and everything moves and turns about it, about that point. And only think that it must be like that up to the last quarter of a second, when his head lies on the block and he waits and . . . *knows*, and suddenly he hears the iron slithering down above his head!" (I.5)

In these execution scenes, the threat of punishment implicit throughout the novel and enacted symbolically in the epileptic attack appears undisguised. The man who rebels against the paternal authority of state or society is to be shot or guillotined. Once again, however, the idea of punishment is juxtaposed with tremendously heightened mental awareness. Both here and in the pre-epileptic aura, the sense of self-conscious existence reaches its highest pitch at the very moment when the ego is actually threatened with annihilation. In the epileptic seizure, the repressed impulses are first released directly in positive unmodified form, producing an instant of ecstatically heightened consciousness in the aura, which is then followed by retaliation and punishment in the seizure. Here the sequence is reversed. The idea of punishment comes first, arousing excited thoughts and feverish mental activity comparable to the mental intensity of the aura and suggesting the release into the ego of instinctual excitement. It is as if these impulses may justifiably be released now, since they are certain to be punished; in fact, the punishment is finally longed for, as though to end the intolerable tension of instinctual excitement: "this idea [of the value of every minute] turned to such fury at last that he longed to be shot quickly."

The execution is described three times, as if there were a compulsion to repeat it again and again. Each successive repetition contains an increasingly minute attention to the most painful details. The last description of the man on the guillotine ends in this way:

> "And only think that it must be like that up to the last quarter of a second, when his head lies on the block and he waits and . . . *knows*, and suddenly he hears the iron slithering down above his head! You would certainly hear that! If I were lying there, I should listen on purpose and hear. It may last only the tenth part of a second, but you would be sure to hear it. And only fancy, it's still disputed whether, when the head is cut off, it knows for a second after that it has been cut off! What an idea! And what if it knows it for five seconds!" (I.5)

This passage creates and then elaborates upon an unbearably vivid image of the conscious experience of suffering. As if the idea of the head's knowing for one second that it has been cut off were not sufficiently dreadful, the interval is expanded to five seconds, as though to stimulate and increase to the highest possible intensity the terror and the masochistic excitement associated with pain and punishment.

It is significant too that the scene before the firing squad here becomes an execution on the guillotine, a form of death suggestive of castration. This transformation reveals more clearly the meaning of the punishment fantasy that unites the scenes of execution and of epilepsy. Castration would of course be the punishment for wishing to replace the father; but it would also represent a reconciliation with him, a way of at last placating this terrible father and being loved by and united with him in final passivity. At the intrapsychic level, this fantasy of a castration-death means resolving the conflict within the personality in favor of the cruel superego: the ego would give up its claims entirely and allow itself to be annihilated by guilt. The pattern at all levels is one of total submission to authority, of annihilation and absorption by it.

This resolution seems to be exactly the reverse of the narcissistic triumph achieved in the ecstasy of the epileptic aura, in which the superego, the internal authority, is overthrown and absorbed by the omnipotent ego. Actually the problem here is the same, and the same goal is achieved, although by different means. The ego, under the assault of rising instinctual impulses and threatened by the superego, can no longer tolerate the conflict with the superego. It submits to being overwhelmed and absorbed by the superego, as though in this way to participate in the superego's omnipotence. Thus the same goal of omnipotence is achieved, this time paradoxically through submission. The intrapsychic transaction does not seem particularly mysterious when one thinks of the joyful sense of release with which individuals regularly renounce their autonomy in favor of authoritarian religions or governments: the fantasy of the devotee is always one of an enormous increase of power through absorption by and participation in the power of the deity or the state.

In the firing squad scene, the image of this transformation appears in the light flashing from the gilded church dome: "It seemed to him that those rays were his new nature and that in three minutes he would somehow melt into them" (I.5). The imagery of light and of melting resembles the flashes and floods of radiance during the aura. This merging into radiance is regarded here, however, with aversion: the price to be paid for omnipotence is, after all, terrible.

The epileptic scenes and the descriptions of execution are the points in the novel at which experience reaches its highest intensity: these episodes are in a sense the prototypes of the emotional experience of *The Idiot*. In the great scenes of climactic emotion or violent confrontation, the reader is led to participate in a kind of loss of control: the ego of the protagonist, under the assault of repressed impulses, gives way to energies and fantasies usually inaccessible to it and undergoes an enormous expansion of its capacity for perception and feeling. But this momentary expansion also exposes it to the possibility of annihilation through the savage force of id energies and the retaliation of superego: the result is the collapse of the ego in frenzy, loss of consciousness, or epileptic convulsions.

This characteristic mode of emotional response is what might be called the "epileptic pattern" in the novel. Its positive value is in one sense enormous: at its most acute, in the aura, it constitutes the claim that may be made for the "mystical" quality of Myshkin's insight and personality. These moments of heightened consciousness represent a breakthrough beyond the barriers of repression that define the normal conditions of the ego into a state in which the darker regions of personality usually inaccessible to consciousness are illuminated and the sense of existence is immeasurably intensified. The ego experiences these states as an enormous expansion of its capacity: the conscious mind appears to be offered the possibility of penetrating a limitless reality. In these scenes the reader feels as if he is being forced to *know* more and more, as if the mind is being wrenched out of its limits and into those areas of experience of which no rational understanding is possible.[13] The aim of these passages seems to be to push consciousness to and beyond the breaking point, as if to attain something like the state of that head severed on the guillotine: freed from the limitations of its normal state, perhaps that isolated head achieves some last awful moment of total comprehension, some final transcendence of the barrier between the conscious and the unconscious mind, even between life and death.

The condition of this final knowledge is, of course, annihilation. This is the ambiguity and the fundamental paradox of the moments of greatest intensity in the novel: the most piercing sense of the existence of the conscious self comes at the point of the destruction of personality, at the moment when the ego is about to give way and the mind to return to a primitive and undifferentiated mode of response. The moments of highest meaning in Myshkin's experience—the brilliant awareness of the texture of existence itself—are also the very moments when existence is on the verge of collapse into meaningless emptiness. Myshkin himself knows this: "he often said to himself that all these gleams and flashes of the highest sensation of life and self-consciousness, and therefore also of the highest form of existence, were nothing but disease, the interruption of the normal conditions; and if so, it was not at all the highest form of being, but on the contrary must be reckoned the lowest." And later: "Stupefaction, spiritual darkness, idiocy stood before him conspicuously as the consequence of these 'higher moments' "; but "for the infinite happiness he had felt in it, that second really might well be worth the whole of life" (II.5).

This mysticism is an extremely dubious phenomenon: it

offers a conception of spiritual experience based on a kind of gambler's dialectic of all or nothing, a compulsion toward extreme mental states that is a continual courting of loss of control. In this compulsive gamble, the ego itself is the stake, and the outcome is omnipotence or annihilation. It might be argued that the character of Myshkin's mental life is imposed on him by his disease, that therefore he cannot be said to "court" or to "gamble" anything. But the point is that this kind of mental excitement, whether chosen or inflicted, is presented in the novel as having an incalculable advantage. Nor is it confined to Myshkin. Myshkin's is only the most extreme form of an experience undergone by other characters as well, all of whom participate to some extent in this "epileptic mode of being," which is at the formal and experiential core of the novel, and which is a continual gamble with the precarious structure of personality.

It is into the darkness that lies beyond the controls of the ego, the perilous region of unmodified instinct and savage retaliation, that we are invited by the great scenes of mounting tension and final frenzy and collapse. Nowhere else in Dostoevsky are we taken so far beyond intellectual speculation about and description of these states into the actual experience itself. The wild beauty and terror of the great scenes, the suffocating excitement that we feel through identification with the protagonists and through the dramatic rhythms of tension and abrupt release, are our own experience of the loosening of ego controls as we read; they register our advance into the realm of dangerous fantasies of forbidden sexual gratification and of reunion with omnipotent authority through awful punishment. Again and again the novel leads us out onto this treacherous ground; beyond this precipice is the abyss of total abandonment in frenzy or stupor—the loss of the ego and all its complicated negotiations between the inner world of instinctual drives and the outer world of external reality.

In the compulsion to lean out over that abyss, to abandon differentiated ego controls for the excitement of more primitive mental states, the novel also risks its own existence as an aesthetic object. The aesthetic experience involves a special kind of mental, and to some degree physical, activity in which id and ego responses are alternated and integrated in a particularly satisfying way that provides the opportunity for both release and mastery.[14] The work of art is a sort of artificial world with built-in formal controls that permit the ego of the reader or spectator to relax its own controls temporarily, to enjoy in the safety of the created world the release of repressed instinctual energies and forbidden fantasies. This id aspect of the aesthetic experience goes on largely without specific conscious awareness. The reader typically feels it only as an excitement or pleasure that may be difficult to explain in terms of the explicit content of the work, for the greatest art often deals with experiences of a kind that are painful, repellent, or frightening in real life. The pleasure afforded by this kind of art implies some dim preconscious or unconscious recognition of the content of the work, however unpleasant it might be in real life, as in some way corresponding to the reader's own internal world.

Moreover, the greatest works engage the whole being of the reader, not simply his conscious mind: at deeper levels of personality the reader is responding unconsciously to symbolic transformations of repressed wishes, to disguised representations of forbidden acts, and to repeated patterns that suggest the structure of primal relationships and fantasies about them. This whole aspect of the aesthetic experience, in which pleasure is often mixed with much that is painful or frightening, may be brought to the level of conscious awareness only in some vaguely articulated way, perhaps as a sense of heightened and expanded life, a feeling that the world is more various, more dangerous, more beautiful than it appears in our everyday lives, that it is richer in meanings for us if we could only know them.

But the ego also has its demands: it requires of the work the pleasures of conscious recognition, of internally consistent and plausible representation, of a harmonious image and a controlled form through which the work defines itself against the relatively formless background of real life and offers a coherent vision of that life. Of course, these two aspects of the aesthetic experience shade off into each other continuously and imperceptibly in ways far too complex to be fully described. But the point here is that the work of art cannot *only* provide an opportunity for regressive fantasy and the release of repressed energies; it must also satisfy the demands of the ego. And in fact the deeper levels of personality can only be involved, paradoxically, by a work that is sufficiently under the control of the ego to allow the ego to relax its controls. That is, if the regression induced by the work feels too deep, too violent, or too real, the ego will experience it as unpleasant and will muster its defenses, turning from the work in aversion, boredom, or incomprehension.

In a work of fiction rooted basically in the realistic mode, the ego is likely to make its demands felt in the specific expectation of an interesting and coherent plot, as well as the more general aesthetic expectation of coherent form, of a sense that every part of the work has some necessary connection with every other part. It is here, with the formal controls that satisfy ego demands, that *The Idiot* takes its greatest risks. First, and most obviously, it deals largely with states that are alien and threatening to the ego: dream, hallucination, delirium, madness, epilepsy, death. But what is more significant, it deals with these states not simply by means of objective description and external observation; the truth of *The Idiot* is the truth that is "proved upon our pulses," in Keats's phrase. Dostoevsky is not content to describe the man on the scaffold as he appears from outside; he gives us the very particles of the condemned man's thought and feeling, his every fugitive impression and sensation as his time runs out, up to the moment when the blade descends on his neck—and even after. The language of the scene evokes a stream of preconscious imagery in the reader in which his own fears and fantasies of extinction are contained. Through the power of language to transfer and mediate such preconscious and unconscious thought and imagery, the prisoner's experience takes on the power of the reader's deepest emotions—the terror of the man on the scaffold is fused with the reader's own most primitive fears. Thus the reader is made to share to an extraordinary degree in the subjective experience of extreme states, even being led to imagine having his head cut off.

The compulsion to introduce this kind of excitement into the novel nearly destroys it as an aesthetic experience. The anxieties aroused mobilize the defenses of the reader's ego, which may protect itself by finding the book "unbearable," or "overwritten," or "ridiculous." Moreover, in their explosive force, the great scenes threaten to escape the control of the plot, to disrupt the continuity of the narrative and drive it into incoherence. This dangerous flirtation with loss of form is the analogue in the structure of the novel itself to the courting of loss of ego control in the protagonists, especially Myshkin. Thus the novel in its terrible fidelity to moral and psychological experience almost loses itself in the gamble.

Almost, but not quite. Form and meaning are salvaged perilously, like the hundred thousand roubles Nastasya pulls from the fire at the last moment. It is not the novel but the protagonists who disappear into the abyss—in madness, death, and idiocy. What they find there we cannot know: it is not finally possible for us, or for the novel, to take that last plunge beyond all language and control. But we have been led as far as a meaningful aesthetic structure can take us into the darkest areas of personality and experience. In the brilliance of the great scenes, even that chaotic darkness is lit up for an instant, so that we recognize in it the outlines of meaning. For out of chaos the book does finally achieve the coherence of meaning, although it does not always give its meanings their true names. Like all dark forces, they must sometimes be called holy, as the Furies were named Gracious Ones. In those unfamiliar shapes of suffering and violence, in that fitfully illuminated landscape of illness, we must finally recognize something of our own dark interior, of the roots of our compassion, our identification with suffering, our fascination with pain. Through Myshkin and all that destroys him, we learn again the lesson of tragedy: that the apparently random and cruel external world of things that we suffer, the world that happens to us, is in some mysterious way integral to the world we experience as necessary and inevitable, the internal world of what we desire and what we are.

VIII. PHILOSOPHICAL REBELLION

The Idiot is dominated at every level of meaning by the tension of a single conflict whose terms are transformed in various experiential contexts, but whose fundamental structure remains the same. Most simply described, this basic dilemma is the conflict between rebellious and submissive impulses. On the psychosexual plane, it is an oedipal conflict: the son is torn between the aggressive wish to murder the father and the passive desire to submit to him. In the first part of the novel, which is dominated by the Myshkin-Nastasya-Rogozhin triangle, this dilemma appears in a context primarily of individual relationships. In the middle section, after the scene changes from Petersburg to Pavlovsk, where the young nihilist Ippolit Terentyev becomes an important character, the problem presents itself in a broader context of political, moral, and philosophical speculation. Here it takes the form of a conflict between the wish to overthrow an oppressive political and social order in the name of human justice, and a desire to submit lovingly to state and tsar, to believe in the ultimate goodness of authority and in the redemptive value of the suffering it inflicts. The conflict is ultimately restated in terms of a question about the order of the universe itself and man's role in it, as a struggle between the liberated modern intellect and a religion rooted in irrational guilt and love.

We know the nature of Dostoevsky's explicit resolution of these conflicts in his life and in the novels. In *The Idiot* it is Myshkin, the "positively beautiful man," whose ideas are given the authority of the resolution, and he is unequivocal in his rejection of atheism, liberalism, nihilism, of all the ideas of the "enlightened" West, in favor of religious belief and submission to the established order. He tries to redeem a world of cruelty and destructive passion not by rebellion against the order on which it is founded, but as Christ did, through loving participation in its suffering.

Yet Myshkin's position should not be understood as the ultimate response of *The Idiot* to the questions it poses. To accept the ideas of the protagonist as the meaning of a work, even when the protagonist appears to be the spokesman for the author's point of view, is to misread the work in terms of something like the intentional fallacy. The "meaning" is not Myshkin's message of Christ-like love and reactionary Slavophilism, extracted from its context in the work as a whole. Meaning is a far more complex entity, and it is to be found rather in the entire emotional and intellectual experience of the novel, of which Myshkin's ideas are but a part.[1] That experience is above all one of irreconcilable tension, of a conflict whose scope and power far exceed the resolution proposed for it; thus the meaning resides in the tension and conflict rather than in the resolution. Myshkin's solution is not in any case a very satisfactory one: the lives he touches most deeply are destroyed, and his own life ends in mental collapse. His character is too complex for us to accept at face value either his way of life or his theories: the psychological ambiguities and disguised instinctual gratifications of Myshkin's submissiveness subvert its explicit religious and political meanings.

Moreover, in Dostoevsky's persistently dualistic scheme, the impulses suppressed in one character emerge in another. As Rogozhin acts out openly the rebellious instinctual drives repressed and disguised in the character of Myshkin, so ideas of political, moral, and philosophical rebellion are expressed in other characters, particularly in the person of Ippolit.

Ippolit is a young intellectual, a boy not yet eighteen who is dying of tuberculosis. His first appearance on the scene is at a gathering at the villa in Pavlovsk where Myshkin is staying. He arrives in the company of Antip Burdovsky, the false son of Pavlishtchev, and the group of young men around him who call themselves nihilists. They are in fact represented as *lumpen* hangers-on of nihilism, dirty, ignorant, and perfectly self-confident, who use the new doctrines to rationalize their own insolence and greed. They have concocted and published their slanderous story about an illegitimate son of Pavlishtchev with the intention of redressing the wrongs of the social order by cheating a prince out of his inheritance. They believe that the truths of society and human life are as inflexible and self-evident as the laws of mathematics: "you are a prince and a millionaire!" Ippolit says to Myshkin. "You may possibly be kind and simple-hearted, but even if you are, you can't be an exception to the general law" (II.8). Among this group, only Ippolit, because of his youth, his intelligence, and the pathos of his condition, attracts much sympathy. His second appearance is a few days later at Myshkin's birthday party. Here he reads his "essential explanation," a sort of confession in which he sets forth the conclusions to which his experience has led him and his reasons for deciding to commit suicide.

Ippolit's confession, like the reflections of the man on the scaffold, is a fevered attempt to seize and understand the nature of existence just as it is about to be snuffed out. And despite Ippolit's self-consciousness and pomposity and the irony in which his confession is framed—it is subtitled "*Après moi le déluge!*"—it is a moving presentation of the existential predicament, of man's situation in a chaotic world ruled by a cruel and alien God. Ippolit is explicitly condemned by Myshkin, who is the agent of the novel's dominant idea, and yet his position is presented with a passion and brilliance that give it for a time the full moral and intellectual authority of the strangely divided mind at work in the book. He is Myshkin's antagonist and counterpart at the intellectual level. Ippolit's aggressive, parricidal rebellion against God and Myshkin's passivity and suffering submission are reverse images of each other, rooted in the same terrible perception—the vision of a cruel God in an irrational universe that is set forth in Ippolit's confession.[2]

The essential fact of Ippolit's situation, the premise from which all his thoughts flow, is the certainty of his approaching death. This makes his situation a kind of existential paradigm of the human condition, for we are all, like Ippolit, under sentence of death, although unlike Ippolit we are mercifully ignorant of the precise limit of our allotted time. Ippolit is an intellectual and a rationalist who, even before his illness, had cut himself off from human society and retreated into speculation about life. When he knows he is soon to die he withdraws entirely, spending his time staring out of his window at a brick wall. This wall, "Meyer's brick wall," comes to represent the hopeless certainty of the laws of nature and the despairing and inexorable logic of a view of life based solely on reason. One conclusion that follows from Ippolit's contemplation of the brick wall is that every activity he might undertake in the few months remaining to him is equally pointless, since it can have no effect on the brick wall of his fate. He begins to study Greek, but then throws the book aside when he realizes that he will not even have time to learn the syntax.

Ippolit had been a young humanitarian, an idealist who "wanted to live for the happiness of all men, to discover and proclaim the truth." He believed in the ideal of a society organized upon principles of enlightened self-interest, the laws of nature, and universal brotherhood, all of which would conveniently coincide. It is his contact with the brutal finality of death that shatters this ideal. Evidently nature cares nothing for his humanitarian projects—he will not even be allowed the time to carry them out. He undertakes a complicated good deed for an impoverished doctor and his family, doing everything in a cold and ironical spirit as though to recognize the perfect gratuitousness of such charity in a universe whose final law is death. When a neighbor, a wretched man who has already lost his wife and his money, finds his baby frozen to death, Ippolit sneers at him and tells him that it is all his own fault. It seems to Ippolit that "if he is alive, he has everything in his power!" And yet of course the case of Surikov and his frozen baby torments Ippolit: human freedom is a cruel joke in this brutally indifferent universe.

The laws of nature and reason are evidently not designed to lead mankind to the achievement of the Enlightenment ideals of rational happiness and universal brotherhood, as Ippolit had believed. Rather, they suggest quite different possibilities—the idea, for example, that in fact "men are created to torment one another." It occurs to Ippolit that it might be amusing to commit an awful crime, kill a dozen people, just to observe the predicament of the authorities. How could they punish a man already condemned to death? He is surprised "that the idea doesn't strike people in my position, if only as a joke. But perhaps it does; there are plenty of merry people, even among us" (III.7). As the death sentence has already been passed and good and evil acts are equally incapable of altering it, Ippolit concludes that one may as well commit crimes. In his view there is nothing in reason alone that would restrain the criminal impulse.

During this period Ippolit has paid a visit to Rogozhin's house; there he is struck, like Myshkin, with the Holbein painting of the crucified Christ, which suggests to him the terrible power of the law of nature, which is simply death.

"Looking at that picture, one conceives of nature in
the shape of an immense, merciless, dumb beast, or
more correctly, much more correctly, speaking,
though it sounds strange, in the form of a huge machine of the most modern construction which, deaf
and insensible, has aimlessly clutched, crushed and
swallowed up a great priceless Being, a Being worth all
nature and its laws, worth the whole earth, which was
created perhaps solely for the sake of the advent of
that Being. This picture expresses and unconsciously
suggests to one the conception of such a dark, insolent,
unreasoning and eternal Power to which everything is
in subjection." (III.6)

Later, in a delirium, he has a vision of the dark Power that
rules nature as a "huge and loathsome tarantula." This vision is followed by the apparition of Rogozhin, who simply
stares sarcastically at Ippolit. It is after these visions that
Ippolit decides to kill himself: "I haven't the strength to
submit to the dark force that takes the shape of a tarantula"
(III.6). Ippolit's rationalism has led him to a vision of nature unredeemed, and the vision is horrible. Without the
light of spirit or faith, nature becomes simply a cruel machine or a loathsome spider. In the apparition of Rogozhin
this "nature" is embodied in the form of human passion,
the brutal lust that will eventually lead Rogozhin to murder.

Ippolit never questions the existence of God; it is God's
justice that he doubts, and that he rejects unequivocally because of the suffering it inflicts. He makes an absolute claim
for the innocence of man in an unjust world: "But this I do
know for certain: that if I have once been allowed to be
conscious that 'I am,' it doesn't matter to me that there are
mistakes in the construction of the world, and that without
them it can't go on. Who will judge me after that, and on
what charge? Say what you like, it's all impossible and unjust." (III.7)

Ippolit's rebellion tells us something about the violently polarized and dualistic quality of Dostoevsky's vision, and helps to explain why the rebellious position in politics and religion must be rejected in favor of submission. It is significant that Ippolit is *not* an atheist. An atheist might take the position that the suffering in the world is in some way random and fortuitous, or at least not the fault of a God whose plan for the universe requires it. But Ippolit's world-view demands the image of a Supreme Being against whom his rage may be directed. The relationship of God to man as Ippolit conceives of it is that of a cruel and arbitrary father to a son on whom he inflicts terrible suffering. It is in fact the image of the crucified son of God that becomes for Ippolit the symbol of innocent suffering, evoking his final terrible visions of the brutal power that rules the world and driving him to suicide. For Ippolit as for Myshkin, the bruised body of the dead Christ is the ultimate representation of the relationship of son to father. Myshkin responds to this image of the dead and mutilated son with overt submission; Ippolit responds with rage and defiance.

He plans to kill himself as the sun rises: "I shall die looking straight at the source of power and life; I do not want this life! If I'd had the power not to be born, I would certainly not have accepted existence upon conditions that are such a mockery. But I still have power to die [. . .]" (III.7). Ippolit's suicide is to be an act of defiance in the face of God, a last seizure of power over his own fate. In killing himself, he will be destroying in the only way he can the arbitrary life-and-death authority of the Father.

Thus Ippolit's relationship to God and the universal order assumes the structure and imagery of the oedipal conflict that dominates the novel. Ippolit expresses in the form of rebellion against God the aggressive rage of the son directed at the despotic father; in his philosophy all the feelings denied and repressed in Myshkin's piety find expression. But Ippolit's confession functions within the overall structure of the novel to control as well as to express these feelings. For within that overall structure Ippolit and his ideas are rejected, at least at the level of conscious meaning and explicit moral ideology: the aggressive rage of the son may be expressed only if it is placed in a larger context that condemns it. Ippolit's rebellion *must* be rejected: to endorse it would mean to defy the father, whose cruelty and power are vividly represented in the painting of the dead Christ.

But there is another danger internal to Ippolit's position and more or less independent of the threat of the father's retaliation. That danger is the emergence of uncontrolled aggression in the rebel himself. Cruelty is a powerful stimulus to cruelty. Ippolit's vision of a universe ruled by a cruel God makes the control of his own aggressive impulses more difficult. Indeed part of Ippolit's suffering is his inability to love, his gradual withdrawal from human fellowship into irony and malice. His insult to the father of the frozen baby and the "amusing" idea of the mass murder he might commit are examples of the aggression implicit in his philosophy. They suggest that Ippolit's rebellion might unleash the force of uncontrolled aggression, making real his vision of the world as a place in which "men are created to torment one another."

Every attack upon the established order in society and religion, not only Ippolit's radical nihilism but the vaguer liberal and Western ideas that circulate among the characters, is persistently associated in the novel with violence and crime. When Burdovsky and his friends try to cheat Myshkin in the name of justice, Yevgeny Pavlovitch cites the case of a man who murdered and robbed six people, and whose lawyer uses his client's poverty in his defense, saying "It was natural [. . .] that in my client's poverty the idea of murdering six people would have occurred to him; and to whom indeed would it not have occurred in his position?" (II.9). This is the Zhemarin case, which haunts the entire novel. It is of Zhemarin that Myshkin thinks when he looks at Rogozhin's knife, and Nastasya sees in the

Zhemarin case the prophetic shape of her own death. The Zhemarin murder provides a kind of spectral link between the intellectual protest of the nihilists and the brutal crime of Rogozhin, suggesting the identification of intellectual and instinctual rebellion. *The Idiot* is full of images of violence; the Zhemarin case, the fears and fantasies of Myshkin, Nastasya, and Ippolit, and the final crime of Rogozhin all create a sense of aggression as a force of demonic power, a wild destructive energy originating in an archaic layer of personality but always threatening to break through the barrier of repression into consciousness and action. The extremity of Ippolit's rebellion, its oedipal structure, and the imagery of aggression in which it expresses itself suggest that to rebel against the authority of God, religion, and the social order in the intellectual sphere is to let loose a terrifying and uncontrollable instinctual force as well: thus the fear of philosophical rebellion is rooted in a fear of instinctual rebellion. The demand for submission to an absolute paternal authority at every level suggests the fear of instinct and the need for repression in a personality where murderous and parricidal impulses are barely under control.

Ippolit is subject to bad dreams, and in his confession he describes one of them. This dream shows the connection between Ippolit's mental life and the central psychological concerns of the novel; it reveals rather clearly the nature of the forces at work in Ippolit and the reason for the horror and repugnance his ideas inspire in Myshkin.

In the dream, Ippolit is in his room when he suddenly notices a dreadful animal:

> "it was brown, and was covered with a shell, a crawling reptile, seven inches long [. . .] . The beast was running about the room, very quickly, on its legs and its tail, and when it ran, the body and legs wriggled like little snakes, with extraordinary swiftness in spite of its

shell, and that was very terrible to look at. I was aw-
fully afraid it would sting me: I had been told it was
poisonous, but what worried me most of all was the
question who had sent it into my room, what they
meant to do to me, and what was the secret of it?"
(III.5)

Ippolit cringes in terror from the creature, drawing his
legs up, when suddenly he hears it behind him:

"the reptile was crawling up the wall, and was already
on a level with my head and was positively touching
my hair with its tail, which was twirling and wriggling
with extraordinary rapidity."

At this point Ippolit dreams that his mother enters the
room with a male "friend."[3] "They began trying to catch
the creature, [. . .] and were not, in fact, afraid of it." His
mother opens the door and calls the dog, "Norma," a big
black Newfoundland. Trembling with fear, Norma confronts the creature.

"All at once she slowly bared her terrible teeth and
opened her huge red jaws, crouched, prepared for a
spring, made up her mind, and suddenly seized the
creature with her teeth. The reptile must have tugged
violently in order to slip away, so that Norma caught it
once more, already in midair, and twice over got it full
in her jaws, both times in midair, seeming to gobble it
up as it ran. Its shell cracked between her teeth, the tail
and legs hanging out of the mouth were moving with
terrible rapidity. All at once Norma gave a piteous
squeal: the reptile had managed to sting her tongue.
Whining and yelping she opened her mouth from the
pain, and I saw that the creature, though bitten in two,
was still wriggling in her mouth, and was emitting,
from its half-crushed body on to the dog's tongue, a
quantity of white fluid such as comes out of a squashed
black-beetle." (III.5)

Ippolit is not, of course, a patient on the couch who can supply the associations that would lead from this manifest dream to the unconscious dream thoughts. But if Ippolit's experience is taken to have an internal psychological coherence, and is related as well to the novel of which it is a part, then that context will provide points of correspondence, analogous to relevant associations, that will elucidate the dream. In any case, the dream has essentially the same status as the rest of the text, and may be interpreted by the same methods.

It is, of course, an anxiety dream of an intensely terrifying kind. Anxiety is the response of the ego to danger either from the external world or from within, in the latter case in the form of repressed instinctual impulses that threaten the control of the ego.[4] The anxiety in this dream is plainly aroused by the emergence of an instinctual threat from within. The chaotic and terrifying quality of the dream and the bizarreness of its imagery make it difficult at first to see what the nature of this instinctual threat might be. However, if we look closely at the figures in the dream and at the pattern of the action, some familiar motifs emerge.

The principal figures are a reptilian animal and a female dog: the climactic action is a violent encounter between the two, in which the reptile, caught in the dog's mouth, stings her tongue, and is itself crushed and bitten in two. A number of features of this encounter suggest that we are dealing once again with the primal scene. The presence of primal scene material elsewhere in the novel, of course, establishes a context within which it is reasonable to look for this theme. However, the symbolic and structural features of the dream itself confirm the interpretation. The monster of the dream obviously suggests the tarantula that rules the world in Ippolit's other vision. However, this creature that he fears so terribly and that seems to have come expressly for him may also be associated with the penis, especially the father's penis. The reptilian details of the creature's appearance suggest this connection: snakes and lizards are familiar phallic symbols. Moreover, the symbolism is densely overdetermined: the animal is a sort of reptile, and its legs are themselves like little snakes. The most terrifying part of the creature is its tail, which has a disturbingly autonomous power of movement and activity; the creature threatens to touch Ippolit with this tail, which evidently carries its sting. The tail, too, is a common symbolic substitute for the penis.

The confrontation between the creature and the dog takes place only after the mother and her male companion enter the room; evidently their appearance on the dream-scene triggers the events that follow.[5] In fact, the entrance of the man and woman at this point suggests that the encounter between the two beasts is a symbolic transformation of an encounter between the human couple, a sexual scene imagined or, more likely, observed by the frightened child whom the parents consider too young to notice what they do.

When the mother summons Norma to her aid in dealing with the monster, the dream reaches its climax. Norma confronts the creature, opens her jaws, then seizes it in her teeth. Here we have a violent representation of intercourse, with the vagina seen as a mouth, a pair of "huge red jaws" with "terrible teeth"; this is the familiar motif of the *vagina dentata*, the female genital perceived as a castrating orifice equipped with teeth. As Norma holds the beast in her mouth, its legs and tail move frantically, suggesting the rapid motion of intercourse, or the child's confused and terrified perception of intercourse as violent activity. After this encounter, the reptile is seen to have been bitten in two and crushed, but not before it has stung Norma, making her howl in pain, and leaving in her mouth "a quantity of white fluid"—evidently the semen.

In this appalling dream the sexual act becomes a purely aggressive and sadistic transaction in which both partners are injured. The threat of castration, which in the staircase sequence seems to emanate primarily from the father, is here associated with the mother's body as well, through the act of intercourse itself. There was some indication of this in the ambiguity of the representation in the staircase scene, where the column inside the staircase, the niche in the column, and the man in the niche suggested the child's confusion about who has the penis and what happens to it during intercourse. Here the penis is bitten in two in the dog's mouth. But the reptilian monster is the more terrifying of the two beasts in the dream, and the more frightening to the dreamer. It seems to have come expressly to pursue the boy; it moves in a violent and utterly unpredictable way; it penetrates; it stings Norma and makes her howl. It is worth noting that the creature is about seven inches long. The only other object in the book whose size is specified is the blade of Rogozhin's knife, which is also approximately seven inches long.[6] This correspondence strengthens the connection between the reptile and the knife as representations of the sadistic penis.

Perhaps the most disturbing aspect of the dream is the extremely primitive quality of the representation—the activity and the principal actors are not even recognizably human, but bestial and utterly alien. This primitive quality of the conception and of the affects it arouses suggests that we are seeing in as nearly "raw" a state as possible representations of instinctual forces themselves. The wild, unpredictable motility of the monster is an image of the terrifying power and energy of the forces of the id, which the ego perceives as monstrous and alien.

In Freud's later instinct theory, he groups the instincts under the two main headings of Eros and death, or sex and aggression. This theory includes the assumption that both kinds of instinct are involved in all human activity in varying proportions, and that they must regularly be "fused, blended, and alloyed with each other." Part of the function of Eros is to neutralize the destructive force of aggression.

Once we have admitted the idea of a fusion of the two classes of instincts with each other, the possibility of a—more or less complete—"defusion" of them forces itself upon us. The sadistic component of the sexual instinct would be a classical example of a serviceable instinctual fusion; and the sadism which has made it-self independent as a perversion would be typical of a defusion.[7]

Freud goes on in the same paragraph to say "we suspect that the epileptic fit is a product and indication of an in-stinctual defusion."

It seems that in Ippolit's dream the same forces are pres-ent as in the staircase scene where Rogozhin attacks Mysh-kin with a knife and Myshkin falls in the epileptic seizure. Both episodes represent a defusion of instinct under the influence of a sadistic conception of the primal scene. The aggressive instinct has overpowered Eros, transformed the erotic act into one of aggression, and emerged as an inde-pendent component. Although the dreamer, like Myshkin on the staircase, is terrified of the act of intercourse and of the father's penis, the anxiety is ultimately aroused by something in the dreamer himself: the dream images come from him, the forces they represent are within himself. What most terrifies Ippolit is the force of his own aggres-sion. In the dream the deadly aggression more or less im-plicit in his vision of a world where there is no control of cruelty appears undisguised. What makes Ippolit's position so dreadful to Myshkin is that it leaves Ippolit at the mercy of his own aggression: it provides no protection against the emergence of those forces with which Myshkin is also ac-quainted, and from which he takes refuge in repression and submission to authority. It is interesting that Ippolit is led finally to attempt not murder but suicide: his attitude toward his own aggression has more in common with Myshkin's than is at first apparent. In both young men the rage stimulated by a paternal imago is turned round upon the self in a masochistic re-enactment of the father's cruelty to the son.

In real life there exists a wide range of possible attitudes toward authority in political, religious, and philosophical matters. What is striking in *The Idiot* is the way the novel structures the problem of authority and the possible responses to it so that the whole range of alternatives is somehow polarized toward the extremes of total rebellion and absolute submission. Even the qualified opposition to authority associated with the liberal position and with Western ideas is lumped together with the most extreme form of rebellion and rejected along with it.

It is aggression—the strength of aggression and the fear of aggression—that causes this polarization. Aggression has a particularly disturbing quality in *The Idiot*. One does not of course actually see the instinct or the drive itself; but its effects are felt everywhere in the novel. Violence is a constant brooding threat in the dark coloration and atmosphere of the novel; it appears explicitly in imagery and action, and in the ideas and fantasies of the characters. The final action toward which everything in the novel tends is murder. The aggression in *The Idiot* is marked by a quality of savage extremity, and by a terrifying unpredictability; it is capable at any time of breaking through a thin surface of safe, predictable behavior. Moreover, sadism and aggression are linked in a disturbingly explicit way with sexuality. In its strength, its extreme lability, and its resistance to control, aggression as it is represented here seems to have retained its originally powerful and primitive character. Stimulated and shaped by the severity of the oedipal conflict, it has remained relatively unmodified; it has not been successfully "fused" with or neutralized by Eros. On the contrary, a sadistic conception of the sexual act has increased its strength with an added increment of sexual excitement.

In the presence of such an intensified aggression, the ego must maintain a regime based on repression to preserve its authority. The order of the state and the universe is perceived in an old and familiar analogy as a macrocosmic image of the order of the individual personality; thus anything that attacks the absolute control of repressive authority in any sphere is felt as a threat to the integrity of personality as well. An attack on the social or religious order becomes an oedipal revolt that will let loose a torrent of repressed rage and destroy the perilous internal equilibrium of repression, threatening the control and even the existence of the ego.

Thus even the liberals, with their relatively moderate criticisms, are perceived as violent and rebellious children. Yevgeny Pavlovitch says, "Russian liberalism is not an attack on the existing order of things, but is an attack on the very essence of our things . . . not merely on the order of things, but on the established Russian order, on Russia itself. My liberal goes so far as to deny even Russia itself, that is, he hates and beats his own mother" (III.1). If the tsar represents paternal authority, then suffering Russia itself is evidently the mother, a mother whom one must love and identify oneself with in suffering, however ambiguous and debased her character. In such a conception, the only alternatives are violent and destructive rebellion or idealized and mystical suffering.

This polarization of alternatives in *The Idiot* is, of course, a distortion of the real world of moral and political choice. But it is through just this distortion that the novel achieves its brilliant penetration of the darkest energies of both revolution and submission. *The Idiot* is mercilessly accurate in its presentation of the brutal ambiguities of revolutionary morality. Yevgeny Pavlovitch describes the nihilists' ideas as "the theory of the triumph of right before everything and setting everything aside, and even to the exclusion of everything else, and perhaps even before finding out what that right consists in. . . . from that position one may easily

make a jump to the right of might, that is, to the right of
the individual fist and of personal caprice [. . .]" (II.10).
Like *The Possessed, The Idiot* forecasts with uncanny presci-
ence a century of the politics of rage and terror. To point
out some of the elements of unconscious conflict in the
dramatization of political and philosophical attitudes in *The
Idiot* is by no means to "reduce" the novel or the importance of its ideas, but on the contrary, to show that those
ideas are, in analytic language, "overdetermined," and thus
immensely *more* complex in their origins and meanings
than is often assumed.

IX. RELIGIOUS SUBMISSION

Like Ippolit, Myshkin too makes a public statement of his
principles, in a situation corresponding closely to that of
Ippolit's "essential explanation." The setting of Myshkin's
confession is the Epanchins' party, at which Myshkin is
presented to society as a possible fiancé for Aglaia. Like
Ippolit, Myshkin is stimulated by the presence of other
people and by a feverish excitement associated with illness
to articulate his ideas about the bonds between men and
the relation of man to God. Both young men are in that
frame of mind in which it seems possible finally to explain
oneself and the world, to achieve truth and reconciliation.
    Before the party Myshkin has been terrified into silence
and circumspection by Aglaia, who is afraid he will dis-
grace himself and the family by some outlandish behavior;
she is in particular convinced that he will somehow contrive
to break her mother's precious Chinese vase. Myshkin is
drawn into conversation in spite of his resolutions by a
story about his benefactor, Pavlishtchev. The story is that
Pavlishtchev, just before his death, was on the point of becoming a Roman Catholic and a Jesuit. Myshkin is out-
raged at this story; he declares that the Catholic church is
the Antichrist, that it has bartered the true Christian mes-

sage for political power and so given birth to socialism and atheism. Such cases as Pavlishtchev's, if the story is true, grow out of the Russian thirst for spiritual intensity, a craving that will turn to perversions and negations such as Catholicism and atheism if Russia itself does not satisfy it. "The man who has renounced his fatherland has renounced his God," says Myshkin; but show the Russian "the whole of humanity, rising again, and renewed by Russian thought alone, perhaps by the Russian God and Christ, and you will see into what a mighty and truthful, what a wise and gentle giant he will grow [. . .]" (IV.7).

As Myshkin expounds these ideas before the astonished company, he grows more and more excited. Just as he is in the midst of this salvation of humanity through Russia and Christ, he swings his arm, and—in a moment brilliant with horror and ghastly comedy—knocks over and shatters the Chinese vase. As Myshkin stands transfixed with terror, mute and motionless "like someone invisible in a fairy tale," what most impresses him about the disaster is his foreknowledge. After Aglaia's warning, he had been tormented all the preceding night by the conviction that he would break the vase; he had deliberately seated himself as far as possible from the vase, and approached it only in the heat of his tirade. An unconscious intention is clearly visible in this "foreknowledge": Myshkin has done the one thing he was told not to do, just *because* he was told not to do it. The defiant intention of the act must also be applied to its more immediate context, the speech about salvation through Russian Christianity. In his speech, Myshkin rejects Catholicism, atheism, and socialism and the oedipal rebellion they imply for him and embraces his country and its orthodox belief. He intends consciously to be good, to love his "fatherland" and Christ, and to avoid breaking the vase. If all these conscious intentions are associated, then the unconscious gesture, the rebellious jerk of the arm that sends the vase flying, also knocks over the obedient and orthodox principles Myshkin has articulated. Clearly

Myshkin's message of salvation through the Russian Christ is not the final meaning of the book; that message has to be accompanied by the rebellious and destructive gesture that contradicts and undoes it even as it is articulated. The conflict between submission and rebellion goes on even within Myshkin's own position.

The second half of this scene has much the same structure as the first. After smashing the vase, Myshkin is petrified into silence, but the Epanchins and their guests behave kindly toward him. In his naïveté and confusion, Myshkin mistakes their aristocratic tact and good manners for true goodness of heart, and is overwhelmed with gratitude and love for them. He launches into a kind of ecstatic eulogy, praising the good deeds, real or imagined, of each one, and exhorting them to the fulfillment of their historic responsibilities:

> "I came here to-day with curiosity, with confusion. I wanted to see for myself [. . .] whether this upper crust of Russian society is really good for nothing and has out-lived its time, is drained of its ancient life and only fit to die, but still persists in a petty quarrel with men . . . of the future, getting in their way and not conscious that it is dying itself.[. . .]
>
> "And what do I find? I find people elegant, simplehearted, and clever. [. . .] I find people ready to understand and to forgive, Russian, and kind-hearted [. . .] ." (IV.7)

Now that he has come back to Russia and met Russians, Myshkin is convinced that despite the shallowness and evil habits of the upper classes, "it's all living material!"

> "You think that I was afraid for *them*, that I'm *their* champion, a democrat, an advocate of equality? [. . .] I'm afraid for you, for all of you, for all of us together. I am a prince myself, of ancient family, and I am sitting with princes. I speak to save us all, that our class

may not vanish in vain; in darkness, without realising anything, abusing everything, and losing everything. Why disappear and make way for others when we might remain in the vanguard and be the leaders? If we are in the vanguard we shall be the leaders. Let us be servants in order to be leaders." (IV.7)

In this mood of increasing exaltation, Myshkin is offering to these worldly and corrupt people a vision of what they *might* be, a vision of themselves transformed by Christian love into servants of those they rule. If this will only happen, there will be no need of strife with the "men of the future." In the world Myshkin wants, the poor and oppressed will not rebel against the rich and powerful, because the rich will give up to the poor all that is needful, freely and without coercion.[1] The only defect in this beautiful vision of social harmony is that, so far as we know, things have never come to pass in that way, nor ever will. It is a utopian vision of a world ruled by love, from which the conflicts of interests and classes that we know to be inescapable in the real world would be eliminated.

This rejection of the real world, with its social and political conflicts, in favor of a fantasy of perfect harmony between selfless rulers and docile masses, brings us back again to the oedipal conflict and the failure to resolve it. The power to deal with reality as it exists, to live in an adult world of inevitable conflict, has to do with resolving the Oedipus complex and reaching a modus vivendi with the internal image of the father. It means being able to tolerate a certain amount of internal tension between loving and aggressive feelings with the confidence that the aggression will not be overwhelming. Myshkin's horror of political and social strife is rooted in his inability to tolerate aggression. His vision of the perfect world is a wish-fulfilling fantasy of total infantile concord with authority, a Garden of Eden in which Adam would never want to eat an apple. It also has in it elements of the pre-lapsarian relationship to the world of the primitive ego of the infant, which is at the back of all paradisal visions, and which Myshkin re-experiences in the pre-epileptic aura.

In Myshkin's paradise, all men would live together like happy and innocent children. Myshkin prefers the company of children, and looks for the childlike qualities in adults, partly because the child represents for him this vision of harmony with authority and freedom from aggression.

In this enraptured speech, Myshkin has been speaking primarily to a dignitary who is General Epanchin's patron and the most important guest at the party, "an old man who is ready to listen to a boy like me and be kind to him." As he goes on, Myshkin stands up, becoming more and more excited: "Look at a child!" he exclaims. "Look at God's sunrise! Look at the grass, how it grows! Look into the eyes that gaze at you and love you! . . ." (IV.7). At this point, the wild epileptic scream breaks from Myshkin, and he falls in a fit. The ecstatic vision of a world without conflict, of happy submission to generous authority, delivered in the presence of an old man who is himself a figure of authority, evidently triggers again in Myshkin the fantasy of erotic submission to the father with its dreadful corollary of castration in the giving up of all aggressive and competitive strivings. The last image of Myshkin's speech is, significantly, "the eyes," which played so important a part in the sequence preceding the first fit. The image is followed here again by the eruption of repressed sexual and aggressive energies.

The breaking of the Chinese vase and the epileptic seizure both function to contradict and undo the sentiments that Myshkin has consciously articulated. They are a kind of protest on the part of the unconscious, signaling the unreality of Myshkin's ideal, the impossibility of a world without tension, conflict, or aggression. The fantasy of such a world is a regressive flight from the social, political, and psychological reality of adult life into the idyllic world of the child before the oedipal crisis. But that idyllic conception is itself not only a regression but a falsification, for its vision of childhood as a state without conflict or aggression is idealized and unreal. The flight from conflict and aggression is evidently hopeless: Myshkin's fit shows that in fact the conflict with authority he so dreads in the external world of society and politics goes on inside him, in the politics of his own being.

Within the particular context of the Epanchins' party, the breaking of the vase and the fit have further significance. For the party is given to acknowledge Myshkin as Aglaia's fiancé, a circumstance that can only heighten his anxieties. Marriage to Aglaia would represent a positive, heterosexual resolution of the Oedipus complex, a commitment by the ego to sexual maturity and an entry into the world of adult society. Myshkin's disastrous behavior, which exceeds the most ominous previsions of an anxious hostess, demonstrates to everyone that he is *not* able to function in this world. To choose Aglaia would mean to abandon the relationship with Nastasya and Rogozhin, with all its infantile and oedipal meanings, and Myshkin's tie to the conflict represented there is far stronger than his tenderness for Aglaia.

The Christian submission that Myshkin chooses in answer to the problems of evil and suffering in God's universe, and that apparently avoids the conflicts aroused by rage and aggression, in reality contains within itself those very elements it seems to reject. These negative elements are present not only in the unconscious attitude toward his own vision of religious harmony betrayed by the convulsive responses of Myshkin's body; they are also present in his understanding of Christianity itself. It is Russian Christianity, specifically, that Myshkin sees as the means to salvation—a combination of the traits of the Russian national character with the doctrines of Christ and the Orthodox church. In the long conversation between Myshkin and Rogozhin in Petersburg on the day of Myshkin's first epileptic attack, Rogozhin asks Myshkin whether he believes in God. In answer, Myshkin describes two incidents that define for him the essence of Russian religious feeling. In the first incident, Myshkin has a long conversation on a train with a learned atheist. Myshkin has the sense during this conversation that the man is somehow not talking about the real issue of belief, but about something quite different. That evening, Myshkin stays in a hotel in which a murder has just been committed; this is the murder of the peasant by his friend for the sake of the silver watch. As he raises his knife to kill his friend, the murderer "turned his eyes heavenwards, crossed himself, and muttering to himself a bitter prayer, 'God, forgive me for Christ's sake!' he cut his friend's throat at one stroke like a sheep and took his watch." On hearing this story, Rogozhin says, "I do like that! . . . One man doesn't believe in God at all, while the other believes in him so thoroughly that he prays as he murders men!" In the second incident, a drunken soldier sells Myshkin his tin cross, claiming that it is silver. Myshkin thinks, "Yes, I'll put off judging that man who sold his Christ. God only knows what's hidden in those weak and drunken hearts" (II.4). An hour later he sees a young mother cross herself when her baby smiles. Myshkin speaks to her, and the woman says something that strikes Myshkin:

" 'God has just such gladness every time he sees from heaven that a sinner is praying to Him with all his heart, as a mother has when she sees the first smile on her baby's face.' That was what the woman said to me almost in those words, this deep, subtle and truly religious thought—a thought in which all the essence of Christianity finds expression; that is the whole conception of God as our Father and of God's gladness in man, like a father's in his own child—the fundamental idea of Christ! A simple peasant woman! It's true she was a mother . . . and who knows, very likely that woman was the wife of that soldier. Listen, Parfyon. You asked me a question just now; here is my answer. The essence of religious feeling does not come under any sort of reasoning, and has nothing to do with any crimes or misdemeanours or with atheism. There is something else here, and there will always be something else—something that the atheists will for ever slur over; they will always be talking of something else. But the chief thing is that you will notice it more clearly and quickly in the Russian heart than anywhere else. And this is my conclusion." (II.4)

The structure and sequence of these two anecdotes suggest the paradoxes of the conception of Christianity put forward in *The Idiot*. The first point to be noted is that true religious feeling has nothing to do with the conclusions of reason about the existence or non-existence of God, but originates rather in an emotion. The second point, which the two stories have in common, is that religious feeling does not preclude criminal behavior. In fact, the two incidents chosen by Myshkin to demonstrate the quintessence of religious feeling, that very Russian Christianity that he expects to save the world, both involve the commission of a crime. The man who cuts his friend's throat is actually demonstrating the strength and comprehensiveness of his religious feeling, by showing that even in the midst of the act apparently most alien to religion, the thought of God does not desert him. The young mother says, when her baby smiles, "God has just such gladness every time he sees from heaven that a sinner is praying to Him with all his heart [. . .]." Presumably the murderer is praying with all his heart, and thus God is glad, even though the murderer is slitting his friend's throat at the moment of his prayer— perhaps just *because* he is doing this.

The men in Myshkin's stories—the murderer who prays and the soldier who cheats Myshkin by selling him his tin cross—are in a sense "holy sinners," who honor God, paradoxically, not by virtue but by sin. Myshkin refrains from condemning them, for "God only knows what's hidden in those weak and drunken hearts," and in any case religious feeling "has nothing to do with any crimes or misdemeanours." The type of the holy sinner is familiar in Dostoevsky's work; in *The Idiot* both Nastasya and Rogozhin are holy sinners, "great souls" who are deeply implicated in evil but whose sin remains within and helps to define a fundamentally religious conception of experience. They resemble certain figures in Christian hagiography who were great sinners before their conversions. St. Augustine and St. Mary Magdalen, who is the religious prototype of Nastasya, are figures of this kind. Their great sinfulness suggested the capacity of their souls for good, and they bring with them into their converted lives and into their images in hagiography the passion and energy of sin. The aura surrounding these flamboyant souls illustrates another paradoxical aspect of Christianity that is derived from the Gospels: at the Last Judgment, according to St. John, Christ will save the virtuous and damn the wicked, but His contempt is reserved for the mediocre: "So then because thou art lukewarm, and neither cold nor hot, I will spue thee out of my mouth." The judgments passed on the characters in *The Idiot* come from this kind of moral vision. Ganya, who never succeeds in doing anything particularly harmful, is nonetheless judged more harshly than anyone else by Myshkin: "In my opinion you are simply one of the most ordinary men that could possibly be, only perhaps very weak and not at all original" (I.11). Rogozhin, however, villainous as he is, is never treated with contempt by Myshkin. Nastasya prefers him to Ganya: "Anyway," she tells him, "you are not a flunkey" (II.3). This preference for total moral commitment, for the hot or the cold over the lukewarm, amounts almost to an encouragement to sin. In Dostoevsky's peculiar moral and religious vision, this paradox is so fully exploited that crime becomes integral to his conception of religious feeling. Although the criminal breaks God's law, his crime paradoxically honors God. And his sin involves him with God in the one vivid and authentic relationship, that of aggression, punishment, and suffering.[2]

It is striking that Dostoevsky's criminals are not generally punished very harshly in any legal or material way: for the murder of Nastasya, Rogozhin is sentenced to only fifteen years of penal servitude—"in view of extenuating circumstances" (IV.12). The real punishment of the sinner is internal, for the relationship with God, like that with the father, is internalized. By sinning, the sinner provokes punishment, and he experiences that punishment not only through imprisonment in Siberia but through psychological suffering, both before and after the crime. But punishment and suffering are felt paradoxically as the expression of love: "Whom I love I chastise." Through suffering the sinner feels himself literally "at one," in his atonement, with the terrible power that he has caused to be visited on himself. Thus the sinner and God are locked together in a continual struggling embrace, a perverse love that expresses itself through the provocation and infliction of pain. It is the transposition onto the highest plane of the central fantasy and the central relationship of the book. The act of love is seen as a struggle; thus struggle becomes the expression of love. Defiance of God is followed by the guilt and suffering that internalize and perpetuate the relationship with a loved and punishing parent. Myshkin's conception of religious feeling is by no means simply the Christianity of the Gospels, but his own image of that Christianity rooted in the need to defy and be punished by the father, and to experience pleasure in the punishment.

X. THE COMPULSION TO REPEAT

The action of the middle and last sections of the novel becomes somewhat confused; there is some obscure and ultimately insignificant intrigue involving letters between

Aglaia, Ganya, and Nastasya, and the machinations of Ippolit, Lebedyev, and Ganya's sister. The notebooks show that during the writing of these chapters, Dostoevsky was not at all certain of the ultimate direction of the novel, nor of the resolution of the relationships. The scurrying about and the hints of secret communications evidently served to keep the options open while he decided how to proceed. Up until a few months before the last chapter appeared in print, the author was still entertaining in the notebooks possibilities disconcertingly at variance with the finished novel. In April 1868 he is planning to have Myshkin marry Aglaia and rehabilitate Nastasya; then a few pages later this startling note appears: "N.B. (The Prince loves Adelaide.)"[1] Adelaide is Aglaia's sister, an entirely insignificant character. In July, Dostoevsky decides to have the Prince marry Nastasya, and as late as October 1868, Aglaia is said to be in love with Ganya.

In spite of this uncertainty and the wavering of the plot line concerning minor characters or insignificant actions, the major scenes and the larger structure of the novel show a powerful coherence. The resolution that is finally chosen, in which Nastasya runs away from Myshkin on their wedding day, Rogozhin murders Nastasya, and Myshkin reverts permanently to idiocy, is repeatedly forecast from the beginning. The tensions of the novel could not have been resolved otherwise, and the hesitations and vacillations of the author may signify his reluctance to recognize consciously the terrible necessity implicit in the situation he had created. The last scene, in which Rogozhin brings Myshkin to his house and the two men lie down by the body of Nastasya, has behind it the weight of the entire novel; it embodies with agonizing finality the dominant unconscious motif, the sadomasochistic primal scene, which is repeated over and over, each time with greater clarity, as if under a compulsion toward fuller expression.[2] The inexorable pressure of this fantasy and the wish it embodies overcomes the hesitations recorded in the journals and drives the novel toward the only conclusion consistent with its deepest unconscious meaning.

What is immediately striking about the last day's action is its repetition of a number of details from the day of Rogozhin's attack on Myshkin on the staircase and Myshkin's fit. Once again Myshkin arrives in Petersburg on the train;[3] again it is a hot, bright day, and Myshkin goes back to the same hotel. In the hotel, he begins to feel unwell and confused, and at the same time to experience the familiar tormenting impression of an idea pressing for consciousness. After searching for Nastasya and Rogozhin, Myshkin returns to the hotel, where he remembers Rogozhin, his eyes, and the knife. As he goes out again, he expects to see Rogozhin hiding in the same spot. In its setting and in Myshkin's mood and expectations, this sequence is organized to correspond to the earlier one, suggesting that the action that follows is the full and final working out of the meaning concealed in the earlier episode.

Rogozhin accosts Myshkin not on the staircase but in the street; he asks the Prince to accompany him to his house, "so that," as he says later, "we may spend this night together." They go together to his study; at one end of the room a curtain has been drawn across the alcove containing the bed. Trembling, Myshkin asks, "Where is Nastasya Filippovna?" Rogozhin motions him inside the curtain: " 'It's dark here,' he [Myshkin] said. 'One can see,' muttered Rogozhin. 'I can scarcely see . . . there's a bed.' 'Go nearer,' Rogozhin suggested softly" (IV.11).

As in the scene on the staircase, the emphasis here is on darkness and the difficulty of seeing. In the staircase episode, Myshkin "wanted to pass by without looking" but "he could not resist turning round." When he looks round, he sees Rogozhin's raised knife, the symbolic instrument of the sexual act and of punishment for sexual curiosity. Here, however, he is invited by Rogozhin to gratify his desire to see. And what he sees this time is the object into which that raised knife has been plunged; he sees on the bed the result of sexual passion—the dead body of a woman. The gratification of his curiosity is also the fulfillment of his fear: this is what the father is capable of, what is done to the mother in the sexual act; this is the fate from which Myshkin was saved on the staircase by his fit. He would otherwise have become like this abject thing on the bed:

> the tip of a bare foot peeped out from under the sheet; it seemed as though it had been carved out of marble and it was horribly still. Myshkin looked and felt that the more he looked, the stiller and more death-like the room became. Suddenly a fly that had just awakened buzzed; it flew over the bed and settled at the head of it. The prince started. (IV.11)

The utterly deathly quality of the imagery—the marmoreal foot, the stillness, the fly—links this corpse with the other intensely dead body in the novel—that of the crucified Christ in the Holbein painting.[4] Both represent the effects of the brutal passions of the father.

Rogozhin notices Myshkin's trembling and expects him to have a fit. But significantly, Myshkin does *not* have a fit. Myshkin's fits have functioned in fact to *protect* him from what happens here: they have served to ward off the vision he has in this scene, to substitute for a conscious idea an unconscious process through which the content of the idea is symbolically acted out without reaching awareness. In the fit, a rising instinctual excitement is suddenly discharged somatically through the seizure that causes loss of consciousness. Here no fit intervenes to save Myshkin, and he is exposed consciously to the fearful result of the act that his convulsions at once imitate and conceal.

In the negative resolution of the Oedipus complex that may be associated with this conception of the sexual act, the role the son must play to win the father's love and avoid his wrath is that of the mother herself. In the rest of this episode, that consequence is played out. Up to this point,

Myshkin has by his impotence and by a kind of active passivity—"I won't hinder you anyway"—implicitly conspired to permit Rogozhin to work his will upon Nastasya. Nastasya represents for Myshkin the abused mother, and his identification with her in her masochism is so strong that he can do nothing to prevent her from being destroyed. Now, in the remainder of this last sequence, Myshkin himself replaces the dead woman with Rogozhin. Rogozhin makes up a couch for himself and Myshkin:

> there was not room for two on the sofa, and he was set on their sleeping side by side, that was why, with much effort, he now dragged, right across the room, the various cushions off the two sofas and laid them by the curtain. He made the bed after a fashion; he went up to Myshkin, tenderly and eagerly took him by the arm, raised him and led him to the bed [. . .]. (IV.11)

The two men lie down together, and Myshkin begins to ask questions in a feverish way:

> "Listen!" said the prince, as though he were confused, as though he were looking for what he meant to ask and at once forgetting it again, "listen, tell me what did you do it with? A knife? The same one?"
> "The same one."
> "There's something else: I want to ask you something else, Parfyon . . . I want to ask you a great many questions, all about it. . . ." (IV.11)

The eagerness and naïveté of Myshkin's questions are weirdly inappropriate to the real situation, and indicate that the scene excites in him the childish curiosity to know "all about it." But the details with which Rogozhin satisfies this curiosity are just those that would confirm in the child's mind his worst fears about the sexual act:

> "And . . . and . . . another thing seems strange: the

knife went in three or four inches . . . just under the
left breast . . . and there wasn't more than half a
tablespoonful of blood flowed on to her chemise, there
was no more. . . ."

"That, that, that," Myshkin sat up suddenly in great
agitation, "that I know, I've read about it, that's called
internal bleeding. . . . Sometimes there's not one drop.
That's when the stab goes straight to the heart."
(IV.11)

A bloodstain on the mother's nightdress can only mean to
the child an injury, a wound inflicted during those mysterious nighttime struggles; sometimes even a small flow of
blood from the right place can mean death. The father
who does such fearful things to the mother could also inflict the wound of castration and death on the son.

The dilemma posed by this conception of the primal
scene is insoluble. In this episode the terrifying and exciting fantasy of replacing the mother, the homosexual wish
that has stood behind Myshkin's half-hearted competition
with Rogozhin for Nastasya, is finally acted out. Myshkin
lies down with his face next to Rogozhin's in an imitation of
the embrace between father and mother. But when they
are found the next day, Myshkin is unable to recognize
anyone or understand what is said to him. The acting out
of the forbidden fantasy has destroyed the repressions on
which his character was based: he has reverted permanently to the state in which Dr. Schneider, the physician
who educated him in Switzerland, first found him. He has
become once again "An idiot!"

Myshkin's idiocy at the end is a return to his original
condition, the state of mental confusion and stupor associated with his epilepsy from which Schneider rescued him.
If the reversion to illness is a repetition of an original response, it must be assumed that the cause of the reversion
is also a repetition of the cause of the original illness.

Throughout the novel Myshkin is repeatedly haunted by the peculiar impression of a thought striving to become conscious, or the sense of familiarity with something apparently unknown, as when he first meets Nastasya or sees the Holbein painting at Rogozhin's. This sense of *déjà vu*, of being on the point of recognizing something that one is yet continually forgetting, indicates the presence of a repressed memory striving to break into consciousness. The recurrence of the memory is a function of the "repetition compulsion," the tendency to repeat past experience and to return to earlier states that Freud, in *Beyond the Pleasure Principle*, identifies as the fundamental characteristic of all instinctual life. In the compulsive reproduction of painful experiences, the repetition compulsion assumes a demonic character associated with masochism and the death instinct. Myshkin's inability to seize the elusive thought in certain scenes is an unconscious attempt to keep the memory of a painful experience in repression. Consciously, Myshkin tries to move forward toward adulthood and marriage with Aglaia; unconsciously, he is drawn inevitably backward toward the past, childhood, and the figure of Nastasya. His attraction to children and his own childishness are signs of this regressive tendency, indicating that a part of Myshkin's psychological development has been fixated in childhood; an event of his early mental life has stamped itself irrevocably on all his later experience, causing him to seek out situations that recreate that event. All the principal characters, especially Nastasya, resemble Myshkin to varying degrees in the way they seek pain, as though trying to recreate and exorcise an original experience of it. Myshkin's return to the hotel in Petersburg is an attempt to re-experience Rogozhin's attack on him, which is in turn a repetition of the repressed childhood experience at the root of Myshkin's illness.

In the last scene, the experience emerges from repression and reveals itself nearly undisguised as the wish and

the fear aroused in the child by a scene of parental intercourse. The question whether the memory is of something
actually seen or only fantasized is meaningless in this context: the primal scene is psychologically significant insofar
as it is a *mental* event, a complex of curiosity, fears, specula-
tions, and fantasies aroused by the unavoidable evidence of
adult sexuality. Moreover, to describe the last scene as the
repetition of a childhood event that is the genesis and the
meaning of Myshkin's illness is not to attribute to the character an experience prior to or outside of the text. It is
rather to point out certain aspects of the text itself: first,
that it contains everywhere primal scene material of a
traumatic and sadistic kind; and second, that the last episode, in which this primal scene material appears clearly,
has in itself the quality of a repetition or a replication.

The sadomasochistic primal scene and the ambivalent attitude toward the father associated with it are acted out
symbolically and unconsciously in Myshkin's fits. At the
level of religious and political conflict, this configuration
appears in the dualistic alternation of rebellious and submissive attitudes among the characters, and in the inextri-
cable combination of such attitudes within each character.
Myshkin finally gives up the struggle in favor of submission
to the father and total loving reconciliation to the point of
identity with him, powerfully represented in the image of
their last embrace. With respect to the structure of personality, Myshkin's submission to his murderous rival means
the collapse of the mature ego, which maintains the internal tension of the psychic structure and negotiates the conflicts between the inner and outer worlds, in a return to a
perfect infantile harmony with the image of the father.
The conflict between ego and superego is annihilated
along with all structural differentiation. But this tensionless
submission turns out to be not the paradise of love that the
escape from conflict has represented for Myshkin, but an
entirely negative state, a place beyond speech or recognition, a plunge into the abyss of nonbeing.

XI. AMBIVALENCE AND THE PRE-OEDIPAL MOTHER

The principal psychological conflict of the novel takes place at the oedipal level, between submissive and murderous wishes toward the father. However, behind and within that conflict can be seen the outlines of a more primitive conflict with a still earlier object. It is, after all, not a man who is murdered at the end of the novel, but a woman.

The peculiar nature of the love relationships in *The Idiot* is based on a sadistic conception of the primal scene. But there is something even deeper and more pervasive here, a pattern that derives from the infant's earliest relation to objects and that may influence the primal scene fantasy itself. One of the most original and disturbing aspects of Dostoevsky's work is his exploration of the phenomenon of ambivalence—that is, love and hatred for the same object. Ambivalence is manifested in the divided and contradictory philosophical attitudes in the novel, but it is expressed most intensely in the sexual relationship. Sexual love is invariably accompanied by hostility: in Ganya's feeling for Nastasya, "passion and hatred were strangely mingled in his soul." Hatred is even the gauge of the intensity of love: Nastasya says of Rogozhin, "he loves me so much that he can't help hating me." This destructive component of passionate love so frightens Myshkin that he takes refuge in chastity.

In his later works Freud accounts for ambivalence as the defusion of erotic and aggressive instincts in regression.[1] Indeed, in Dostoevsky's novels love appears not as a single unified emotion, but rather as an unstable synthesis of partial and contradictory impulses: tenderness, desire, and delight in the object are combined with a compulsion to dominate, injure, and destroy.

However, in an earlier explanation, somewhat different though by no means contradictory, Freud sees ambivalence as the persistence of infantile forms of love:

As the first of these aims we recognize the phase of incorporating or devouring—a type of love which is consistent with abolishing the object's separate existence
and which may therefore be described as ambivalent.
At the higher stage of the pregenital sadistic-anal organization, the striving for the object appears in the
form of an urge for mastery, to which injury or annihilation of the object is a matter of indifference. Love at
this preliminary stage is hardly to be distinguished
from hate. . . . Not until the genital organization is established does love become the opposite of hate.[2]

The peculiar form taken by love in *The Idiot*, the compulsion to possess the object even at the price of its destruction, seems very like the primitive, pregenital love-hate,
particularly the devouring love of the oral phase. Whether
aggression and Eros are seen as "defused" or as aspects of
an undifferentiated wish for closeness through incorpora-
tion, the effect is the same: in this archaic relation to the
object, what we call love and hate are inseparable. As
Myshkin says to Rogozhin, "there's no distinguishing your
love from hate."

The principal object of this early ambivalence is the
mother, who is in the first years of life an immensely powerful figure, the source of both the satisfaction and the
frustration of instinctual needs. The feeling for the pre-
oedipal mother must influence the development of the
Oedipus complex. The earlier ambivalent emotion, whose
contradictions become less tolerable as the ego matures,
may be split up, the father endowed with much of the
negative component. The vision of the oedipal father as
cruel and all-powerful then defends against the more
frightening primary recognition of such attributes in the
mother. Even the form taken by the primal scene is determined by this evolution: the sadistic conception of intercourse may be in part the fulfillment of a wish to see the

mother punished, as in Myshkin's fantasy of the loved woman under the warder's rod.[3]

In *The Idiot*, the oedipal conflict must inherit something of its peculiar form and intensity from a strongly ambivalent relationship with the pre-oedipal mother. The ambivalent quality of this attachment can of course be much intensified by the mother's real behavior. In the novel, both of the principal female figures are given to baffling alternations between tenderness and cruelty. Nastasya especially is capable of real savagery, and finally is thought to be insane.

The attitude toward the father in the novel is itself extremely ambivalent and primitive in quality, a mixture of feelings of rage and terror with a wish for total union in the form of a fantasy of homosexual intercourse. But the imagery connected with this negative oedipal fantasy—the impression of ecstatic merging and synthesis in the epileptic aura—is strongly "oceanic," suggesting its origin in an earlier phase of development and a more primitive relationship—that of the child in oral union with the pre-oedipal mother.

As the pre-oedipal mother is a partly fearful figure, and as the wish for fusion with her also implies the sadistic wish to devour, so her overpowering image suggests the possibility of a masochist reversal of that wish, the danger of being devoured. In a discussion of sadistic murders, Fenichel writes, "the ideas of avoiding a terrible passive experience by actively perpetrating it on others and of establishing a mystical union with the victim must be decisive."[4] Beneath the oedipal fear of castration by the father in *The Idiot* must lie a more primitive fear of total passivity and vulnerability in relation to the mother. In the murder of Nastasya, the possibility of a passive experience is warded off and reversed. The mother and all she represents is finally possessed for good. Nastasya has lived with and promised to marry both Myshkin and Rogozhin; again and again she has tormented, frustrated, and abandoned

both men. In death she is no longer free to give and with-
hold her affection capriciously. After the murder,
Rogozhin wishes not to be discovered, not because he is
afraid of the police, but because he is determined above all
to keep Nastasya's body.

> "So we won't confess and let them take her away."
> "Not for anything!" decided the prince, "No, no,
> no!"
> "That's what I decided, lad, not to give her up on
> any account to any one." (IV.11)

The infantile love described by Freud as "consistent with
abolishing the object's separate existence" has triumphed.
Nastasya is dominated and immobilized, and the separate
existence and the wayward individual will that have caused
such pain to both Myshkin and Rogozhin have been annihilated.

In that last scene, the culmination of the homosexual
fantasy in the embrace between Myshkin and Rogozhin beside the dead body of Nastasya also suggests oral fusion
with the mother: the two men are so closely united that
Myshkin's tears flow down Rogozhin's cheeks. Through
the murder of Nastasya, the power of the pre-oedipal
mother is mastered, and there is a kind of reunion in
death. In addition to its other meanings, Myshkin's reversion to the "idiocy" of his childhood is a regression to the
earliest relationship with the mother, a re-entry into that
oceanic oneness so strongly suggested in the epileptic aura.

The murder of Nastasya, in which Myshkin and
Rogozhin have collaborated, does succeed in symbolically
incorporating the figure of the mother and in perpetuating
the mother-child relationship, for it reduces both men to
an infantile state. Rogozhin is at least temporarily mad, and
Myshkin will require a kind of maternal care for the rest of
his life. By the end of the last scene, Myshkin seems to have
become both mother and child. He is uncomprehending

and speechless, like an infant; but when Rogozhin begins playing the part of the child by screaming and babbling, Myshkin strokes his hair and cheeks, "as though caressing and soothing him," like a mother.[5]

There is a curious little episode set into the long sequence leading up to Rogozhin's attack on Myshkin that seems full of some mysterious significance. The incident takes place at Rogozhin's house after the long conversation between the two men. Rogozhin asks Myshkin to change crosses with him. Then he leads Myshkin into a separate part of the house, through a locked door and a series of dark rooms, into a small drawing-room, where Myshkin finds a little old woman, obviously quite senile, who nods and smiles childishly at him. This is Rogozhin's mother. "Bless him, mother, as though it were your own son you were blessing," says Rogozhin. And the old lady silently makes the sign of the cross three times over Myshkin. The blessing seals the bond of brotherhood between the two young men. Perhaps it also suggests that the love-hate between them is derived from the relationship of mother to child. Rogozhin's dark, old-fashioned house with its small dirty windows has for Myshkin the appearance of "keeping something dark and hidden." The house holds the darkness and brutality of Rogozhin's soul, and later it will hide the body of Nastasya. But in this scene the innermost secret of the house seems to be this little old lady, seated like a dumb idol in the very womb of the house, suggesting the importance of the maternal figure in the novel's deepest meaning. Here the mother is childish, powerless, and benign—an idiot, like Myshkin himself at the end. Thus "idiocy" is here, as in the last scene, the annihilation of conflict, the fusion of mother and child in a single image.

In the shifting ambiguities and the densely overdetermined meanings of the novel's central relationships, the principal motifs of psychic life are contained. Intermingled with the adult strivings of the characters are the passions of the oedipal conflict, and within and beneath these passions are still older and more primitive feelings of the first years and months of life. All of these motifs are condensed in the last scene, although when spelled out in the language of rational analysis this tangle of meanings may seem more tortuously complex than anything the mind could produce.

It is interesting to try to imagine the effect of the novel had Dostoevsky been able to give it the happy ending he considered at times in the notebooks, with Myshkin marrying Aglaia and rehabilitating Nastasya. The result would have been utterly unconvincing and at odds with the characters and the atmosphere as they are established from the beginning. Despite its comic elements, the novel is fundamentally tragic in feeling and structure, and in tragic art the revelation of truth involves the acting out of regressive desires.

In *The Idiot*, regression goes as far as it can. The novel is like a shaft sunk vertically through the strata of psychic life; at the very bottom is the last and most primitive image—Myshkin and Rogozhin in each other's arms by the body of Nastasya. Here is a terrible peace: every wish is gratified, and the price of gratification is paid. The infantile desires on whose repression and transformation the whole course of psychic development depends have been acted out; a complex psychic evolution has been undone and lived backward, so to speak, to reveal the first sources of love and hate. This descent into the oldest layers of psychic life is inseparable from regression: it is surely that dangerous regression, in which author and reader as well as protagonists participate, that inspired in Dostoevsky the "unnatural fear" of which he wrote to Maikov. In this novel the earliest relation to objects is revived, and it is perhaps the experience of that archaic emotion in which love is bound up with destruction that gives us the sense in *The Idiot* of having endured some fundamental mystery of human life and suffering.

XII. THE END OF INTERPRETATION

We have come, then, to the end of interpretation, the most deeply buried layer of meaning. Or have we? This deepest meaning may be only a sort of false bottom, beneath which lie still further meanings; at the heart of the maze there may be still another maze. The complexity of *The Idiot*, its mystery, its possibilities of meaning are potentially endless. Psychoanalytic interpretation does not lead to a single, final notion of meaning. Rather, it is a means of exploration, a way of tracing and articulating the ramifications of the novel's internal structure. It is in that whole web of internal relations that meaning consists, rather than in any single part of it or any statement that can be extrapolated from it. The story of Myshkin, Rogozhin, and Nastasya, enacted in the midst of the intellectual ferment of nineteenth-century Petersburg, is no mere allegory for some other, more "real," psychosexual drama. Rather, that story is in itself fully meaningful: its conscious and unconscious meanings are everywhere intermingled and inseparable.

Psychoanalysis is committed to the conception of mental life and mental productions as complex, dynamic, and overdetermined. The goal of psychoanalytic criticism, then, should be to suggest the complexity and the protean ambiguity of the great works, which are as rich in significance as the workings of the living mind itself. And like the mind, the great work never yields entirely to rational understanding; somewhere, beyond all analysis, it retains its vital mystery.

After this examination of *The Idiot*, what can be said of the author's conscious intentions for it? Do they bear any relation at all to the result, the novel as it is actually experienced? Those intentions were strongly moral and even didactic. Dostoevsky wished to create a "positively beautiful man," a Christ figure who would point the way to the moral regeneration of Russia and even the world. But the formal and dramatic imagination of the great writer follows its own laws. The unconscious impulses and fantasies in which creative imagination originates are amoral; they seek only gratification, and so they are profoundly subversive of the ideals that are developed to oppose and control their expression. The uniqueness of *The Idiot* is that it contains the two poles of this dialectic within a single conception: the figure of Myshkin. The goodness of Dostoevsky's most sublime vision of the good, his "Prince Christ," is rooted in the darkest human impulses, in the very lust and cruelty of which his conscious personality is the negation. Behind and within the explicit moral ideals proposed by the novel and its central character—compassion, purity, religious submission—one is made to feel the attraction of the forbidden impulses that contradict those ideals: cruelty, perverse erotic excitement, and rebellion.

In the person of Myshkin, the novel poses a radical question. We are presented with an apparently "good" man whose character embodies Christian ideals of self-sacrifice and compassion, and whose charm and sweetness cannot be destroyed by all the analysis his darker side invites; yet this figure is treated in such a way as to raise the most disturbing questions about the origins of his goodness and the concealed gratifications afforded by his self-abnegation. By its presentation of the good man, the novel calls into question the very nature of goodness, and its relation to what we call evil.

If the novel does achieve a moral effect, that effect is at once humbler and more radical than Dostoevsky intended. *The Idiot* demonstrates the dangers of "goodness," and the equivocal nature of all moral choice. Like Tiresias in his great speech to Oedipus, it tells us, "You have your eyes but see not where you are in sin." And like the story of Oedipus, it suggests that our deepest motives are finally unknowable. The ambiguity of the novel's central conception is inexhaustible: its depths are lost to view, in some darkness at the roots of personality and moral action where good and evil cannot be separated.

Appendix

THE CREATIVE PROCESS IN THE NOTEBOOKS FOR "THE IDIOT"

The notebooks Dostoevsky kept during the planning and writing of *The Idiot* are a rich source of information about the interests and ideas and the creative process out of which the novel emerged. However, their existence creates something of a dilemma in a study of this kind. To draw on them extensively in the body of the book would have been inconsistent with its fundamental premise: that unconscious meaning is contained, and conveyed to the reader, in the internal structures of the text. Notebooks and letters can tell us what the author wanted to do or thought he was doing; but what he actually did is to be found only in the work itself. Moreover, in the notebooks characters and ideas are seen in primitive states of development. While certain patterns concealed in the work may appear more clearly in these crude early stages, these patterns are altered by the later modification they undergo. Thus the configurations of meaning in the notebooks are not necessarily those of the novel.

Nonetheless, in a psychoanalytic study, a record of the creative process is bound to be of the greatest interest. The notebooks are the best means of access to what was going on in Dostoevsky's mind during those agonizing months when he went through plan after plan, struggling to arrive at a workable conception. In the notes we find Dostoevsky's first thoughts for the novel—the first bits of character and plot, the first conception of the personality of the Idiot himself, and the real-life story from the newspaper that, as so often happened, stimulated his imagination. Dostoevsky traveled an extraordinary distance from the characters and plot of the first sketch to those of the novel itself. And yet he was, after all, going somewhere. The material in the notes is thrown out, retrieved, remolded and transformed time and time again. In the rejections and transformations we see processes very like the repression, condensation, displacement, and secondary revision that go on in the formation of a dream. Moreover, by that law of conservation that operates in the unconscious, virtually none of the ideas in the notebooks is lost. The violent, sexual, incoherent material Dostoevsky consciously rejects turns up later in the novel, disguised and buried, but animating *The Idiot* with the power of repressed idea and impulse. Thus although the notebooks are not a secret key to the novel, the material they contain is certainly connected with the conscious and unconscious processes out of which it emerged, and with its unconscious structure and meaning.

The notebooks, then, had to be dealt with. But in order to ensure that my interpretation of *The Idiot* would be based entirely on the novel itself, I avoided the notes (literally: I did not read them) until my own conception of the text had been worked out. When I did turn to the notebooks, it was with some trepidation. Obviously I hoped they would contain some confirmation of my understanding of the novel. They did confirm my reading of the text—in such striking ways that not even wish-fulfillment seems sufficient to account for the correspondences. In the body of this study, I refer to the notebooks only occasionally, where they have some direct relevance to a specific point in the text. In looking at them separately in this essay, I hope to show that they support the psychoanalytic interpretation of the novel as a whole. And they are in their own right a fascinating record of the dynamics of literary creation.

The notebooks contain at least eight different plans for the novel: the earliest date in the first plan is 14 September 1867, and the last plan was written at the end of November. Each plan contains a number of variant or contradictory versions of the action. The atmosphere of the notes is chaotic; the author seems to be trying desperately to impose order on material that continually escapes his control. *"New and definitive plan for the novel,"* he writes, only to follow this with still more definitive plans. The notes are full of expressions of confusion and dissatisfaction and self-exhortations to "hurry up." In texture the notes are dense and fragmented. On a single page a plot is sketched out and then abolished; characters are killed off and then reappear a few lines later, or change families or personalities. There are passages of fragmentary jottings—apparently unconnected words, phrases, names. The quality of the notes seems close at times to that of primary process thinking. The author is simply recording rapidly whatever comes into his mind, without much attempt at order or coherence. We are certainly not seeing unconscious motifs in their original forms in the notes. But without the strictures of continuous narrative and its requirements of coherence and plausibility, ego controls are somewhat relaxed, contradiction is permitted, fantasy encouraged. Violent and sexual ideas emerge more freely in this fluid atmosphere, and unconscious material is less fully disguised. The need to placate both external and internal censors is also diminished: there are, for example, many explicit allusions to sexual matters in the notebooks that are suppressed in the novel.

Although a number of important themes run throughout all the plans, there is no clear conception of an action or character that could dramatize and unify them. Even the last plan, written at the end of November 1867, little more than a month before serial publication was due to begin, has quite a different plot and cast of characters from the novel that somehow took shape almost immediately afterward. In letters to his niece and to Maikov written in January 1868, after the first chapters of *The Idiot* had been sent off to the publisher, Dostoevsky says that in December he destroyed everything he had done and started "a new novel." Although *The Idiot* is indeed in many ways a new novel, different from anything in the plans that preceded it, the process of creation was nonetheless going on in those fragmentary and confusing notes; something was happening that enabled Dostoevsky after months of frustration to produce in three weeks the seven brilliant opening chapters.

The first plan outlines a situation quite remote from that of the finished novel. Here the principal characters are a family of ruined gentry headed by a ne'er-do-well father resembling General Ivolgin. The family also includes a mother, a spoiled elder son referred to as "the handsome youth," a daughter who is engaged to be married, and a foster daughter named Mignon, who has been abused by both her own parents and her adoptive family. The most enigmatic figure is the younger son, "the Idiot," an epileptic despised by the family although he is their sole financial support. This family appeals for help to "the uncle," the father's wealthy younger brother, who also has a son. The center of the intrigue in this version is "the heroine," called throughout the notes "Héro," a beautiful and arrogant cousin of the daughter's fiancé. Héro, who prefigures Nastasya, is courted by the handsome youth, the Idiot, the uncle, and the uncle's son. The fiancé wants to get her profitably married off, and so he "sells" her to the uncle's son. The son, a person of noble character, really does love her and is about to tell her so when his father, the uncle, proposes to her. The son withdraws in favor of his father, and although the heroine begs the son to take her away, "the son cannot decide to deal his father this wound, and he renounces her."[1] To show her contempt for both father and son, the heroine elopes with the Idiot. This plot is surrounded by a bewildering tangle of variants and subplots, some of them involving Mignon, the abused foster daughter, who is raped by the Idiot.

The competition between father and son over a woman that is a hidden component of the struggle between Myshkin and Rogozhin for Nastasya is central to this plan, and quite explicit; the oedipal motif will emerge again clearly in the third and eighth plans. But what is most striking in the first plan is the character of the Idiot. Under psychoanalytic scrutiny, the chaste and compassionate character of Myshkin in the novel appears to have developed out of the repression and transformation of violent and lustful impulses. This interpretation is borne out by the notebooks. The Idiot of the first plan is a savage creature: "He is ripe for horror, crimes, villainy" (41). He rapes Mignon, and breaks the heroine's hands. His "idiocy" is a pretense and a weapon: "the Idiot speaks haughtily, laconically (he pretends to be an idiot out of mockery)" (34). In the novel the gentle Myshkin and the violent Rogozhin seem somehow intimately related: here it is clear that they did in fact grow out of a single conception. In the first plan the Idiot is very like Rogozhin, particularly in his relationship with Héro:

> From the outset he frightened her to such a terrible degree that she would suddenly be seized with an urge to run away from him and hide; but also she would have a sudden urge to play with fire or leap off a tower: the voluptuousness in a sinking of the heart. (42)

Like Rogozhin, the Idiot excites the wish for suffering and destruction.

However, Dostoevsky also plants the seeds of a possible metamorphosis:

> N.B. *The Idiot's basic character.* Domination of himself out of pride (not morality) and rabid self-license in everything. As yet, however, self-license is but a dream, whereas at the moment he has only convulsive impulses. Consequently, he could turn into a monster, but love saves him. He becomes imbued with the most profound compassion and he forgives faults in others. [. . .] In compensation he progressively develops a high moral sense, and performs a heroic action. (37)

The transformation of violent impulses into compassion and morality described here suggests to the psychoanalytic interpreter the process of reaction-formation. Out of this process the character of Prince Myshkin finally evolves. Myshkin is also prefigured in Plan I by the uncle's son. The son is interested in social problems; he preaches about happiness—"each moment is a happiness"; he is carried away by compassion for others; and he is identified explicitly with Christ.

Rogozhin's attack on Myshkin on the staircase, which brilliantly dramatizes significant unconscious motifs in the novel, may also be faintly prefigured here in a little scene sketched out in two sentences: "The heroine [. . .] is enthralled by him [the son], and his indifference merely enflames her the more. Once she runs to see him, but the Idiot waits for her on the stairs" (43). In the novel, of course, Myshkin takes the place of the heroine on the stairs, and Rogozhin has assumed much of the character first ascribed to the Idiot. This first glimpse of that scene suggests something of the ambiguities of sex and identity that persist at the unconscious level in the final version.

Another important feature of Plan I is the role of the character called Mignon. Mignon is central to the first plan, and reappears throughout the notebooks. In the novel itself she has disappeared, but the theme associated with her has been assimilated into the experience of the three principal characters. Mignon was based upon a real person, a girl of fifteen named Olga Umetskaia, who figured in a case being tried in the courts in September of 1867. Umetskaia had been tortured, starved, and sexually abused by her parents, and had in turn tried several times to burn down their house. Dostoevsky's wife describes in her memoirs her husband's interest in the case, and in the notes for Plan I, Dostoevsky writes, "Mignon's history is altogether like that of Olga Umetskaia" (32). Mignon is the victim of several sexual assults in Plan I: she is raped by the Idiot, and the father of the principal family, Mignon's foster-father, also makes advances to her. In a later plan, the Umetskaia character is seduced by her own father. Thus the motif of the sadistic and sexual abuse of a child that is deeply buried in the experiences of Myshkin, Rogozhin, and Nastasya proves in the notebooks to have been one of the generative ideas behind *The Idiot*. When he began the actual writing of the novel, however, Dostoevsky dropped the Umetskaia story. Evidently a process of repression and transformation took place, and the theme went underground, to create a network of linked derivatives in the childhood experiences of the three central characters. The sadomasochistic and incestuous features of the Mignon-Umetskaia motif emerge most clearly in the story of Nastasya, who is derived from Umetskaia as well as from "Héro." In the first plan Mignon is, like Nastasya, proud, vengeful, and masochistic: "as soon as she gets her revenge on them all, she will kill herself at once" (36); she wants to become a "woman of the streets," as Nastasya threatens to do.

The first plan also contains another more generalized pattern connected with infantile experience, which seems to have disappeared entirely from the explicit narrative in the novel: this is the theme of the rejecting mother who arouses such painful ambivalence in her child. This motif can be retrieved in the novel only at the deepest level of unconscious meaning, concealed behind the homosexual fantasy and in the murder of Nastasya. In Plan I, the Idiot's mother "detests him and constantly complains of him" (31). The uncle too was "an unloved child" (33). The pattern is repeated in the life of the uncle's son, who is "unloved and unacknowledged by his father" (37).

On first reading, Plan I seems to bear very little relation to *The Idiot*; the explicit forms of character and action are quite different from those of the novel. On closer examination, however, one finds themes that will become important elements in the unconscious structure of the novel already present in the sketch, often quite openly.

What Dostoevsky seems to have been struggling for in the notebooks, without of course consciously articulating the problem in this way, was a configuration of characters and a dramatic structure that would at once disguise these themes and permit them some degree of expression.

The second plan, written around the middle of October 1867, is essentially a variation and elaboration on the first. The character of the Idiot remains violent and even demonic, although there continues to be a possibility of moral regeneration. The specific threat of murder that haunts the novel is introduced here: "The main point: the reader and *all the characters* in the novel must remember that *he can kill the heroine* and that everyone is expecting him to kill her" (54). The original Idiot was conceived of as a potential murderer, and although the actual execution of the murder is later delegated to Rogozhin, who is a split-off part of this original Idiot, murderous wishes remain in the personality of Myshkin even as it evolves in the direction of goodness.

There is also a hint in this plan of the relationship between "idiocy" and the familiarity with forbidden experience or the exposure to forbidden sights: "In the beginning they treated the Idiot as if he were a madman in a physical sense, short of flogging him. They looked on him as a nonentity. They talked about everything before him. Not even the needs of nature deterred them in his presence" (56). As a child, then, the Idiot is allowed to hear and see things that are usually concealed. The masochism that is so strong an element in Myshkin begins to emerge here in response to these experiences:

> His own attitude conduced to this treatment by the family. He remained silent, peering up at them all, though inside he was seething.
>
> [. . .] *he* [. . .] *let it be understood* that he was quite aware of his own delight in this inordinate humiliation and the thirst for revenge it incited. "I have subdued myself." That's voluptuousness. (56)

The cast of characters remains much the same in Plan III, written in the second half of October, although there is a significant change in relationship. The Idiot is moved from the family of the General to that of the uncle—he becomes the uncle's son, and thus the brother of the good son. All three of these men, along with the General and his son, the "handsome youth," compete for the heroine. As before, she runs away from the uncle with the Idiot (now the uncle's son). Olga Umetskaia (she is given her real-life name here) continues to play the part of the oppressed girl longing for revenge. In all three plans she becomes involved with the uncle and/or the Idiot after each loses the heroine.

Perhaps the most interesting feature of this plan is the intensification of the relationship among the principal male characters. The Idiot and the good son are now brothers, suggesting the intimacy of the hidden connection between Myshkin and Rogozhin. And a father, "the uncle," and his two sons are now all in competition for the same woman, suggesting the oedipal aspect of the love story in the novel. The forging of these links was evidently part of the process by which Dostoevsky groped his way toward the form of the novel itself. Connections had to be established before they could be broken and forced into the unconscious, where they remained alive. The relationships among the three men are ambiguous, and highly ambivalent. The uncle has in the past rejected or refused to acknowledge the two sons. Yet he feels the most intense attraction for the Idiot: "He worships the Idiot" (67). At the beginning of this plan, in a passage sketching out incidents involving the Idiot, this cryptic note appears: "Romantic relations with the uncle" (61). The homosexual theme is in fact suggested in the very first plan, where the uncle is described as "simply fanatically attached to the Idiot" (40).

In Plan III the two sons, who have been raised separately, meet for the first time in a railway carriage, prefiguring the opening of the novel. Their relationship has the same erotic intensity as that of the uncle and the

Idiot. At first the Idiot behaves hatefully to his brother, but gradually he is won over by the good son's gentleness. "The Idiot *grows enamored* with the son, though he laughs at himself" (70). This ambiguous relationship of brothers survives in the novel, in the "double" relationship between Myshkin and Rogozhin.

The intense and eroticized feeling between men recurs in the fourth plan, which was done at the end of October:

> N.B. He [the Idiot] has a terrible love for the son. A queer passion.
> N.B. Queerest of all, he loves the uncle too.

The Idiot "subjugates the uncle to the point of enslavement and crazy fanaticism" (82).

In this sketch the Idiot becomes once again the son of the General, rather than of the uncle. As before, Héro is courted by all the men. The most striking feature of this plan is the emergence of "Ganechka." Ganechka is the name given here to the handsome youth, the eldest son of the General, who in the earlier plans is a minor figure, a pampered, venal, and selfish young man like Ganya in the novel. Here his character is transformed; he becomes "pure, beautiful, virtuous, strict, very nervous, with a profoundly Christian, compassionate lovingness" (84). The role of the uncle's son, who had previously had these qualities, is diminished here in proportion to the increased importance of Ganechka.

The way in which traits of character are shifted in these notes from one figure to another reveals a significant aspect of Dostoevsky's conception of *The Idiot*. The novel seems to have originated not in the idea of a specific character or action, but rather in the sense of a psychological and spiritual conflict. The terms of this conflict remain relatively constant from the beginning, although the forms in which it is presented change. This is particularly obvious in the treatment of the male characters. Taken together, the young men in the notes make up a kind of composite personality whose conflicting traits and emotions are allotted differently from one plan to another, although the emotions and the conflict itself remain essentially unchanged. This sense of a subterranean connection among the young male characters remains in the novel, where Myshkin, Rogozhin, Ganya, Ippolit, and even some of the lesser figures often function as repressed or split-off parts of one another.

The conflict being worked out among these characters is most fully embodied, of course, in the Idiot himself, whose nature remains polarized between the extremes of good and evil. In Plan III, he was a malicious schemer and manipulator—there Dostoevsky compares him to Iago. In Plan IV, he begins increasingly to resemble Raskolnikov or Stavrogin. Elements of boredom, alienation, and perversity in his character are emphasized: "an anguished, contemptuous, endlessly proud personality who delights in his own superiority and others' worthlessness; he hates and despises his success and his pleasures to the point of loathing [. . .]" (85). His intellect is severed from his feelings, and he seems to exercise his will in an emotionless void: "Out of boredom he sets fire to the house and rapes Umetskaia" (81). However, *"in the end he is agonized by his own role,* and suddenly he perceives a solution in love" (85).

In the fifth plan, written early in November, the Idiot is placed in a situation very like that of Stavrogin two years later in *The Possessed.* He is secretly married to a woman who is considered debased—she has had an illegitimate child; he feels both pitying love and contempt for her. He then falls passionately in love with the beautiful and aristocratic heroine, who "loves him to distraction." He tells the heroine jeeringly, "I am a monster" (100). In one version of the action, he rapes the heroine, and in another he apparently poisons his wife, or she poisons herself. Intellectually and emotionally, he is torn by conflict. Dostoev-

sky's conception of him appears most clearly in this sequence of notes:

> He is a Christian yet at the same time he does not
> believe.
> *The dualism of a deep nature.*
> N.B. *The tongue in the mirror.* (107)

The last image seems to stand for all the corrosive irony,
self-hatred, and perversity of the Idiot of this plan.

The theme of ambivalence emerges most openly in Plan
V. Throughout the notes, the Idiot has behaved hatefully
and violently to those he loves, as in breaking the heroine's
hands in the first sketch. In Plan IV, Dostoevsky writes
"The entire novel is built on the struggle between love and hate"
(80). And in Plan V, even more explicitly: "love, alternating
with unconscious hatred" (114). In a letter to the Idiot, the
heroine writes "I never loved you . . . . except with a
hate-love" (114). Plan V is entirely dominated by the conflict in the Idiot between love and hatred, in his feelings for
both his wife and the heroine.

In the novel, loving and hateful impulses coexist in all
the principal characters, even in Myshkin with his "double
thoughts." The violently polarized nature of the original
Idiot, who was to begin in hatred and to be transformed by
love, is divided in the novel between the characters of
Myshkin and Rogozhin. However, although Myshkin has
none of the overt violence and hatred of the Idiot of the
notebooks, his love has results at least as disastrous: the
woman he loves is murdered.

Plan VI is quite brief. The essential situation is the same
as in the preceding plan. This sketch was prepared early in
November, about two months before the completion of the
first chapters of the novel; and yet the character of the
Idiot and the projected plot are radically different from
what was to appear in January. There are, however, several
hints of the coming change in the central character that will

open up a whole new conception. At the beginning of the plan this note appears: "*Enigmas.* Who is he? A terrible scoundrel or a mysterious ideal?" (124). And toward the end there is an allusion to the conception of the *yurodivyi*, or holy fool, the Prince Christ who loves children: "Prince *Yurodivyi*. (He is with the children.)?!" (129).

In the seventh plan, written during the last three weeks of November, the crucial change occurs: the demonic and violent Idiot is finally transformed into the character who will become Myshkin in the novel. He is gentle, compassionate, deeply Christian. "A son rejected since childhood, the Idiot is wrapped up in his passion for children. Everywhere he has children about him" (143). The son, Ganechka, now becomes violent and passionate. Dostoevsky writes of him "This is the character that was formerly the Idiot's: magnanimous, bitterness, pride, and envy" (141). From the beginning the Idiot has had good qualities that would lead eventually to his regeneration, but they were always overshadowed in action by his spiteful and violent tendencies. Evidently it was necessary, in order for the novel to take final shape, to divide these two sides of the Idiot's nature into two characters. Myshkin had been foreshadowed at various stages by the good son, the earlier Ganechka, and the good side of the Idiot; Rogozhin grows principally out of the original conception of the Idiot himself.

We also have in Plan VII the basis for the relationship of Myshkin and Nastasya. Nastasya is prefigured here by a character called Nastia, a daughter of the Umetsky family. Nastia has been seduced and left in the country alone and pregnant. The Idiot takes her in and offers to marry her. Nastia, however, considers herself defiled, and runs away from the Idiot with Ganechka, as Nastasya runs away from Myshkin with Rogozhin.

Throughout the notebooks Olga Umetskaia has played a significant but subordinate part. In this draft, the Umetsky family and the themes associated with them move to the center of the story. The original figure of the daughter is split or multiplied; the Umetskys now have two or even three daughters: Nastia, Olga, and Ustinia, who is at times identified with Olga. As the Umetsky women, especially Nastia, take over the center of the stage, the girl called "Héro" disappears: her wild and unpredictable character is largely assimilated by Nastia.

The themes of incest and seduction of a very young girl by a much older man dominate this plan. Olga Umetskaia has a baby, presumably by her father. (Earlier, in Plan V, we are told "Several times VI. Umetsky makes attempts on Umetskaia" [94]). A note in Plan VII, partly crossed out, reads: "~~Nastia is 22. The father was already running after~~ her when she was only 20, when he could still—." Nastia ran away, but the father caught her and "beat and tortured her like a wild animal" (142). She then set the house on fire, like the real Olga Umetskaia. The third girl in this group, Ustinia, is either Umetsky's daughter or his ward. In either case she has lived with him and had his child. In another note, Ustinia is kept by a man called Trotsky; this liaison points the way to that of Nastasya and Totsky in the novel. Another relationship in this plan also leads to that of Nastasya and her guardian: the General, the father of the principal family, here and in several other drafts wants to marry his young ward. This substitution of the guardian, with his obviously paternal responsibilities, for the real father will make it possible to treat the theme of incest in the story of Nastasya, retaining its emotional resonance while avoiding too direct a confrontation with forbidden material.

Surprisingly, in the eighth and last plan, written at the end of November 1867, only two and a half weeks before he began the novel itself, Dostoevsky seems almost to abandon his new vision of a compassionate and Christlike Idiot. Instead, this plan is dominated by a violent struggle between the General and his son Ganechka over Ustinia Umetskaia. Ustinia seduces the son and then taunts him with her intention to marry his father. As in the preceding plan, Ustinia has been seduced by a rich landowner, Trotsky, and has had his child. The explicitly incestuous stories of Plan VII have been replaced by this relationship. However, Vladimir Umetsky, Ustinia's father, is very important here. He whips Ustinia and tries to kill her child, and he savagely beats his son, a "spindly, frail youth." Umetsky is characterized by "his gloating sadism toward his wife, his daughter, his children, and especially his schoolboy son" (151). The General says of him, "I know him, in the regiment he used to like flogging" (156). In Vladimir Umetsky we have something very like the shadowy composite father-figure of the novel. In Plan VII Umetsky seduces his daughter, as Totsky does Nastasya; in Plan VIII he has a reputation for flogging his subordinates in the army, like Myshkin's father, and he actually flogs his son, like Rogozhin's father and Myshkin's lady guardian. In terms of the explicit story, Plan VIII appears to be a retreat from the advances toward the final plot made in Plan VII—the saintly character of the Idiot and the relationship between the Idiot and Nastia. However, this last plan may have been an essential prelude to the writing of the novel itself. Plan VIII is dominated by the oedipal rivalry and by the figure of the sadistic and sexually seductive father. These two motifs are of crucial importance: they lead to the negative Oedipus complex and the sadomasochistic conception of the primal scene that are central elements in the unconscious structure of *The Idiot*.

In his editorial commentary on Plan VIII, Edward Wasiolek writes of the re-emergence of the Umetsky story,

The Umetsky affair had influenced [Dostoevsky] greatly, and he tried mightily, with minimal success, to work it directly into his novel. Now, on the eve of the publication of the first part, he returned to it again,

with the same lack of success. . . . When one surveys
the multiple efforts he made to use the theme of the
maltreated child, the cruel and ugly environment of
childhood and its effects upon the soul of the adult,
the horrifying prospect of a father's betrayal of his
God-like trust, one is struck even more how little
finally found its way into the finished novel. (149)

In the most obvious and literal way, this is true. The story
of Olga Umetskaia was an essential part of the inspiration
for the novel: it appears in one form or another throughout all the plans, and assumes central importance in the last
two. Then it disappears, suddenly and completely. The
eighth plan is dated 30 November; four days later, on December 4th, Dostoevsky threw it out. In a phrase from a
letter, he "threw it all to the devil" and began a new novel.
The painful and dangerous Umetsky material is emphati-
cally repressed. And yet in the "new novel" that began to
take shape in the next few days, the themes of the violated
child and the sadistic father are nevertheless present,
worked into its very texture. The Umetsky case seems to
have functioned in the genesis of the novel in somewhat
the same way as the day's residue works in the creation of a
dream: a real-life incident triggers a complex of unconscious memories and associations, and is itself transformed
by the unconscious processes it evokes. The Umetsky story
could not be used just as it was—a case of undisguised incest and sadism. Before it could enter the novel it had to be
buried and transformed: barred from direct expression, it
is forced into disguised and derivative forms; it undergoes
that "proliferation in the dark" of which Freud writes,
helping to create the web of organic connections that
makes up the emotional texture of the novel.
    The first notes, written in September 1867, are domi-
nated by two powerful characters: The Idiot and Mignon-Umetskaia, both profoundly sinned against, both violent and vengeful personalities, full of the wish to suffer

and to injure others. Dostoevsky did not, of course, literally throw out in December everything he had done in the intervening months. The notebooks show the characters of Myshkin, Rogozhin, and Nastasya evolving gradually, if erratically, out of the original figures by processes of condensation, displacement, splitting, and secondary elaboration very like what occurs in the formation of a dream, as the "day's residue" is subjected to the powerful influence of unconscious memories and associations. The process transcribed in the notebooks also resembles the formation of a dream in another way: the notes record not only the movement toward expression of the ideas they contain but also, paradoxically, the struggle to repress those ideas. Between the last plan and the beginning of the novel itself, an act of creative repression has taken place. The novel is a compromise formation; the material emerges in a disguised and sublimated form in which both repressed and repressing tendencies are given some expression.

The muting of the explicit sexuality and sadism of the Umetsky story and the evolution of the violent and demonic Idiot in the direction of goodness were necessary. Blocked from open expression, energies that might otherwise have erupted directly and quickly are forced to cut new channels, creating an intricate capillary network of major and minor characters, of plots and subplots, of ambiguous actions and hidden meanings. The whole densely peopled and intricately constructed world of the novel takes shape. And, as Freud points out in his essay on repression, a repressed idea loses none of its original force. On the contrary, its strength is augmented by being dammed up. The enormous emotional energy that infuses the novel even down to the least significant levels of character and action must come largely from this containment and transformation of forbidden ideas and impulses.

There is a hiatus in the notes between November 1867 and March 1868 while Dostoevsky was writing Part I of the novel—the sixteen chapters that were published in the January and February issues of *The Russian Messenger*. Early in March Dostoevsky began making notes for Part II and for the whole novel, of which he still had no coherent conception. These notes continue in the intervals of the work on Part II, which was completed in July 1868. The notebooks end with a small group of entries made during the composition of Parts III and IV.

The notes made after the writing of the novel had actually begun are, of course, different from the chaotic and fragmentary early sketches. However, even though a large part of the novel had already been published, in the notebooks things are still in a fluid and indeterminate state. With the completion of Part I, which ends with the brilliantly climactic episode of Nastasya's birthday party, Dostoevsky found that he had no idea how to continue. The identities and personalities of the principal characters had been established, but their actions and their destinies seemed to their creator unpredictable, almost like those of real persons.

The major issue to be dealt with was the relationship among Myshkin, Rogozhin, and Nastasya; the roles of Aglaia and Ganya were subsidiary to this problem. The notes sketch out almost every conceivable combination of these elements. One possibility to which Dostoevsky returned again and again was a marriage between the Prince and Nastasya. This marriage always leads to disaster: after the wedding Nastasya "plunges into debauchery," becomes a laundress, goes into a brothel, and dies or kills herself there. In one version she incites Ganya and Rogozhin to seduce Aglaia, who is rescued by the Prince (167). Or else Nastasya is engaged to the Prince—"her total rehabilitation, and her total downfall" (203); she then runs away from him with Rogozhin on her wedding day. Dostoevsky tried several times to find a way to save Nastasya; in one version Rogozhin marries Nastasya, Aglaia marries the

Prince, and together Aglaia and Myshkin rehabilitate Nastasya. However, quite early in this set of notes, a week after they begin, Dostoevsky sketches out a plot close to what finally occurs in the novel: Myshkin and Nastasya become engaged, but Nastasya "plunges into wild depravity" and goes to a brothel; she marries Rogozhin, and he cuts her throat.

The treatment of Aglaia in the first pages of these notes is surprising. The first day's entry contains these lines:

> The Prince understands N.F.'s behavior and wants to give Aglaia up.
> Frank discussions with Aglaia. Aglaia says all right and to avenge herself runs away with Gania—on the eve of the wedding.
> The Prince is engaged to Aglaia.

And a few lines farther down:

> On the eve of the wedding Aglaia breaks everything off or else runs away with the count. (165)

Dostoevsky's idea here is unclear: is the wedding in question Aglaia's wedding to Myshkin? And is the count with whom she elopes Totsky? In any case, these notes point up the connection between Aglaia and Nastasya and between Ganya and Rogozhin that emerges in the interpretation of the novel. Aglaia acts here as Nastasya will act in the novel: she elopes with Ganya, as Nastasya does with Rogozhin. Indeed, on the next page, "Rogozhin falls in love with Aglaia" (166). And a few pages later, "Gania strangles Aglaia" (169). The two women are at this point almost interchangeable. Dostoevsky writes one name, then another, then crosses one out: "The Prince is married to N. F. ~~Aglaia~~. N. F. ~~Aglaia~~ could not endure the night at Rogozhin's" (166).

The theme of sadomasochistic sexuality emerges clearly in these pages: the woman is debased by the sexual relationship, and she punishes herself by becoming a laundress (with the implication of prostitution), or she is murdered. As in the early sketches for the novel, the psychological pattern precedes the specific embodiment in character and action. The notes also treat the development of the secondary characters. Ippolit takes shape here and becomes an extremely important figure—even more so than in the novel. Dostoevsky writes: "Ipolit—the main axis of the whole novel" (236). And "Write tersely and powerfully about Ipolit. Center the whole plot on him" (238). And "Ipolit kills" (239). Ippolit was meant to be implicated profoundly in the central conception.

Ganya's character and role remain problematic throughout these notes. At times he is seen as a violent personality like Rogozhin: "Gania's terrible disposition, gloomy, passionate" (178). "Toward the end he kills himself" (184). At other times the conception of his character draws closer to that of Myshkin. "N. B. Gania too is like a Sphinx" (200). "Gania. Ill, almost an idiot. [. . .] His role = a slave's role. (N.B. This is a role that can be made very genuine, beautiful, and gentle.)" (215) The question "What to do with Gania?" appears again and again, and in fact his role is never satisfactorily resolved in the notes or in the novel, where he begins as a kind of minor Rogozhin, then becomes for a time a somewhat unconvincing investigator and agent for Myshkin, and later a petty conniver and intriguer.

The uncertainties regarding Ganya, like the difficulties with the relations between Myshkin, Rogozhin, Nastasya, and Aglaia, are a continuation of the struggles recorded in the early sketches for the novel. The central conflict is always between impulses of love and hatred; its roots are in childhood, in the dilemma of the child for whom love is inextricably bound up with contradictory fantasies of murderous vengeance and of gentle, even slavelike, submission.

This study of the notebooks raises a paradoxical problem: the notes contain in recognizable form motifs that are deeply concealed in the novel and that can be brought to light there only with painstaking analysis. The presence of this material in the notebooks seems, then, to support the psychoanalytic interpretation. From another point of view, however, the evidence in the notebooks might point to another conclusion. Perhaps in fact the references to such matters as incest and sadism in the notebooks do not support, but contradict the psychoanalytic interpretation, which bases its claims on the presence of *unconscious* material in the novel. The notebooks might be taken to indicate that Dostoevsky was in fact conscious of these themes and of their indirect and disguised expression in the novel. If this is true, then the concept of an unconscious structure created by the ramification of ideas forced into repression cannot be substantiated.

This argument can be refuted, however. First and most obvious: the highly charged themes that surface in the notes, such as incest, sadism, and the ambivalent relationship with the mother, are so thoroughly disguised and transformed in the novel that a good deal of interpretation is required to bring them to light. It is absurd to imagine Dostoevsky settling on these themes and then undertaking consciously to conceal them, a task so fantastically complex, with such unpredictable results, that it could never be accomplished by conscious, rational processes. Moreover, assuming that the notes are a true record of Dostoevsky's thoughts and not a deliberate effort to mislead posterity, it is inconceivable that they would contain not a single reference to the problem of disguising the forbidden material.

There is a more important point to be made here, however. The argument that "unconscious" motifs in the novel must in fact be conscious because derivatives of them appear in the notes would be based on a fundamental misunderstanding of the nature of repression. The repressed or unconscious quality of an idea does not mean that the idea has never been present in consciousness in some form. In the essay on repression, Freud writes "it is not even correct to suppose that repression withholds from consciousness *all* the derivatives of what was primally repressed."[2] Freud also points out that the amnesias filled in during analysis are in many cases not true gaps in memory: the original experience that gave rise to the repression may be present in consciousness, but the connection between that incident and other materials related to it has been broken.[3] It is then this connection, rather than the incident itself, that has undergone repression; although the disturbing experience may be remembered, its meaning and effects remain unknown.

This kind of repressive breaking of connections seems to have occurred most effectively in the interval between the completion of the eighth plan and the beginning of the novel itself. There is absolutely no indication in the notes or the letters that Dostoevsky recognized consciously the connection between the sadistic and incestuous themes in the notebooks and the novel he finally wrote. On the contrary, he was furiously discontented with the ideas in the notebooks. The material that appears there seems to assail him quite against his will; what comes to mind is not at all what he is consciously striving for.

As the deadline approaches, he tries one plan after another, without finding an idea that enables him to embark on the novel. On November 1, he ends the fourth plan with the note, "No good. The main idea as to the Idiot does not emerge" (89). In the letter of January 12 to Maikov we have his own evaluation of the work in the notebooks:

> Well: all summer and autumn I was putting together various thoughts (some were most ingenious), but some experience always let me feel either the falsity, the difficulty, or the unworkability of a particular idea. Finally, I settled on one [evidently Plan VIII] and

began to work; I had written a great deal, but on the 4th of December [. . .] I threw it all to the devil. I assure you that the novel could have been satisfactory, but it became repulsive to me to an incredible extent precisely because it was satisfactory and not *positively good*.[4]

In a way, Dostoevsky had come full circle: he had returned after various detours to the Umetsky theme with which he had begun, as though he could not escape it. And then as he wrote, it became "repulsive" to him and he threw it "to the devil," where such dangerous stuff apparently belonged.

Then began the extraordinary two weeks of feverish mental activity in which the decisive transformation of the earlier ideas took place.

Then (since my whole future was at stake) I began to torment myself over the invention of *a new novel*. [. . .] I thought from the 4th to the 18th of December inclusive. I must have worked out six plans a day (not less) on the average. My head turned into a mill. I don't understand how I didn't lose my mind. Finally, on the 18th of December I sat down to write a new novel.[5]

Dostoevsky certainly did not think of this new novel as concerned with such matters as incest and sadistic sexuality. On the contrary, it was to present to the world the ideal of the Russian Christ, the "positively beautiful man."

Somewhere, of course, in that shadowy borderland psychoanalysts call the preconscious, Dostoevsky must have suspected something of the nature of the material that had seeped back into the novel. Perhaps his dissatisfaction with *The Idiot*—"my idea that did not succeed"—came from the recognition that he had not in fact achieved the moral purity he had set himself as an ideal. We can be grateful for this failure, however. The richness and excitement of *The Idiot* originate in the tensions between that ideal of order and beauty and the chaotic, ugly, and violent material of the notebooks. The flexibility in the repressions that Freud attributes to the artist allowed some of that disturbing material into the final version, while the "strong capacity for sublimation" of the great writer transformed it. The result is the strangeness, the power, and the brilliance of one of the world's greatest novels.

Notes

1 THEORY

Part 1 I. Introduction

1. Steven Marcus, in an essay entitled "Freud and Dora: Story, History, Case History" (*Representations: Essays on Literature and Society* [New York: Random House, 1975]), has explored in depth the literary qualities and devices of one of Freud's major case histories.

2. "Studies on Hysteria," *The Standard Edition of the Complete Psychological Works of Sigmund Freud*, ed. James Strachey et al. (hereafter abbreviated *S.E.*), 24 vols. (London: Hogarth, 1953-1974), II, 160-61. Dates of individual works cited in the *Standard Edition* are listed in my bibliography.

3. Quoted in Lionel Trilling, "Freud and Literature," in *The Liberal Imagination: Essays on Literature and Society* (1950; rpt. Garden City, N.Y.: Doubleday-Anchor, 1953), p. 32.

4. Ernest Jones, *The Life and Work of Sigmund Freud* (New York: Basic Books, 1953-1957), I, 27.

5. "Leonardo da Vinci and a Memory of His Childhood," *S.E.*, XI, 63.

Part 1 II. Psychoanalysis and the Interpretation of the Text

1. "The Interpretation of Dreams" (hereafter referred to as "Dreams"), *S.E.*, IV, 277.

2. Paul Ricoeur makes this point in *De l'interprétation: essai sur Freud* (Paris: Éditions du Seuil, 1965), p. 18.

3. "Dreams," *S.E.*, IV, 262-63.

4. Frederick Crews discusses the academic resistances to psychoanalytic criticism in an essay entitled "Anaesthetic Criticism," in *Out of My System: Psychoanalysis, Ideology, and Critical Method* (New York: Oxford University Press, 1975). However, in "Reductionism and Its Discontents," the last

essay in the volume, he seems to have succumbed to them himself.

5. "Dreams," *S.E.*, IV, 266.

6. *The Portrait of a Lady* (1908; rpt. New York: Modern Library, 1966), p. xxxiv.

7. Ibid., p. xxxvii.

8. *The Future of the Novel: Essays on the Art of Fiction*, ed. Leon Edel (New York: Vintage-Knopf, 1956), p. 12.

9. Ibid., pp. 19-20.

10. "On the Relation of Analytical Psychology to Poetry," *The Collected Works of C. G. Jung*, trans. R.F.C. Hull (hereafter abbreviated *C.W.*), Bollingen Series XX, 18 vols. (New York: Pantheon, and Princeton: Princeton University Press, 1953—), XV, 80.

11. *C.W.*, IX, part I, 83.

12. One need only read the newspapers to find stories of maternal savagery that surpass the exploits of the witches and ogres of childish imagination, and from his perspective of total dependency, even the most fortunate child must see an angry mother as threatening his very existence. As for the hermaphroditic mother: children are invariably confused about the genitals and about who has what. Little boys find it almost impossible to think that everyone is not made as they are, and may believe quite tenaciously, even against the evidence of their own eyes, that the mother has a penis, perhaps hidden inside her body. A funny and pathetic story in Frank O'Connor's autobiography, *An Only Child* (New York: Knopf, 1961), shows that this belief can persist to a surprisingly late age. When at twelve he began perusing art books in the Carnegie Library in Dublin, O'Connor was puzzled by the female nudes, and finally concluded that the painters, out of respect for women, had simply not depicted the penises of the female figures.

13. Jung, "Introduction to the Religious and Psychological Problems of Alchemy," *C.W.*, XII, 10.

14. "The Practical Use of Dream-Analysis," *C.W.*, XVI,

149. In "On the Nature of Dreams," *C.W.*, VIII, 291, Jung cites an example. A young man dreams of a great snake guarding a golden bowl in an underground vault. This dream embodies an archetypal episode, an ordeal in the life of the hero, and according to Jung this is its meaning for the dreamer. It is not necessary, evidently, to consult the young man's associations to the dream elements.

15. Jung, "On the Relation of Analytical Psychology to Poetry," *C.W.*, XV, 80.

16. *Freud or Jung?* (1950; rpt. Cleveland: World-Meridian, 1956), p. 184. Glover's book contains a thorough and devastating analysis of Jung's ideas and a comparison of Jung and Freud on the major issues.

17. One interesting work of literary criticism—Maude Bodkin's *Archetypal Patterns of Poetry* (London: Oxford University Press, 1934)—was influenced by Jung's theories. Bodkin was also indebted, however, to the studies of Frazer and the other Cambridge anthropologists, who treat universal mythic and religious patterns in relation to the specific human biological and social needs from which they arise, rather than as quasi-mystical manifestations of an inherited racial unconscious.

18. *C.W.*, XV, 68.

19. Ibid., p. 80.

20. Ibid., p. 69.

21. *C.W.*, X, 85.

22. See Freud, "Civilization and Its Discontents," *S.E.*, XXI, 79-80.

Part 1   III. Repression, the Unconscious, and the Structure of the Literary Work

1. Freud, "Dreams," *S.E.*, V, 553n.

2. Freud, "Creative Writers and Day-dreaming," *S.E.*, IX, 151.

3. See "Some General Remarks on Hysterical Attacks," *S.E.*, IX, 227-34.

4. "Dreams," *S.E.*, V, 515.

5. "Repression," *S.E.*, XIV, 149.

6. "Dreams," *S.E.*, V, 513.

7. This unconscious structure is no guarantee, of course, that the total effect of the work will be unified and coherent, or artistically successful.

8. Preface to *Portrait of a Lady*, p. xxxviii.

9. "Dreams," *S.E.*, V, 499.

10. Freud, "Dreams," *S.E.*, IV, 247.

11. In "Introductory Lectures on Psycho-Analysis" (*S.E.*, XV, 114), Freud writes: "For the remembered dream is not the genuine material but a distorted substitute for it, which should assist us, by calling up other substitutive images, to come nearer to the genuine material."

12. "Creative Writers and Day-dreaming," *S.E.*, IX, 150.

13. Marie Bonaparte's classic *Edgar Poe: étude psychanalytique* (Paris: Denoël et Steele, 1933) might be cited here: Bonaparte achieves brilliant insights, but she identifies characters in the stories in too literal and limiting a way with figures in Poe's life.

14. "Freud—and the Analysis of Poetry," *The American Journal of Sociology*, 44 (1939), rpt. in William Phillips, ed., *Art and Psychoanalysis* (Cleveland: World-Meridian, 1963), pp. 419, 427.

15. For example: in detective and crime fiction of the "tough," Mickey Spillane school, there is an avid preoccupation with violence. A frequent pattern is the sadistic beating of a woman by a man. It is difficult to understand how such material gets by the superego without arousing more guilt and anxiety than most readers, at least male readers, seem to experience. Perhaps the language and form of such scenes has become so conventionalized as to mute the reality of the action. It seems, however, that one of the functions of the convention itself is to permit the guiltless enjoyment of sexual sadism under cover of the thinnest of rationalizations, such as "she had it coming, she was no good." Entirely different sets of conventions prevail in

other types of crime fiction, such as the genteel detective stories of Agatha Christie. The various conventions by which potentially dangerous material is made acceptable in all kinds of popular literature merit much fuller analytic examination. The issues raised by the subject can only be suggested here.

16. Many comic works do arouse considerable anxiety: for example, the novels of Dickens. Irish writers also come immediately to mind: the works of Swift and Beckett are clearly comic in intention and effect, and yet they grow out of a darker and more frightening vision than most tragedies. In some of Shakespeare's romances and comedies, the comic universe comes perilously close to disintegration. This is particularly true of *Measure for Measure*. The threatening elements in the play—Claudio's death sentence, Angelo's villainy, and the whole atmosphere of hypocrisy and diseased sexuality—are perhaps too disturbing to be fully accommodated by the comic vision or convincingly resolved by the happy ending. A somewhat similar pattern of danger exists in *The Tempest*, where it is handled in more typical comic fashion. Although the malice of Antonio, Sebastian, and Caliban is serious, their murderous and lustful wishes never seem so close to realization as Angelo's, partly because the power of Prospero is always in evidence, while in *Measure for Measure* the Duke is a shadowy figure. Our confidence in Prospero's ultimate benevolence allays the anxiety aroused by the villains and their plots.

17. Norman Holland, *The Dynamics of Literary Response* (New York: Oxford University Press, 1968), p. 189.

18. Ibid., p. 130.

19. Ibid., p. 111.

20. "Dreams," *S.E.*, V, 352-53.

21. *Psychoanalysis and Literary Process*, p. 10.

22. Ibid., p. 23.

23. "The Moses of Michelangelo," *S.E.*, XIII, 212.

24. This process is described by Ernst Kris in *Psychoanalytic Explorations in Art* (1952; rpt. New York: Schocken, 1964), pp. 61-62.

25. See ibid., p. 62.

26. Kris, pp. 243-64.

Part 1   IV. The Ambiguity of Language

1. "Dreams," *S.E.*, V, 340.

2. See Victor H. Rosen, "Introduction to Panel on Language and Psychoanalysis," *International Journal of Psycho-Analysis*, 50 (1969), 113. Rosen writes: "The development of Freud's structural theory had its forerunners in his monograph *On Aphasia* (1888) and in *The Project [for a Scientific Psychology]* (1895). In these monographs he first stressed the unique potential of the auditory modality for the development of language. He was aware that only in the auditory sphere is there a simultaneous communication with the object and feedback of the centrifugal stimuli to the self, so that interpersonal and intrapsychic communication become important mirrors of each other."

3. "Dreams," *S.E.*, V, 340.

4. See Ricoeur, *De l'interprétation*, p. 15.

5. "Dreams," *S.E.*, V, 362.

6. Ibid., 362-63.

7. Ibid., 347-48.

8. Ibid., 352.

9. *Papers on Psycho-Analysis* (Baltimore: William Wood, 1938), pp. 129-86.

10. See Henry Edelheit, "Speech and Psychic Structure," *Journal of the American Psychoanalytic Association*, 17 (1969), 381-411.

11. "Sign Phenomena and Their Relationship to Unconscious Meaning," *International Journal of Psycho-Analysis*, 50 (1969), 197-207. My discussion of language in this and the three succeeding paragraphs draws heavily on this article, and to a lesser degree on the article by Edelheit cited above.

12. The terms "symbol" and "symbolic" are used in this portion of the discussion, not in the usual psychoanalytic or literary ways, but in a purely linguistic sense, in which every word is a symbol in that it stands for a referent.

13. See Edelheit, p. 401.

14. Rosen, "Sign Phenomena," p. 204.

15. *S.E.*, XIX, 20.

16. See Edelheit, p. 403.

17. Exception must obviously be made here for certain kinds of thought that cannot be expressed in discursive language, but only in such special "languages" as musical notation or the numbers and symbols of mathematics.

18. Simon O. Lesser discusses the relaxation of ego control, the importance of visual imagery and primary process thinking, and other aspects of the emotional and psychological experience of literature in *Fiction and the Unconscious* (Boston: Beacon Hill Press, 1957). See especially chap. VI, "The Language of Fiction."

Part 1   V.   Literature and Psychopathology

1. "Delusions and Dreams in Jensen's *Gradiva*," *S.E.*, IX, 44.

2. "Introductory Lectures on Psycho-Analysis," *S.E.*, XVI, 376.

3. "Three Essays on the Theory of Sexuality," *S.E.*, VII, 238.

4. *A Writer's Diary* (1953; rpt. New York: New American Library, 1968), p. 161.

5. See "Approaches to Art," in Kris, *Psychoanalytic Explorations*, pp. 13-63.

6. Kris, pp. 103, 25, 26ff.

7. K. R. Eissler, *Discourse on Hamlet and "Hamlet": A Psychoanalytic Inquiry* (New York: International Universities Press, 1971), pp. 520, 547.

Other writers have taken positions similar to Eissler's on the relationship between mental disorder and creative genius, among them William Barrett in "Writers and Madness" (*Partisan Review*, 14 [1947], rpt. in William Phillips, ed., *Art and Psychoanalysis*, pp. 390-411). Edmund Wilson, in *The Wound and the Bow* (New York: Oxford University Press, 1947), emphasizes the sickness of the artist: "genius and disease, like strength and mutilation, may be inextricably bound up together" (p. 289).

8. *Goethe: A Psychoanalytic Study* (Detroit: Wayne State University Press, 1963), I, 24.

9. *Leonardo da Vinci: Psychoanalytic Notes on the Enigma* (New York: International Universities Press, 1961), pp. 217-18.

10. *Hamlet*, p. 525.

11. "Formulations on the Two Principles of Mental Functioning," *S.E.*, XII, 224.

12. See Hanns Sachs, "The Community of Daydreams," in *The Creative Unconscious* (Cambridge, Mass.: Sci-Art Publishers, 1942), pp. 11-54.

13. Henry Lowenfeld, in "Psychic Trauma and Productive Experience in the Artist" (*Psychoanalytic Quarterly*, 10 [1941], 116-30), attempts to trace the connections between childhood trauma and later artistic production in the case of a painter.

2 DEMONSTRATION

Part 2 I. "A Kind of Unnatural Fear"

1. Trans. Boris Brasol (New York: George Braziller, 1954), p. 35.

2. F. M. Dostoevskii, *Pis'ma*, ed. A. S. Dolinin (Moscow: Gosudarstvennoe izdatel'stvo, 1928-1959), II, 1/13 January 1868; 71.

3. Ibid., 25 January/6 February 1869; 160.

4. Ibid., 26 February/10 March 1869; 170.

5. See Konstantin Mochulsky, *Dostoevsky: His Life and Work*, trans. Michael A. Minihan (Princeton: Princeton University Press, 1967 [1947]), pp. 402-403.

6. *Dostoevsky, The Making of a Novelist* (1940; rpt. New York: Vintage-Knopf, 1962), p. 218.

7. *Dostoevsky, The Major Fiction* (Cambridge, Mass.: MIT Press, 1971), p. 108. The ambiguities of this scene are modified in a significant way by Wasiolek's description of it, for Myshkin actually shares a bed not with the dead Nastasya, but with her murderer, Rogozhin.

8. This failure of criticism before the novel comes in part from the notion of Dostoevsky as primarily a religious prophet and philosopher rather than a novelist, an idea that informs a great deal of the writing on his work. Philip Rahv argues persuasively against this misconception in "The Other Dostoevsky," *New York Review of Books*, 20 April 1972, pp. 30-38.

9. *The Tragic Vision* (New York: Holt, Rhinehart, and Winston, 1960), pp. 209-27.

10. *Dostoevsky: Essays and Perspectives* (Berkeley: University of California Press, 1970), pp. 84, 88, 83. Lord's essay goes astray partly because he misuses the notebooks for *The Idiot* in interpreting the novel itself. In the early plans for the novel, the hero is a character much like Stavrogin or Raskolnikov. This earlier vision of the Idiot's character did influence the final conception, but in modified and disguised form. In ignoring this transformation, Lord loses the tension and ambiguity of the novel as surely as do the critics who give us a perfect and saintly Prince.

11. Edward Wasiolek, ed., *The Notebooks for "The Idiot,"* trans. Katharine Strelsky (Chicago: University of Chicago Press, 1967), p. 193.

12. *Pis'ma*, II, 16/28 August 1867; 25.

13. This period is described in harrowing detail by Dostoevsky's second wife in her diary. See *Dostoevsky Portrayed by His Wife: The Diary and Reminiscences of Mme. Dostoevsky*, ed. S. S. Koteliansky (London: George Routledge & Sons, 1926).

14. *Pis'ma*, II, 31 December 1867/12 January 1868; 60.

15. Ibid., 9/21 October 1867; 47.

16. Ibid., 31 December 1867/12 January 1868; 61.

17. Ibid., 2/14 March 1868; 95.

18. Ibid., 9/21 March 1868; 115-16.

19. Ibid., 2/14 March 1868; 95-96.

Part 2 II. Prince Christ

1. Quotations from *The Idiot* are generally from Constance Garnett's translation (New York: Random House-Modern Library, 1935); where the translation departs significantly from the Russian text, it has been amended to bring it closer to the literal meaning. The novel is divided into four parts: quotations in this study are followed by parentheses with a Roman numeral for the part and an Arabic numeral for the chapter. Where a single paragraph of my text contains several quotations from the same chapter, only the last is followed by the reference to part and chapter. Dostoevsky often uses a series of dots to punctuate. In order to avoid confusion with the ellipses that indicate deletions, in all quotations from Dostoevsky I have put brackets around ellipses standing for matter deleted by me.

2. A number of characters in the novel are related psychologically to Myshkin, acting out openly tendencies only suggested in him. An unattractive minor character named Ferdyshtchenko, a sort of court baffoon in Nastasya's circle, has an unconventional and "honest" personality that demonstrates the aggressiveness of some childish behavior. Ferdyshtchenko says of himself, "You see, [. . .] every one has wit, but I have no wit. To make up for it I've asked leave to speak the truth, for every one knows that it's only people who have no wit who speak the truth. Besides, I am a very vindictive man, and that is because I have no wit. I put up with every insult, but only till my antagonist comes to grief" (I.13). In this self-description, Ferdyshtchenko sounds like a parody of Myshkin. Myshkin too has "no wit" and so speaks the truth—this is the essence of the role of

"idiot" or holy fool; and Myshkin too puts up with every insult.

In a story about himself that Ferdyshtchenko tells at Nastasya's birthday party, he describes a sort of *acte gratuit*, an inexplicably malicious action resulting in the dismissal of an innocent maid servant, which represents the eruption of childish—indeed extremely primitive—aggression.

3. Through his use of Myshkin as protagonist, Dostoevsky accomplishes what the Russian formalist critic Viktor Shklovsky called "making it strange" (*ostranenie*). Myshkin's naïveté and his unfamiliarity with Russian life call into question the habitual and unthinking assumptions of the society in which he finds himself, and of the reader of the novel as well. His innocent vision destroys the familiar image and the automatic response, and creates a "sphere of new perception." For a discussion of Shklovsky's theory, see Victor Erlich, *Russian Formalism* (The Hague: Mouton, 1955), pp. 149-54.

4. *The Notebooks for "The Idiot,"* p. 193.

5. In *"The Idiot*: A Rage of Goodness"* (*Eleven Essays in the European Novel* [New York: Harcourt, Brace & World, 1964], p. 151), R. P. Blackmur writes of Dostoevsky's "emphasis on humiliation as the necessary preface and absolute condition of humility."

6. *S.E.*, XIX, 165.

7. Ibid., 169-70.

8. Ibid., 170.

9. Ibid., 169.

10. Ibid.

11. Simon O. Lesser has done a psychoanalytic study of *The Idiot* entitled "Saint and Sinner—Dostoevsky's *Idiot*" (*Modern Fiction Studies*, 4 [1958], 211-24, rpt. in Leonard and Eleanor Manheim, ed., *Hidden Patterns: Studies in Psychoanalytic Literary Criticism* [New York: Macmillan, 1966], pp. 132-50). Lesser also finds evidence of moral masochism in the Prince. His essay deals mainly with the

character of Myshkin, whom he sees as suffering from the conflict between an overdeveloped superego and a weak ego, and with the sadistic and masochistic aspects of his relations with other characters, especially Rogozhin. My interpretation coincides at several points with Lesser's.

12. *S.E.*, XIX, 170.

Part 2   III.   The Saintly Whore

1. See Freud, "The Psychopathology of Everyday Life," *S.E.*, VI, 265-68.

2. "(Contributions to the Psychology of Love I)," *S.E.*, XI, 165-75. The Dumas novel and the sensation it made in fashionable Russian society are referred to explicitly in *The Idiot* in an anecdote contributed by Totsky to the "game of the worst action" at Nastasya's birthday party. Nastasya is also associated with another literary prototype when Myshkin goes to her rooms on the day of her death and finds a copy of *Madame Bovary* lying open on a table. Dostoevsky's wife mentions in her diary (*The Diary of Dostoyevsky's Wife*, p. 255) that Dostoevsky bought the Flaubert novel in July 1867, shortly before he began working on *The Idiot*. Harold Rosenberg, in his introduction to the Henry and Olga Carlisle translation of *The Idiot* (New York: New American Library-Signet, 1969), pp. vii-xxii, points out the influence of prototypes from continental romantic fiction on Dostoevsky's conception of all the major characters in the novel, and on their conceptions of themselves.

3. Freud, "A Special Type of Choice of Object," *S.E.*, XI, 171.

4. "(Contributions to the Psychology of Love II)," *S.E.*, XI, 183.

5. *The Notebooks for "The Idiot,"* p. 170.

Part 2   IV.   "Whom I Love I Chastise"

1. Here is an instance in which the difference between the Garnett translation and the original text is important. Twice in this passage, and in several other passages, Gar-

nett changes the brutally specific and psychologically significant image of being knifed to the more general idea of murder. She translates here as follows: "To be drowned or murdered! [. . .] Ha! Why that's just why she is marrying me, because she expects to be murdered! . . ."

2. Freud's most thorough treatment of the primal scene is in the case of the Wolf Man—"From the History of an Infantile Neurosis," *S.E.*, XVII, 7-122. See especially sec. IV, pp. 29-47. Aaron H. Esman, in "The Primal Scene: A Review and a Reconsideration" (*The Psychoanalytic Study of the Child*, 28 [1973], 49-81), questions the universality of the sadistic conception of the primal scene. He asserts that the nature of the child's response to primal scene experiences or fantasies is determined primarily by the cultural and familial context in which they occur. Thus children of parents who quarrel frequently or who are physically violent with each other or the children will be most likely to develop a sadistic conception of the sexual act. Freud makes the same point in the interpretation of a primal scene in a dream. ("Dreams," *S.E.*, V, 584-85.) In any case, the conception of the primal scene in *The Idiot* is certainly sadistic; here, as so often in Dostoevsky's work, sexuality and aggression are closely associated.

3. This discussion of the vicissitudes of the Oedipus complex is derived in part from Freud's essay "Dostoevsky and Parricide," *S.E.*, XXI, 183-84. See also the discussion of the "complete" Oedipus complex in chap. III of "The Ego and the Id," *S.E.*, XIX.

4. It is not necessary here to take up the controversy over whether female sexuality is really passive and masochistic. What does seem clear is that the child who observes parental intercourse often misunderstands the mother's sexual role as one of suffering. This misunderstanding is reinforced by the child's first ideas about the difference between the genitals of the two sexes, and by the opportunities for masochistic excitement often afforded the child by parental attempts at discipline.

5. Freud, "Masochism," *S.E.*, XIX, 170.

6. *S.E.*, XIV, 248.

7. Ibid., 251.

8. See "A Short Study of the Development of the Libido, Viewed in the Light of Mental Disorders," *Selected Papers of Karl Abraham*, ed. Ernest Jones (London: Hogarth, 1927), p. 438.

9. It might seem that the seduction of a girl of sixteen comes too late in her life to have so devastating an effect on her personality as Totsky's seduction of Nastasya apparently has. However, this is no ordinary seduction, but one that represents the fulfillment of a guilty childhood wish; an event of this kind could in real life contribute to the formation of a neurosis. Moreover, the loss of Totsky has an earlier parallel in the deaths of Nastasya's father and mother when she was seven. A loss of that kind is often interpreted by the child as rejection and abandonment by the parents, and Nastasya's later guilt and self-hatred after the loss of Totsky can be seen as a re-activation of those earlier feelings. It is tempting to pursue this kind of analysis, because Dostoevsky's treatment of Nastasya is so rich in detail and so realistic psychologically.

10. Lesser also points out the function of Rogozhin and Nastasya in acting out repressed tendencies in Myshkin's personality (*Hidden Patterns*, ed. Manheim, p. 142); however, he does not consider the lives of Nastasya and Rogozhin themselves. Nor does he discuss oedipal and primal scene material.

11. "Masochism," *S.E.*, XIX, 169.

Part 2   V. The Scene on the Staircase

1. See Freud, "Instincts and Their Vicissitudes," *S.E.*, XIV, 111-40.

2. Some of the symbols that appear frequently in dreams, with their most common meanings, can be found in chap. VI (E) of "The Interpretation of Dreams," *S.E.*, V, 350-404. As it happens, almost all of the images in the

staircase scene and the preceding sequence appear there. A male patient's dream of being attacked by a man with a hatchet ("Dreams," *S.E.*, V, 584-85), together with the patient's associations, bears some striking resemblances to the staircase scene. Freud interprets the dream as the transformation of a primal scene memory.

Part 2 VI. Fathers and Children

1. The similarity between the stories told of Myshkin's father and the personality and fate of Dostoevsky's own father is too striking to resist here. Biographers are in agreement that Dostoevsky's father was a harsh, despotic man. Mochulsky writes of him: "A man of extremely difficult temperament, sullen, contentious, suspicious. . . . His personality was a fusion of cruelty and sensibility, piety and avarice" (p. 3). Dostoevsky's brother Andrey recalls in his memoirs: "When my brothers were with my father [for Latin lessons], which was frequently for an hour or more, they not only did not dare sit down, but even lean their elbows on the table." (Quoted in Mochulsky, p. 4.) After the death of his wife, the elder Dostoevsky retired to his country estate, where he took to drink and debauchery and began abusing his peasants, quite in the style of old Fyodor Karamazov. One of his peasants recalled him in these words: "The man was a beast. His soul was dark,—that's it. . . . The master was a stern, unrighteous lord, but the mistress was kindhearted. He didn't live well with her; beat her. He flogged the peasants for nothing." (Quoted in Mochulsky, p. 6.) In 1839, when Dostoevsky was eighteen, his father died. It has always been thought that he was murdered by his rebellious serfs. A recent biography by Joseph Frank (*Dostoevsky: The Seeds of Revolt, 1821-1849* [Princeton: Princeton University Press, 1976]) contains new material suggesting that the death may in fact have been due to natural causes (p. 86n). However, what is psychologically significant is not what actually happened but what Dostoevsky believed, and he believed that his father

had been murdered. The new evidence casting doubt on the murder theory makes it all the more suggestive that the family apparently accepted that theory. Evidently the elder Dostoevsky's personality was such that the idea of a violent uprising against him was quite credible. Frank is at some pains to rehabilitate the character of Dostoevsky's father; he emphasizes that the father did not believe in corporal punishment for his children—as if actual blows were the only means of evoking fears and fantasies of punishment in a child. Nothing he says, however, substantially changes the picture of a difficult and rather frightening personality.

2. In "Dostoevsky and Parricide," *S.E.*, XXI, 175-94, Freud advances a formulation like this one to explain Dostoevsky's own epileptic seizures. During his mid-twenties Dostoevsky suffered from a mysterious "nervous disorder" probably related to his epilepsy. It was manifested in periods of lethargic somnolence and fear of death, followed by a strange deathlike experience: he told his friend Solovyev, "it often seemed to me that I was dying, and really—actual death came and then went away." (Quoted in Frank, *Dostoevsky: The Seeds of Revolt*, pp. 387-88. For a discussion of the variety of bizarre hallucinatory experiences sometimes associated with epilepsy, see chap. 18 of Redlich and Freedman, *The Theory and Practice of Psychiatry* [New York: Basic Books, 1966], especially the section on "psychic seizures.") Dostoevsky's brother Andrey relates that Fydor used to leave notes about before going to bed during this period; fearing that he would fall into a deathlike sleep, he asked that his burial be postponed for five days. (Frank, pp. 387-88.) In specifying that Kolpakov was actually buried, Ivolgin's story alludes to the fear of premature burial, which Kolpakov miraculously survives.

3. The motif of the seduction of a very young girl appears over and over, in one form or another, in Dostoevsky's work, sometimes quite openly, as in "Stavrogin's Confession." In a letter to Tolstoy after Dostoevsky's death, his friend Strakhov wrote that Dostoevsky had boasted in con-

versation of having himself raped a little girl in a bath-house. Dostoevsky's second wife denied this story indig-nantly, saying that her husband had indeed related such an incident, but as something that had only been described to him and that he intended to use in creating the character of Stavrogin. See *Dostoevsky Portrayed by His Wife*, p. 240.

4. The theme of the abused child was central to the first plan of *The Idiot*. Dostoevsky was interested at the time in an actual case being tried in the courts: a girl named Olga Umetskaia, who had been beaten, starved, and sexually abused by her parents, had tried to burn down their house. For further discussion of the influence of the Umetsky case, see the appendix to this study.

5. The allusion to Siberia in conjunction with hostility to the father recalls again the experience of Dostoevsky him-self. Freud speculates that Dostoevsky was able to endure his nine-year Siberian imprisonment and exile because he equated his rebellious projects against the tsar, the "little father" of the Russian people, with the parricidal wishes against his own father, which were realized in the father's supposed murder. Dostoevsky accepted his punishment as deserved, as though his wishes had in fact brought about the father's death. See "Dostoevsky and Parricide," *S.E.*, XXI, 186-87.

Part 2   VII. The Epileptic Mode of Being

1. I have taken this phrase from Robert Lord (*Dostoevsky, Essays and Perspectives*), who entitles his chapter on *The Idiot* "An Epileptic Mode of Being." Lord sees Myshkin's epilepsy as "metaphysical" in origin (p. 98), and as the fun-damental limitation of his being. Oddly enough, most critics who write on *The Idiot* have little to say of Myshkin's disorder; Lord is among the few who have tried to explore its significance. Although his approach to the epilepsy is in-teresting and suggestive, I disagree entirely with his in-terpretation of the novel.

2. In an extremely interesting essay on Dostoevsky's mys-

ticism, Derek Traversi points out the "strange vortex-like movement in his writing, as though we felt the life he was considering circling faster and faster until, at the crucial moment, it collapsed." "Dostoevsky," *The Criterion*, 16 (1937), 585-602, rpt. in *Dostoevsky: A Collection of Critical Essays*, ed. René Wellek, Twentieth Century Views (Englewood Cliffs, N.J.: Prentice-Hall, 1962), pp. 159-71.

3. *Pis'ma*, II, 2/14 March 1868; 95.

4. *S.E.*, XXI, 175-94.

5. Although recently discovered records make it uncertain whether the death was actually a murder, this new evidence was not available to Dostoevsky. Insofar as it affected him psychologically the murder, whether or not it actually occurred, was real.

6. It is not clear when Dostoevsky's disease first appeared. From the letters it would seem that true convulsive seizures first occurred in Siberia, over ten years after his father's death, although the earlier "nervous disorder" may well have been epileptic in character. Dostoevsky's daughter Aimée writes in *Fyodor Dostoyevsky*, p. 33n: "According to a family tradition, it was when he first heard of his father's death that Dostoyevsky had his first epileptic fit." This version may be factually inaccurate; however, such a family belief connecting the epilepsy and the father's death is surely significant.

7. *S.E.*, XXI, 66-67.

8. Ibid., 68.

9. Whether Myshkin's experience is truly "mystical" or merely a manifestation of his illness, or whether in fact a meaningful distinction can be made here, is immaterial to this discussion. The point is that during the period of diminished ego control preceding his fits, Myshkin undergoes a peculiar experience that has certain aspects usually identified as mystical.

10. "New Introductory Lectures on Psycho-Analysis," *S.E.*, XXII, 79-80.

11. The disappearance of the superego into the ego is

described by Freud in "Group Psychology and the Analysis of the Ego," *S.E.*, XVII, 129-33. See also the discussion of mania in Otto Fenichel, *The Psychoanalytic Theory of Neurosis* (New York: Norton, 1945), pp. 407-11.

12. The descriptions of execution also correspond to some elements in Victor Hugo's *Le Dernier Jour d'un condamné* (1829).

13. Apropos of the description of the beheading, Traversi writes that such passages "are not concerned with the normal life of the senses at all, but with a desire to transcend experience and stretch the capacity of the mind beyond the limit of the conceivable: they seek in fact to comprehend what we call the infinite." In *Dostoevsky*, ed. Wellek, p. 160.

14. See Kris, *Psychoanalytic Explorations in Art*, p. 45.

Part 2   VIII. Philosophical Rebellion

1. Mikhail Bakhtin makes a similar argument for Dostoevsky's work in general in *Problems of Dostoevsky's Poetics*, trans. R. W. Rotsel (Ann Arbor, Mich.: Ardis, 1973 [1929]). Bakhtin argues against removing the ideas of individual characters from "the interrelationship of events of consciousness" and forcing them into "a systematic monological context" (p. 7). "The plurality of independent and unmerged voices and consciousnesses and the genuine polyphony of full-valued voices are in fact characteristics of Dostoevsky's novels" (p. 4).

2. Joseph Frank also notes the relationship between the views of Myshkin and Ippolit. He points out that Ippolit's "Necessary Explanation" contains "all the major features of Myshkin's *Weltanschauung* combined with an *opposite* human attitude." "A Reading of *The Idiot*," *Southern Review*, 5 (1969), 320.

3. Although the Garnett translation does not specify the sex of the "friend," in Russian the word is in the masculine form. The Carlisle translation makes this clear: "My

mother came into the room with some man she knew" (p. 410).

4. See Freud, "Inhibitions, Symptoms, and Anxiety," *S.E.*, XX, 77-174.

5. The indistinctness of the male figure in the dream, referred to as the mother's "friend," or "some man she knew," suggests that this figure arouses anxiety that must be repressed: Freud writes, "There is a causal connection between the obscurity of the dream-content and the state of repression (inadmissibility to consciousness) of certain of the dream-thoughts." ("Dreams," *S.E.*, V, 672.) The conspicuous casualness and vagueness of the reference may indicate that "some friend of hers" (Garnett) or "some man she knew" (Carlisle) is in fact the man the mother knows best—the father. The anxiety aroused by this male figure, which cannot be admitted to consciousness, is displaced from the man in the dream and associated with the terrifying reptile.

6. The Garnett translation makes both the knife-blade and the reptile seven inches long, although in Russian they are not exactly the same size. The knife-blade is "about three and a half *vershki* long" and the reptile is "about four *vershki* long."

7. Freud, "The Ego and the Id," *S.E.*, XIX, 41.

Part 2   IX. Religious Submission

1. Dostoevsky himself expressed a view of Russian political life quite like Myshkin's in a letter dated April 2, 1868—while he was in the midst of writing *The Idiot*: "our constitution signifies the mutual love of the Monarch for the people and of the people for the Monarch. Yes, the principle of our State is love and not conquest (which the Slavophiles were, it seems, the first to discover) and it's the highest idea on which much can be constructed." (*Pis'ma*, II, 20 March/2 April 1868; 100.) At this point in his life, Dostoevsky could evidently put such sentiments in a letter without irony; fortunately, in the "polyphonic" texture of

the novel, this dubious conception is undermined to some extent by Myshkin's unconscious reaction against it, and counterpointed by the ideas of Ippolit.

2. Blackmur and Traversi both take up in their essays other "heretical" aspects of Dostoevsky's Christianity.

Part 2   X. The Compulsion to Repeat

1. *Notebooks*, p. 203.

2. Edwin Muir comments on Dostoevsky's masterful handling of the repeated foreshadowings of the murder and its shocking effect when it finally happens: "Dostoevsky's intention seems to be to suggest so often and so openly that Rogojin will end by murdering Nastasia that it becomes the one thing that nobody expects because everybody says it." *The Structure of the Novel* (New York: Harcourt, Brace, 1929), p. 77.

3. Robert Hollander, in "The Apocalyptic Framework of Dostoevsky's *The Idiot*," *Mosaic*, 7 (1974), 123-39, points out the many references in the novel to the new railways, which are usually associated with modern greed and materialism. Lebedyev interprets the star Wormwood in the Apocalypse as "the network of railways spread over Europe" (II.11).

4. Allen Tate, in "The Hovering Fly," *Collected Essays* (Denver: Allen Swallow, 1959), pp. 146-62, sees the fly as an image of the conversion of life into death, and of the degradation and nobility of Nastasya. "The fly comes to stand in its sinister and abundant life for the privation of life, the body of the young woman on the bed" (p. 158). Dostoevsky's use of the fly becomes in this essay the focus of an argument in support of the power of dramatic imagination to create for us the "actual world" of lived experience, as opposed to the "occult" and abstract world of the positivistic "religion of science."

Part 2   XI. Ambivalence and the Pre-oedipal Mother

1. See especially "The Ego and the Id," *S.E.*, XIX, 42-43.

2. "Instincts and Their Vicissitudes," *S.E.*, XIV, 139.

3. Edmund Bergler develops this ramification of the Oedipus complex in *The Writer and Psychoanalysis*, 2nd ed. (New York: Robert Brunner, 1954).

4. Fenichel, p. 356.

5. This scene duplicates almost exactly the earlier one in which Myshkin comforts Nastasya after the confrontation between the two heroines in which he chooses her over Aglaia: "He said nothing, but listened intently to her broken, excited, incoherent babble [. . .] he began [. . .] tenderly passing his hands over her cheeks, soothing and comforting her like a child" (IV.8). Here too the roles of mother and child are mingled and fused in Myshkin.

Appendix

1. Edward Wasiolek, ed., *The Notebooks for "The Idiot,"* trans. Katharine Strelsky (Chicago: University of Chicago Press, 1967), p. 39. Subsequent page references to *The Notebooks* will be in parentheses following quotations.

2. "Repression," *S.E.*, XIV, 149.

3. "Fragment of an Analysis of a Case of Hysteria," *S.E.*, VII, 17.

4. *Pis'ma*, II, 31 December 1867/12 January 1868; 60-61.

5. Ibid., 60.

Selected Bibliography

The following bibliography lists most of the works referred to or quoted in this study. Only works mentioned in passing or quoted briefly by way of illustration are omitted.

Abraham, Karl. "A Short Study of the Development of the Libido, Viewed in the Light of Mental Disorders." *Selected Papers of Karl Abraham*. Ed. Ernest Jones. London: Hogarth, 1927.

Bakhtin, Mikhail. *Problems of Dostoevsky's Poetics*. Trans. R. W. Rotsel. Ann Arbor, Mich.: Ardis, 1973 (1929).

Barrett, William. "Writers and Madness." *Partisan Review*, 14 (1947). Rpt. in *Art and Psychoanalysis*. Ed. William Phillips. Cleveland: World-Meridian, 1963.

Bergler, Edmund. *The Writer and Psychoanalysis*. 2nd ed. New York: Robert Brunner, 1954.

Blackmur, R[ichard] P. "*The Idiot*: A Rage of Goodness." *Eleven Essays in the European Novel*. New York: Harcourt, Brace & World, 1964.

Burke, Kenneth. "Freud—and the Analysis of Poetry." *The American Journal of Sociology*, 44 (1939). Rpt. in *Art and Psychoanalysis*. Ed. William Phillips. Cleveland: World-Meridian, 1963.

Crews, Frederick. "Anaesthetic Criticism." *Out of My System: Psychoanalysis, Ideology, and Critical Method*. New York: Oxford Univ. Press, 1975.

Dostoevskii, F. M. *Pis'ma*. Ed. A. S. Dolinin. 4 vols. Moscow: Gosudarstvennoe izdatel'stvo, 1928-1959.

Dostoevsky, Anna Gregorevna. *Dostoevsky Portrayed by His Wife: The Diary and Reminiscences of Mme. Dostoevsky*. Ed. and trans. S. S. Koteliansky. London: George Routledge & Sons, 1926.

Dostoevsky, Fyodor. *The Diary of a Writer*. Trans. Boris Brasol. New York: George Braziller, 1954.

Dostoevsky, Fyodor. *The Notebooks for "The Idiot."* Ed. Edward Wasiolek. Trans. Katharine Strelsky. Chicago: Univ. of Chicago Press, 1967.

Dostoyevsky, Aimée. *Fyodor Dostoyevsky: A Study.* London: William Heinemann, 1921.

Dostoyevsky, Fyodor. *The Idiot.* Trans. Constance Garnett. New York: Random House-Modern Library, 1935.

Edelheit, Henry. "Speech and Psychic Structure." *Journal of the American Psychoanalytic Association*, 17 (1969), 381-412.

Eissler, K[urt] R. *Discourse on Hamlet and "Hamlet": A Psychoanalytic Inquiry.* New York: International Universities Press, 1971.

————. *Goethe: A Psychoanalytic Study.* 2 vols. Detroit: Wayne State Univ. Press, 1963.

————. *Leonardo da Vinci: Psychoanalytic Notes on the Enigma.* New York: International Universities Press, 1961.

Erlich, Victor. *Russian Formalism.* The Hague: Mouton, 1955.

Esman, Aaron H. "The Primal Scene: A Review and a Reconsideration." *The Psychoanalytic Study of the Child*, 28 (1973), 49-81.

Fenichel, Otto. *The Psychoanalytic Theory of Neurosis.* New York: Norton, 1945.

Frank, Joseph. *Dostoevsky: The Seeds of Revolt, 1821-1849.* Princeton: Princeton University Press, 1976.

————. "A Reading of *The Idiot.*" *Southern Review*, 5 (1969), 303-31.

Freud, Sigmund. *The Standard Edition of the Complete Psychological Works of Sigmund Freud.* Ed. James Strachey et al. 24 vols. London: Hogarth, 1953-1974.

"Beyond the Pleasure Principle." (1920). Vol. XVIII.

"Civilization and Its Discontents." (1930 [1929]). Vol. XXI.

"Creative Writers and Day-dreaming." (1908 [1907]). Vol. IX.

"Delusions and Dreams in Jensen's *Gradiva*." (1907 [1906]). Vol. IX.

"Dostoevsky and Parricide." (1928 [1927]). Vol. XXI.

"The Economic Problem of Masochism." (1924). Vol. XIX.

"The Ego and the Id." (1923). Vol. XIX.

"Formulations on the Two Principles of Mental Functioning." (1911). Vol. XII.

"Fragment of an Analysis of a Case of Hysteria." (1905). Vol. VII.

"Some General Remarks on Hysterical Attacks." (1908). Vol. IX.

"Group Psychology and the Analysis of the Ego." (1921). Vol. XVIII.

"From the History of an Infantile Neurosis." (1918 [1914]). Vol. XVII.

"Inhibitions, Symptoms, and Anxiety." (1926 [1925]). Vol. XX.

"Instincts and Their Vicissitudes." (1915). Vol. XIV.

"The Interpretation of Dreams." (1900). Vols. IV and V.

"Introductory Lectures on Psycho-Analysis." (1916-1917 [1915-1917]). Vols. XV and XVI.

"Leonardo da Vinci and a Memory of His Childhood." (1910). Vol. XI.

"The Moses of Michelangelo." (1914). Vol. XIII.

"Mourning and Melancholia." (1917 [1915]). Vol. XIV.

"New Introductory Lectures on Psycho-Analysis." (1933 [1932]). Vol. XXII.

"The Psychopathology of Everyday Life." (1910). Vol. VI.

"Repression." (1915). Vol. XIV.

"A Special Type of Choice of Object Made by Men (Contributions to the Psychology of Love I)." (1910). Vol. XI.

"Studies on Hysteria." (1895 [1893-1895]). Vol. II.

"The Theme of the Three Caskets." (1913). Vol. XII.

"Three Essays on the Theory of Sexuality." (1905). Vol. VII.

"The Unconscious." (1915). Vol. XIV.

"On the Universal Tendency to Debasement in the Sphere of Love (Contributions to the Psychology of Love II)." (1912). Vol. XI.

Glover, Edward. *Freud or Jung?*. 1950; rpt. Cleveland: World-Meridian, 1956.

Holland, Norman. *The Dynamics of Literary Response*. New York: Oxford Univ. Press, 1968.

Hollander, Robert. "The Apocalyptic Framework of Dostoevsky's *The Idiot*." *Mosaic*, 7 (1974), 123-39.

James, Henry. "The Art of Fiction." *The Future of the Novel: Essays on the Art of Fiction*. Ed. Leon Edel. New York: Vintage-Knopf, 1956.

————. "Preface" to *Portrait of a Lady*. 1908; rpt. New York: Random House-Modern Library, 1966.

Jones, Ernest. *Hamlet and Oedipus*. New York: Norton, 1949.

————. *The Life and Work of Sigmund Freud*. 3 vols. New York: Basic Books, 1953-1957.

————. *Papers on Psycho-Analysis*. Baltimore: William Wood, 1938.

Jung, C[arl] G[ustav]. *The Collected Works of C. G. Jung*. Trans. R. F. C. Hull. Bollingen Series XX. 18 vols. New York: Pantheon, and Princeton: Princeton University Press, 1953—.

"Introduction to the Religious and Psychological Problems of Alchemy." (1944). Vol. XII.

"On the Nature of Dreams." (1948 [1945]). Vol. VIII.

"The Practical Use of Dream Analysis." (1934) Vol. XVI.

"Psychological Aspects of the Mother Archetype." (1954 [1938]). Vol. IX, part 1.

"Psychology and Literature." (1950 [1930]). Vol. XV.

"On the Relation of Analytical Psychology to Poetry." (1922). Vol. XV.

"The Spiritual Problem of Modern Man." (1931 [1928]). Vol. X.

Krieger, Murray. "Dostoevsky's Idiot: The Curse of Saintliness." *The Tragic Vision.* New York: Holt, Rhinehart, and Winston, 1960. Rpt. in *Dostoevsky: A Collection of Critical Essays.* Ed. René Wellek. Twentieth Century Views. Englewood Cliffs, N.Y.: Prentice-Hall, 1962.

Kris, Ernst. *Psychoanalytic Explorations in Art.* 1952; rpt. New York: Schocken, 1964.

Lesser, Simon O. *Fiction and the Unconscious.* Boston: Beacon Hill Press, 1957.

———. "Saint and Sinner—Dostoevsky's *Idiot." Modern Fiction Studies,* 4 (1958). Rpt. in *Hidden Patterns: Studies in Psychoanalytic Literary Criticism.* Ed. Leonard and Eleanor Manheim. New York: Macmillan, 1966.

Lord, Robert. *Dostoevsky: Essays and Perspectives.* Berkeley: University of California Press, 1970.

Lowenfeld, Henry. "Psychic Trauma and Productive Experience in the Artist." *Psychoanalytic Quarterly,* 10 (1941). Rpt. in *Art and Psychoanalysis.* Ed. William Phillips. Cleveland: World-Meridian, 1963.

Marcus, Steven. "Freud and Dora: Story, History, Case History." *Representations: Essays on Literature and Society.* New York: Random House, 1975.

Mochulsky, Konstantin. *Dostoevsky: His Life and Work.* Trans. Michael A. Minihan. Princeton: Princeton University Press, 1967 (1947).

Muir, Edwin. *The Structure of the Novel.* New York: Harcourt, Brace, 1929.

Rahv, Philip. "The Other Dostoevsky." *New York Review of Books,* 20 April 1972, pp. 30-38.

Redlich, Frederick C., and Freedman, Daniel X. *The Theory and Practice of Psychiatry.* New York: Basic Books, 1966.

Ricoeur, Paul. *De l'interprétation: essai sur Freud*. Paris: Éditions du Seuil, 1965.

Rosen, Victor H. "Introduction to Panel on Language and Psychoanalysis." *International Journal of Psycho-Analysis*, 50 (1969), 113-16.

———. "Sign Phenomena and Their Relationship to Unconscious Meaning." *International Journal of Psycho-Analysis*, 50 (1969), 197-207.

Rosenberg, Harold. "Introduction" to Fyodor Dostoevsky, *The Idiot*. Trans. Henry and Olga Carlisle. New York: New American Library-Signet, 1969.

Sachs, Hanns. *The Creative Unconscious*. Cambridge, Mass.: Sci-Art Publishers, 1942.

Simmons, Ernest J. *Dostoevsky, The Making of a Novelist*. 1940; rpt. New York: Vintage-Knopf, 1962.

Tate, Allen. "The Hovering Fly." *Collected Essays*. Denver: Allen Swallow, 1959.

Traversi, D[erek] A. "Dostoevsky." *The Criterion*, 16 (1937). Rpt. in *Dostoevsky: A Collection of Critical Essays*. Ed. René Wellek. Twentieth Century Views. Englewood Cliffs, N.J.: Prentice-Hall, 1962.

Trilling, Lionel. "Art and Neurosis." "Freud and Literature." *The Liberal Imagination: Essays on Literature and Society*. 1950; rpt. Garden City, N.Y.: Doubleday-Anchor, 1953.

Wasiolek, Edward. *Dostoevsky, The Major Fiction*. Cambridge, Mass.: MIT Press, 1971.

Wilson, Edmund. *The Wound and the Bow*. New York: Oxford University Press, 1947.

Woolf, Virginia. *A Writer's Diary*. 1953; rpt. New York: New American Library, 1968.

Library of Congress Cataloging in Publication Data

Dalton, Elizabeth, 1936-
    Unconscious structure in The idiot.

    Bibliography: p.
    1.   Dostoevskiĭ, Fedor Mikhaĭlovich, 1821-1881.
Idiot.   I.   Title.
PG3325.I33D34   891.7'3'3   78-70287
ISBN 0-691-06364-8

79

√ B

766889